Johannes E. Flade
Erich Tylinek / Zuzana Samková

The Compleat Horse

David & Charles
Newton Abbot   London

Prentice Hall Press
New York

Contents

Introduction

For thousands of years, the horse has been a faithful companion to man. At about the middle of this century it almost seemed that the horse had had its day, yet there came an unexpected revival of interest which restored the horse once again to its established and respected position as man's partner and also as an important element in his recreational and sporting activities. To an ever-increasing extent, the horse fulfils a vital function as a link between nature and man who is so restricted within the confines of civilisation.

People who seek close contact with animals are usually motivated by a love of them—and this seems especially the case with those who wish to care for horses. But that alone is not enough to establish successful and lasting links, and indeed, mistakenly applied, can seriously damage the horse's standard of performance and reduce its life expectancy. The management and employment of horses, particularly in equestrian sport, not only entails a great deal of expense but also requires extensive and specific skills and involves considerable responsibility.

It is the aim of this book to help to provide some knowledge of the demands made by the horse on its environment and on those who manage, care for, ride and drive it, and at the same time to show something of its manifold beauty and grace. Information is provided on the breeding, rearing and care of horses, on their sensory perception and behaviour, based on the latest scientific findings. In addition, the reader is presented with a fundamental account of the origins of horses, their use in past ages, and on the development of horse breeding and equestrian sport in various historical epochs. The story of English thoroughbred breeding illustrates the achievements and the perseverance of the horse breeder. For where would horse breeding be without the work carried out in the stud farms? I would like this book to stand as a tribute to that work. It was no easy matter to make a choice; four important European studs are presented here as representative examples. A catalogue of breeds provides more detailed information on some of the most influential breeds of horses and their development.

Not least, this book will give pleasure through its illustrations which beautifully convey the image of the horse in its natural surroundings in a wide variety of situations and activities.

I would like to express my sincere thanks here to all who have so generously given their co-operation and support in the preparation and production of this book.

Dr Johannes E. Flade

'The horse of today is not a child of nature, it is a ward in the charge of man.' With these words, Hutten-Czapski, a leading authority on the history of horse breeding, writing in the middle of the last century, described the role of domestication. Undoubtedly the horse was not the first animal to be domesticated. Following upon certain preliminary stages of animal management—in the Near East, for example, herds of gazelles and antelopes were maintained—man began to domesticate wild animals of various kinds some twelve thousand years ago. When cultivation of the land began, certain species of animals, initially goats, sheep, dogs and pigs, were cared for and bred. Planned agriculture and animal breeding provided man with a more secure existence, since he could produce more food with less work. The result was a comparatively rapid improvement in the material basis of human life.

In the tenth and ninth millennia BC there were considerable advances in colonisation, great settlements and cities were established, such as those in the valley of the Indus, in Mesopotamia between the Euphrates and Tigris rivers, and on the eastern shores of the Mediterranean, and with them were laid the foundations of our present-day civilisation. Domestication, then, together with agriculture, brought about a fundamental change in material production and, consequently, an acceleration in the development of human society. As far as we know, this process had its beginnings in the region of the Near East or central Asia. It continued there until the end of the eighth millennium, and it was not until the sixth millennium that its centre shifted to the Asian river valleys and the valley of the Nile. This period saw the domestication of further species of wild animals, such as the ox (in the eighth millennium) in Asia Minor and south-eastern Europe, the ass (seventh to sixth millennium) in North Africa, and the bee. With the domestication of the ox, systematic cereal cultivation became possible; semi-nomadism gave way to cattle nomadism. The ox was used both as a pack animal and for riding.

Another two thousand years passed before the horse was added to the household. This happened at approximately the same time as the introduction of artificial irrigation of cultivated land; the resulting increase in yields made it easier for farmers to feed themselves and their livestock. The rapid rise in agricultural production led for the first time to the creation of surpluses, and awakened an interest in forms of produce exchange. Huge herds of domestic animals, particularly of cattle and horses, were evidence of the increasing prosperity.

The beginnings of horse domestication may have been in the early fourth or late fifth millennium BC, and probably occurred almost simultaneously in several regions. Suitable conditions, based on large stocks of wild horses that had survived the Ice Age, existed in particular in the steppe regions of south-eastern Europe and central Asia. Archaeological evidence shows that in the area to the south and east of the middle reaches of the Dnieper and to the east of the Volga, there were domesticated horses as early as the middle of the fourth millennium BC (the Aereolithic site at Dereivka). It was from these regions that the first domestic horses came to central and western Europe, where, however, it was several millennia before a high level of horse breeding was achieved. Here, horses introduced from the East played the dominant role in breeding right up to the development of the English thoroughbred in the seventeenth and eighteenth centuries AD; for example, Turkmenes and Arabs were used to produce fast breeds of saddle and carriage horses.

There is evidence that domesticated horses existed in the fourth millennium BC in Mesopotamia (Iraq); and in the Chinese kingdom of the fourth to third millennia, horses were bred in the area of the Lung-shan culture.

Where climatic conditions made it possible, wild horses and domesticated horses lived alongside one another for thousands of years in many areas. The domestication of wild horses continued into the nineteenth century. Exceptions to this development are seen in the equatorial zone of Africa, and the entire continent of America, where the primitive inhabitants of the north must undoubtedly have known the wild horse (confirmed by archaeologi-

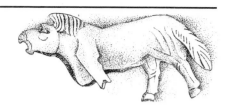

cal finds from the twelfth millennium BC in Colorado) which, however, for reasons not yet known, became extinct long before that society had achieved the stage of maturity necessary for horse domestication. The Aztecs, Incas and Mayas of Central and South America created their advanced civilisations without the horse. The domesticated horse only reached Australia and New Zealand in the eighteenth century, taken there by European settlers.

In the light of present knowledge, the domestic horse can be traced back to a single parent species, *Equus przewalskii*. The term 'species' implies a group of animals which, in conditions of free mate selection, forms a natural reproductive community.

The wild parent species of the horse showed considerable diversity at an early period. This is clear from the Palaeolithic cave paintings in Lascaux in the province of Guienne-Dordogne in France. Archaeological and zoological interpretation of the numerous findings there confirms that skulls and other parts of skeletons can be assigned to this one wild form. The same is true of archaeological finds from the glacial period in western and central Europe, such as the remains of some 40,000 wild horses found in Solutré, in the region of Saône-et-Loire, France, where the bones cover an area of nearly an acre in layers from a few inches to several feet deep.

This wild species can be divided into the following subspecies: *Equus przewalskii gmelini* Antonius, 1912 (southern Russian steppe tarpan); *Equus przewalskii silvaticus* Vetulani, 1928 (forest tarpan); and *Equus ferus przewalskii* Poliakov, 1881 (eastern tarpan). However, some other theories accord these subspecies the status of independent species.

The wild horse, still living today in small residual herds, belongs to the last-named subspecies and is generally known as Przewalski's horse (or the Przevalsky horse), the Asiatic wild horse or the Mongolian wild horse. It is a representative of the largest subspecies, reaching a height of between 12.1 and 14.1 hands. It survives in zoos and research institutes, and in the wild is strictly protected. The International Stud Book of Przewalski's horse published on 1 January 1960, following the first International Symposium for the Conservation of Przewalski's Horse (1959), is held in the Prague Zoological Gardens. It contains information on total stocks and changes in numbers in the stocks in captivity. In 1983 there were some five hundred of them. It is not impossible that, in addition, these horses are still living in the wild in quite small numbers on the Mongolian-Chinese frontier (the Gobi desert); there have, however, been no confirmed reports of sightings since 1969. At the second symposium, it was agreed that a request should be made to the government of the Soviet Union and of the Mongolian People's Republic for the establishment, where feasible, of reserves in which Przewalski's horses could be returned to the wild. This was done with considerable success. The increase in numbers that was achieved, encouraged the idea of returning Przewalski's horse to its original home. In 1980 the Soviet Union made available from its research station, Askania Nova, thirty of

Horses of the Przewalski type

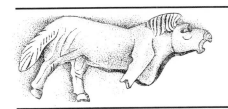

the Przewalski's wild horses that had been foaled and reared there in accordance with the breeding programme of the International Symposium, so that they could be liberated into the Gobi desert.

At the end of the eighteenth century, Peter Simon Pallas, travelling in central Asia, wrote:

The steppeland of Gobi in the Khanate of Lesser Bukharia, so remarkable in the history of zoology, also houses in its leafy, grassy districts and in the higher country round about, the wild horse, the taki as it is called by the Chinese. Its distribution extends well beyond the fourty-eighth degree of latitude, the limit of the wild ass, and extends as far as Dauria, southern Siberia and the Mongolian steppes. Its eye is fiery, its mane short and tightly curled, the mousy-grey hair of its body long and thick like fur, its legs are black. They are smaller and less handsome than the tame horses, have a bulky, curving head, are timid, intractable, extremely fast and wary. They live in herds under the leadership of the most powerful stallion which precedes them at some considerable distance, defiant of danger, they cannot be tamed and they entice the tamed horses from their pastures.

The Russian explorer Przewalski (1830—88), writing of his journeys to Tibet and along the upper courses of the Yellow River in 1879—80, says of this horse which bears his name:

The wild horse was first described quite recently by our zoologist I. S. Poliakov, who named it in my honour *Equus przewalskii*. In its external characteristics, it is still intermediate between an ass and a horse, but since it inclines rather more toward the latter, it is allotted to this genus. This animal, called *kertag* by the Kirghiz and *taki* by the Mongolians, is small in stature (the sole specimen in Europe is in the Museum of the Academy of Sciences in Petersburg); the head is relatively large, the ears smaller than those of the ass; the mane is short, erect, lacking a forelock and dark brown in colour.

The upper half of the tail has short, rough hair while the lower half has long fine black hairs like those of the horse. The colour of the body is whitish-grey, that of the underparts of the belly whitish, the head reddish, the muzzle white. The winter coat is wavy. The legs are conspicuously thick, whitish in the upper half, becoming reddish below the knees to black towards the hooves, while the hind legs are whitish. The hooves are broad and round.

These animals generally live in groups of five to fifteen individuals, led by an older stallion. Apparently the rest of the herd consists only of mares, all of which belong to the stallion. They are lively little creatures, very timid, with an acute sense of smell, a sensitive ear and a keen eye. By preference, they inhabit the wildest of regions and it is very difficult to approach them unobserved. They appear to be particularly fond of saline soils and able to survive for a long time without water . . . Most remarkable is the fact that this horse has not yet been encountered anywhere except in the wildest parts of the Central Asian deserts . . .

Our domestic horses, then, of whatever breed they may be, have a common origin; from the vast hordes of wild horses of the glacial and post-glacial period that lived between the Atlantic coast of western Europe and those parts of Asia adjacent to eastern Europe as far as the China Sea, they have been incorporated into man's rich store of domestic animals.

Characteristics of Domestication

Generally, the term domestication is understood to imply the process by which a species of animal, or an individual animal, is converted from the wild state to the domestic or tame state. It is linked with fundamental alterations in the animal's environmental conditions and brings about far-reaching morphological changes in the animal itself as the direct result of human intervention. Immediately following domestication, the wealth of forms within a species undergo a quite explosive increase. Control experiments carried out on mink have shown that after twenty-five generations diversity (in this case in colour) reaches its maximum, and after that only insignificant extensions occur. Before domestication, natural selection marks out and maintains the boundaries of a species; artificial selection extends its range, producing increased numbers of mutants (individual animals or characteristics in animals that have arisen as a result of alterations in the genetic material). Extreme forms occur, such as the tiny Shetland pony and the heavy draught horse.

Since many of the characteristics of the horse are hereditary, a multiplicity of breeds has been created, particularly in the last 150 years, by deliberately controlled artificial selection carried out to achieve particular breeding results based on economic criteria. At the moment there are more than a hundred breeds of horses, which in turn can be adapted rapidly to new demands. The factors that have brought about this massive biological remodelling can be summarised as follows.

Once in captivity, the horse was kept in reproductive isolation. Random mating such as was possible in the wild state was abolished, resulting in high variability and numerous modifications (alterations in the appearance of an animal brought about by environmental factors and therefore restricted to a single generation). Horses in conditions of domestication were subject to artificial selection, no doubt at first with quite simple intentions for practical purposes (size, behaviour, colour), and this developed later into purposeful selection in the true sense of animal breeding. Direct consequences of domestication were skeletal alterations, changes in the proportions of the body, and alteration in behaviour patterns as a result of selection for passivity. Changed environmental conditions in captivity, eg the absence of natural enemies, high concentration of numbers caused by stabling, and a different diet, brought about psychological and physiological alterations, and organic changes, with all the consequences resulting from them.

It goes without saying that all these factors caused major transformations in the primitive wild horse, both in its form and in its performance and way of life. These phenomena as a whole are known as the characteristics of domestication. Among them, those most important for horse breeding, horse management and equestrian sport might be listed as follows:

Anatomy
More rapid growth in the domestic horse has been promoted by specific selection and more intensive feeding. Examples of early maturation are seen in the heavy draught horse, the English thoroughbred and certain breeds of ponies. There has in general been no selection for size reduction, apart, that is, from the development and maintenance of very small breeds such as the Shetland pony or where the particular effects of insular status have placed a restriction on growth. The reason is that the activities of pulling and carrying loads and participation in sport demand a larger horse than the wild horse.

Physiology
Earlier maturation and, associated with it, earlier signs of senescence (eg hair whitening with age) appear in the domestic horse. It has a more intensive metabolism, particularly when it is descended from high performance breeds (such as the English thoroughbred) but, because it has become accustomed to concentrated feedstuff, it is less well able to utilise liquid food and coarse fodder. (The wild horse, on the other hand, utilises rough fodder more efficiently than concentrates.) Wild horses are harmonious-

ly adapted to their natural environment. As a result of artificial selection, this is no longer the case with domestic horses, and this must be taken into account by those involved in their care, training and use.

Colour of coat
Light colour as a result of loss of pigment in the hair (leucosis) disappears in the wild horse because of natural selection, but in the domestic horse, it is present in a wide range of nuances. It occurs to the greatest extent on those parts of the body that are most radically altered or most heavily burdened by the demands of domestication, for example, the head and the lower extremities. Leucosis occurs totally (in horses born white or, very rarely, albinos), partially, ie as marks on the limbs (very frequently) and on the head (frequently), as light-coloured mane, tail and other hair fringings, or as dappling (rare).

Black coloration (melanism) occurs in the domestic horse in the form of genuinely black hair, though some horses with deceptively dark coats are not truly melanistic. Wild horses are never entirely black, although individual black hairs occur. The coat of the true black horse appears black to mousy-grey in sunlight, while that of the pseudo-black shows up as brown to dark brown. Red coloration (erythrism) is considered to be a typical phenomenon of refinement resulting from breeding, and is unknown in the wild horse because of the extensive nature of its diet and habits. It is also a direct consequence of the intensification of metabolism resulting from selection for performance (racing, competitive sport, etc). Erythrism can be induced to a limited extent in a wild animal simply by intensive (or more intensive) feeding, but it is unstable. An example is the red summer coloration of the roe deer that occurs in conditions of optimal feeding or when the animal is kept in a zoo.

A distinction can be drawn between erythrism with reddish-brown top hair, dark extremities and dark fringes on mane and tail (brown, bay), and erythrism producing yellowish-red to dark brownish-red top hair, with the extremities and the fringing of mane and tail approximating to the basic colour or else lighter, sometimes even white (chestnut, sorrel).

Because, since ancient times, domestic breeds have been bred primarily for strength, vigour and endurance, and so for a high level of performance and intensive metabolism, the red colouring has obviously also become the most widespread one. Moreover, chestnuts mated with chestnuts always produce chestnuts, with the result that the prevalence of this particular colour among high performance breeds is considered by some to be excessive today.

Mixed colouring is found in rough-haired breeds, piebalds, skewbalds, greys and roans. In nature, such colouring is eliminated by natural selection, but in captivity it is more or less widespread, depending upon the breeds, and is a typical characteristic of domestication. This colour nuance is caused by the absence of medulla in some hairs as a result of which no pigment can be absorbed and deposited there. Only air is present inside such hair which is therefore transparent and appears white. This transparency means that, particularly when a horse is wet, the ground colour of the skin gleams through. Grey horses that are born dark coloured become lighter with age, while skin and hooves remain dark.

Hair
Following domestication, the dense, long, coarse hairs of the wild horse disappeared as a result of stabling. This process can to some extent be reversed by again subjecting the horse to natural climatic conditions (with care). Certain breeds, such as the small horses and ponies of northern and north-western Europe, still retain this coarse hair covering which insulates the body from cold and wet, prevents the thawing of snow on the back and reduces heat loss.

Constitution
As a consequence of artificial selection for draught capability and sporting performance, the highly-bred horse is more sensitive to the effects of climate and more susceptible to illnesses, particularly respiratory diseases, that often cause permanent damage. Reduction in resistance to fatigue and overtaxing may be observed unless counteracted by constant training. Here there are distinct differences between large, highly-bred horses on the one hand and the smaller or regional breeds and breeds of Oriental origin on the other, which, because of the condition in which they are kept and used, are in a much more favourable position, or which benefit from more favourable measures of selection.

Sexual sphere
In the horse, as in other animals, domestication brings about a reduction in sexual dimorphism (sexually-determined differences in the characteristics of individual animals). This convergence of the sexes is probably the result of enlargement of the mare (due to selection directed towards greater strength) and reduction in size

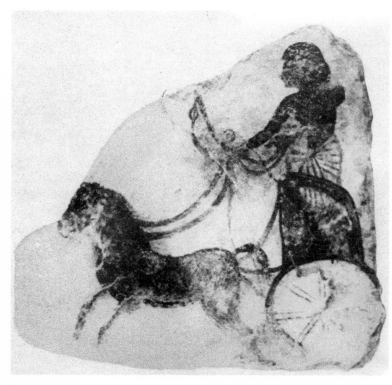

Egyptian ponies drawing a chariot. Ostracon from the time of the nineteenth dynasty (thirteenth century BC)

activity, with a larger number of mares covered over a longer breeding season. In the wild stallion, the testes are enlarged only during the mating period in spring.

The periodic oestral cycles of the domestic mare are spread more or less evenly throughout the year; in the wild state they are restricted to the spring.

In the domestic horse, the normal mating instinct is restricted. This makes artificial insemination possible as well as interspecific hybridisation within the genus of equids (*Equus*) with, for example, an ass or zebra. Without this characteristic of domestication, the mule (offspring of a jackass and a mare), known from as early as the fourth century BC, and the hinny or jennet (offspring of a stallion and she-ass), would not exist, and the crossing of stallions with the females of Asiatic wild asses (hemiones) would have been out of the question.

Behaviour

In addition to reduction in efficiency of the sense organs that followed the loss of natural enemies and of the need to seek out food, the instinct for perceiving danger and taking preventative and strategic measures of self-protection is considerably diminished in the domestic horse. Nevertheless there still exist typical behaviour patterns that must be taken into consideration when keeping and working with horses.

Even as a foal, the domestic horse has lost its fear of man. This is in complete contrast to the behaviour of the wild horse or other wild equids, particularly zebras, which even after generations spent living in zoos retain their antagonism and fear of man. This also illustrates the difference between domestication, the effects of which are usually permanent, and taming, the effects of which persist only in the tamed generation.

in the stallion (due to selection for lightness), similar to that found, for instance, in the ox (the bull and the cow).

In the domestic stallion, the primary sexual organs such as the testes are more highly developed as a result of increased sexual

Ever since domestication began, horse breeding has been carried out purposefully, making use of experience gained in the process. The earliest leaders in this field were the nomadic tribes of south-eastern Europe and central Asia. In the region of Turania (central Asia, between the lowlands round the Caspian Sea and the Kazakh hills), elegant, slender-boned, small-headed horses already lived in early times in the charge of Turkmenian herdsmen.

Descendants of these horses include the Akhal-Teké horses that had almost become extinct at the beginning of this century, but which have been bred systematically since the early twenties and are now strictly protected. They live in the Akhal-Teké oasis where the city of Ashkhabad also lies. These horses have an extremely fine coat, often with an intermingling of golden hairs, and in spite of their small stature—up to 15.1 or 15.3 hands—are capable of a very high standard of performance. In races over exceptionally long distances—more than four miles—they are distinctly superior to the English thoroughbred, and on Derby courses, only slightly inferior. In 1935, Akhal-Tekés were ridden from Ashkhabad to Moscow (a distance of well over two thousand miles) in eighty-four days, all of them completing the course in excellent condition.

Links were also established between Turania and the sedentary races and farther afield to western and south-western Asia and the Near East, so that there were domestic horses in Mesopotamia, for example, and the neighbouring areas including present-day south-western Iran as early as the beginning of the third millennium BC. In this early period, the horses most in demand were small but very robust, being used mainly as pack and draught animals, and possibly also as a source of meat. Although, later, larger breeds were added, these small animals remained dominant in south-west Asia until the middle of the second millennium, and in Egypt until the beginning and in China until the end of the first millennium BC. They resembled the Mongolian horse of today and were represented across the entire area of their distribution between the present-day Ukrainian Republic and the Pacific coast of China. From the evidence of written Egyptian records, supplemented by the discovery of a war chariot, now in Florence, with shafts only two-thirds of the length they would be today, it appears that until the thirteenth century BC, even chariot horses were not very large.

It should be mentioned here that in the Far East—for example, on the islands of Japan and the Ryukyu Islands, in South China and in Korea—small breeds of horses were reared, the descendants of which can be found today in the Tokara pony, the Java pony and in other Indonesian, Japanese or southern Asiatic breeds. The pyramidal temple of Borobudur in Java, built about 800 BC, has reliefs that still show saddle horses the size of ponies. But by that time, the inhabitants of China had, since the end of the second millennium, also known of the existence of larger, more noble horses in lands to the west of their kingdom. They provided the earliest documentation of the Bactrian-Turanian horse, although that was not until the second century BC. They learned that

World stocks of horses (in millions)

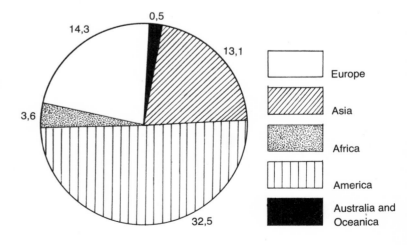

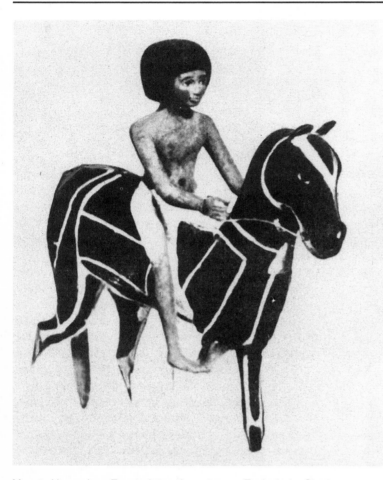

Mounted horse-boy, Egypt, sixteenth century BC, Zoologische Staats-sammlung, Munich

in the region round Ferghana (Ta-yüan, upper Syr-Darja, the present Uzbekistan), particularly elegant saddle horses were bred which sweated blood and which they called 'celestial horses' (Ta-yüans) on account of their beauty. Emperor Han Wu Di (140 to 87 BC) tried in vain to get possession of some of these horses; and it was only when he made his second attack on the Bactrian capital, Bactria—that lay on the Silk-Route and had a galloping horse in its coat of arms as the symbol of commerce—that he captured thirty Ta-yüans together with three thousand 'half-bred stallions and mares', which he used as the basis for breeding a noble horse in China.

Methods of bridling, harnessing and riding employed by horsemen remained for a long time closely based on the practices of cattle management. The development of methods of saddling and bridling and of appropriate equipment specific to the horse had to wait until the second millennium and, even then, gained general acceptance only slowly in certain regions. The same is true of the rider's clothing. In classical antiquity, Greeks and Romans still considered trousers to be a typically 'barbaric' garment, worn by foreign peoples among whom riding was customary, such as Dacians, Teutons, Trojans, and Scythians. Improbable though it sounds, even Charlemagne himself (742–814) was still prevented by court etiquette from wearing trousers on official occasions.

Evidence of the first stage in the development of the domestic horse is provided by what is so far the earliest geological find, the impression of a stamp from Gawra in northern Mesopotamia from the end of the fourth millennium that clearly shows domestic horses at a fodder crib. A fragment of a clay relief found at Ur from the Akkad period, about 2300 BC, shows a rider squatting on a horse. There is archaeological evidence of the use of domestic horses since the third millennium BC in southern Mesopotamia.

2 The wild horse that still lives today in small residual herds belongs
to the subspecies *Equus ferus
przewalskii* Poliakov 1881. Efforts
are being made in many zoos
throughout the world to preserve this
wild form from extinction. The International Stud Book is held at Prague
Zoo
Characteristic features of Przewalski's horse include the short, erect
mane and the absence of a forelock

3 The ass *(Equus asinus)* was domesticated before the horse. It still
has considerable importance as a
draught and pack animal, particularly
in the hot, arid zones of the world.
Some 38 million of these faithful but
frequently maltreated animals exist
today (Photo: Hausmann)

Previous page:
1 Abundant and fine hair in mane
and tail like this is usually an indication of Oriental ancestry; it requires
careful attention

4　Until the beginning of the glacial period, zebra, ass, Asiatic wild ass and wild horse shared a common evolution. They split into independent species early in the Pliocene, that is, more than a million years ago. Of the many subspecies of the zebra that existed, only a few remain, such as Grevy's zebra *(Equus grevyi)*, a species native to eastern Africa

5   The Hanoverian warmblood is a typical show jumper and hunter with an outstandingly fine action (Photo: W. Ernst)

6   The head of a stallion of Trakehner extraction, a special-purpose breed used to stabilise and foster riding qualities in warmblood breeds

7 In addition to the basic paces the Icelandic pony also moves at the amble and *tölt*. Its sure-footedness, even on pathless terrain, is very impressive. It is greatly prized internationally as a riding pony

8 Improvement in riding qualities in Haflingers is brought about by the restricted use of pure-bred Arabs in breeding. The 'Gabion' shown here is half Arab and half Haflinger

9 The internationally-recognised height division between ponies and horses is 14.2 hands. Depending upon their size and weight, ponies are particularly suitable for light harness work and as children's mounts

10 'Pinto' is the name given to a horse with large areas of white marking. Within the group of Western horses, it is considered as an independent breed. Pintos are usually fairly small and are a popular choice as cow ponies

11 Heavy warmblood horse—a great favourite in warmblood breeding, lively, a reliable draught animal and easy to handle

12 Isabelline warmblood stallion from Czechoslovakia. In the Isabella, only the basic dun colour is visible, even in the covering and protective hairs. There is no black marking; at most, a few individual dark or black hairs occur

Previous pages:
13 In the Neustadt paddocks

14 Head of a Kladruber. The distinct Roman nose is typical and a feature inherited from its Spanish and North African ancestors. Another feature often found in greys is described as a 'mealy muzzle'

15 The introduction of Arabian blood into the breeding of Haflingers has particularly affected the shape of the head, and gives this stallion a distinctly elegant appearance

16 The distinctive expression of the
English thoroughbred

17 Arabian horse—perfect harmony in balance and movement (Photo: Flade)

18 Since 1971, the Mecklenburg and Brandenburg warmblood breeds have been combined under the name of 'noble warmbloods of the GDR' and are reared under a common programme. The principal aim is the production of saddle horses

19 This stallion comes from the line of white horses founded by the stallion Generalissimus, foaled in 1797, and is a splendid example of the 'Starokladrubsky Kun' that is lovingly reared today in Czechoslovakia in the Kladruby nad Labem stud, founded in 1572

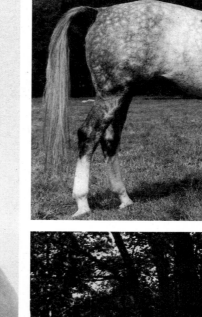

20 The 'dry', expressive head—characteristic of a highly-bred warmblood horse

21 The breeding of Haflingers is particularly encouraged in their original home, the Alpine regions of Europe

22 Descendant of the ancient Iberian horse and the Spanish ancestor of almost all European breeds of saddle horse, the Andalusian in its modern form. The strong influence of Oriental and Barbary horses is still evident in this high-spirited riding horse today

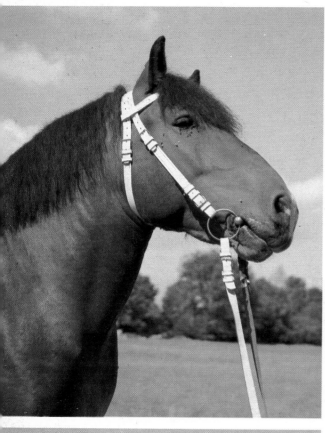

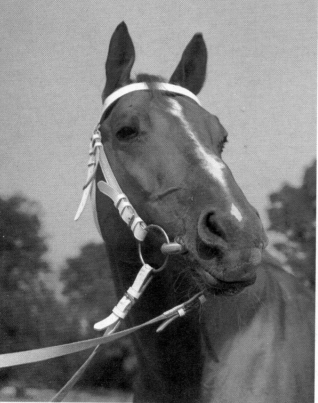

23 A heavy draught horse brings some 800 kg (16 cwt) of weight into play

24 The Noriker is the typical heavy working horse of the Alpine region. It was mentioned by Charlemagne, and in the Middle Ages the Bishops of Salzburg adopted a carefully-planned programme of breeding based on the old breed in the Roman province of Noricum

25 A very highly-bred, fine quality stallion from the Neustadt stud

26 Chestnuts with long, light-coloured manes and tails also occur among heavy draught horses

27 Haflingers' typical colouring—chestnut with long, light-coloured mane and tail—makes them very distinctive and much loved

Previous pages:
28   Federal Austrian stud at Piber: Lipizzaners in the Stubai Alps

29   Haflingers being ridden near the church at Hafling. The small parish on the edge of the Sarntaler Alps south of Merano (northern Italy) gave this breed of ponies its name

30   High-lying mountain pastures provide fodder especially rich in minerals which, together with the intense sunlight, fosters growth and general good health in the horse

31   At an altitude of 2,000 m (6,500 ft) in the Lienz Dolomites

Following page:
32   Herd of Mongolian horses (Photo: A. Vogel)

In the horse, there is a distinction between sexual maturity on the one hand and readiness for use for breeding purposes on the other. Whereas sexual maturity is achieved at an age of about a year to a year and a half, it is well to accept the principle that our leading breeds of horses do not achieve breeding maturity until they are about three to five years of age. This depends upon their speed of growth which in turn is largely determined by breed.

The time at which the stallion is first put to serve and the mare first covered should be chosen to accord with these physiological facts. From a biological point of view it is never a mistake to delay it somewhat. Premature use of the horse (for riding purposes as well) can result in irremediable damage, the consequences of which can be a restriction of the covering capacity because of failure to achieve potential physical development, and reduction in service life, finally affecting the life span of the horse.

The natural mating period for the horse corresponds to the period of increasing daylight following the winter months, that is, it occurs in the spring and early summer. Gestation lasts about eleven months so the foals are born at approximately this same period of the year.

As in many other mammals, the most favourable covering time is determined by the alternation between a short period of darkness and a long period of light in the course of the twenty-four hour rhythm, that is, not solely by the absolute length of daylight. The appropriate light/dark cycle leads to an increase in the production of the follicle-stimulating hormone (FSH) in the anterior pituitary body that in turn triggers off sexual activity and oestrus. Under these conditions, the mares achieve not only maximum readiness for mating but also the most favourable prospect of fertilisation and the production of progeny.

On the basis of these facts, the horse's mating period in the most northerly and most southerly zones of its distribution is only relatively short, while in the tropics as far as about latitudes 20 degrees north and 20 degrees south, where the sun is overhead twice in the year, there are two optimal periods—April/May and October/November. In the countries between about latitudes 50 degrees and 60 degrees north, in central Europe, the months most favourable for successful fertilisation are May to July, at 40 degrees north they are April to July, and at 40 degrees south (New Zealand, Australia) November to December. When mares are taken from the northern to the southern hemisphere or vice versa, the seasons of oestrus adapt to the new locality.

In deciding the date for the mare's covering, both the biological and economic aspects of foaling should be taken into consideration, so it will probably fall in the months of February to April or, at the latest, May. It is most favourable if, at the start of the grazing period, the foals together with the mares are able to feed independently on the fresh green fodder which, especially in the early period of growth, is particularly valuable and rich in proteins, minerals and vitamins. In the climatic conditions of central Europe, this means that a foaling time between February and May is desirable. Under certain circumstances, such as the availability of stable space, the classification of foals into particular age groups, the use of the mares for riding, current stock levels and the labour supply situation, earlier foaling may be desirable.

Successful covering depends upon the mare being in oestrus (in season). Oestrus lasts about five to ten days. Ovulation (rupture of the follicle) takes place about one or two days before the end of oestrus. Chances of fertilisation are high five to two days before the end of the mare's period in season.

After the birth, the mare comes into season again between the fourth and seventh day, irrespective of whether early or late maturity is a characteristic of the breed; depending upon the mare's constitutional tendency, the period of oestrus ends on the tenth to fifteenth day. The normal practice of trying and possibly covering the mare on the ninth day after foaling is correct in principle. In the case of mares with a short period of oestrus, it should be carried out a day or two before that.

It is always advisable to bring the mare to the stallion on the theoretically correct date in order to determine whether or not she is ready to mate, because the possibility of conception is particularly high in the first period of oestrus following a birth. In addition, the mare's contact with another female of her own species or with a male from an unfamiliar stock can trigger off and make visible the external signs of oestrus. While the mare is in season, it is not unusual for her suckling foal to exhibit symptoms akin to diarrhoea as a result of changes in the composition of the mare's milk—a useful indication from which appropriate conclusions can be drawn. The oestrous cycle recurs every three weeks (twenty-one to twenty-five days) but it is clearly dependent upon the individual duration of the period of season, so that each mare establishes her own particular rhythm which can be recorded in tabular form, thus increasing the likelihood of selecting the correct date for covering. If the mare accepts the stallion, covering can follow. It is usually carried out on the second day of oestrus and repeated on the fourth or fifth.

A check is carried out after three weeks (second period of oestrus), or six weeks (third period of oestrus), to determine the success of covering, although the possibility of pseudo-oestrus with existing gestation must be taken into consideration, since abortion of the embryo could be induced. Successful pregnancy can be confirmed by a veterinary surgeon by rectal examination from day 30, from about day 45 to day 120 by the presence of gestation hormones in the blood and, from about day 125, in the urine.

Essential in the handling of a pregnancy are the proper treatment of stallion and mare, regular and appropriate exercise, good physical condition and correct feeding that, in particular, ensures a supply of essential minerals and vitamins.

The stud horse

In choosing a suitable stud horse, it is well worth while seeking the advice of the appropriate breeding organisation. This will have a wide range of information on the stallions that are available, their lineage, and their breeding achievements so far. As a result, it will be possible to establish suitable combinations which allow for selection towards genetic improvement and avoid the possible disadvantage arising from breeding between closely related animals. For the sake of breeding stability, it is as well not to change stallions too frequently, a practice that is understandable if there is a lack of patience and experience, but one that is not to be recommended. A balanced breeding stock can be achieved only if stallions are employed for a long time in one place, even if, as is almost invariably the case, they do not fulfil every requirement. Only in this way it is possible to breed for or correct particular features and characteristics by deliberate planning on a long-term basis.

The keeping of stallions, particularly for breeding purposes, is subject to mandatory government legislation in most countries. In addition, regulations providing for workers' protection and the prevention of epidemics must be observed.

The stud horse should be given as much exercise as possible, being walked, ridden or put with a herd. The practice of bringing the stallion out of the stable only for the purposes of covering, possibly combined with an excessive provision of fodder, is a bad one. It leads to undesirable and dangerous patterns of behaviour, poor performance and a reduced useful life and life expectancy. Loose boxes should be roomy, allowing a reasonable amount of movement. Accredited stallions are valuable breeding animals and every effort should be made to keep them in good health. This means protecting the stallion from injuries resulting from kicks or bites, and from hoof damage and lameness. Quiet handling, cleanliness and good order in the stable are essential.

Successful insemination by the stallion is most likely when spermatozoa of normal quality are ejected through the cervix directly into the mare's uterus. At each copulation the stallion emits some 30 cm^3 (Shetland pony) to 200 cm^3 (heavy draught horse) of fluid containing between 140 and 200 million spermatozoa per cm^3. Quality and quantity of the sperm depend upon the conditions under which the horse is kept, acclimatisation, frequency of use for covering and the degree of sexual stimulation, in addition, the quantity of the sperm is linked to body size which is a function of breed. In their first breeding year, usually at three to five years of age, young stallions should cover only one mare in a day and at intervals of one to two weeks; older stallions serve twice or even several times a day, with at least one rest day a week.

Sperm from the stallion remain viable within the female genital tract for only about forty hours, during which time fertilisation of a mature egg is possible. This is another reason for establishing the exact period of oestrus in the mare. In some mares, the cervix is not fully dilated until towards the end of the period in season, so if she is served before that time, only a small number of the sperm can enter the uterus.

It is, of course, in the interests of the breeder that at the optimal point in the period of oestrus the whole of the seminal fluid ejaculated by the stallion should enter the uterus of the mare. In artificial insemination, with its associated technical potentialities, this is always the case, so that considerably smaller quantities and concentrations of spermatozoa are sufficient to achieve successful fertilisation; the problems lie in assessing correctly that point within the period of oestrus most favourable for fertilisation, and in the quality of the sperm in the semen collected from the stallion.

The period of gestation

It is sensible to breed only from mares of recognised quality that are registered in a stud book and offer good breeding prospects. In the long term, it is necessary to allow only those mares to be served that regularly produce foals and also rear them satisfactorily, and which, for example, have an adequate and lasting supply of milk. The characteristic of fertility is a particularly important one in horses, and in many breeds it has been deliberately fostered by the breeding programme. It is not only hereditary but is also determined by a series of external influences and by the functioning of the mare's sexual organs. So it is advisable to have the mare examined by a vet about two months before the beginning of the stud season. This is particularly recommended in the case of mares who have slipped foals, who have difficulty in conceiving, who exhibit external symptoms of disease of the generative tract or whose foals have suffered from lameness, and in addition, those who have not been served for more than a year and therefore have increased difficulty in conceiving.

In horses, the ratio of the sexes stands at about 98 male births to 100 female. As in all mammals, the sex of the foal is determined at the moment of conception. Since the earliest times, horse breeders have been interested in the possibility of deliberately influencing the sex of the unborn foal; numerous theories have been tested and all manner of advice given to the breeder (see p. 77). But because of a lack of scientific knowledge, none has produced results. As early as 1578, M. Fugger questioned the validity of such traditional practices, but in vain, for even today, incredible notions still circulate concerning sex determination.

There are those who believe they have the secret of deciding the sex of horses. They say that if a mare is covered three days before full moon, she produces a male foal; but if she is served three days after full moon, she conceives a female foal. Others recommend that if a colt is desired, a strip of linen cloth should be tied round the left testicle of the stallion, and round the right testicle if a filly is wanted. Others again believe that a male foal will be born if the mare is mated when the wind is from the north-east; but a female foal if mated when the wind blows from the south (but in these cases, the mare must stand with her hindquarters turned against the wind) . . . And finally, it is claimed by some that the mare will

Mare's oestrous cycle, allowing for constitutional tendency to short or long period of oestrus (five to ten days)

Day	1	2	3	4	5	6	7	8	9	10	11	12	13	14	15	16	17	18	19	20	21	22	23	24	25	26	27	28	29	30
Mares with short period of oestrus	s	s	s	s	s	−	−	−	−	−	−	−	−	−	−	−	−	−	−	−	s	s	s	s	s	−	−	−	−	−
Mares with long period of oestrus	s	s	s	s	s	s	s	s	s	s	−	−	−	−	−	−	−	−	−	−	−	−	−	−	−	s	s	s	s

− = not in season   s = in season

conceive a colt if the stud horse dismounts to her right side but a filly if he gets down to her left.

Many mares have a tendency to express the stallion's sperm immediately after copulation, and should therefore straight away be walked quietly for a short time, because while moving, they are unable to express. Such problems already occupied the Greeks of classical antiquity; their quite simple ideas on these matters were taken over by M. Fugger, among others, whose theories featured in the literature of horse breeding and horse management until this century and had wide practical application. Although many of his ideas are still valid today, the following advice cannot be accepted.

As soon as the act of copulation is over and the stallion withdraws from the mare, one or two stable-lads standing ready with cold water, must immediately pour it on the mare so that she retains the semen and does not allow it to flow out; then the mare's fettered feet are freed rapidly and she is walked slowly and beaten on the croup with a switch so that she contracts her body, bending inwards, the more surely to retain the semen... The stud horse must be led round gently, but neither too close to nor too far from the mare, so that she does not lose sight of him, as a result of which his image is impressed upon her senses to such an extent that the foal resembles the stallion...

Gestation in the mare averages eleven months (336 days) but fluctuates considerably. The following tendencies are general. Duration of gestation depends upon the month of conception; there is a general inclination towards an increase in the period of gestation from November to May/June and a decrease from July/August to October, with a difference of twelve to fifteen days on average at the extremes. With normal foaling, the period of gestation fluctuates between about 320 and 350 days, but pregnancies of more than 365 and under 300 days are not unknown. The mare herself may have an individual tendency towards a particularly short or extended gestation period. The duration also depends upon the characteristic of early or late maturing in particular breeds. Heavy draught horses (coldbloods), for example, are carried for a shorter time than are warmblood breeds, especially those of Oriental origin. A gestation of less than 240 days (thirty-four weeks) is considered an abortion (stillbirth); under certain conditions, it is possible for individual foals born in the thirty-fifth week (premature birth) to be kept alive.

The incidence of twin births in horses can be put at about 1 per cent, although it is rather higher in English thoroughbreds. Most twins are not carried to full term, and because of the often drastic reduction in the period of gestation and the associated underdevelopment of the foetuses, chances of survival are poor. Only some 15 per cent of these foals live more than a year. It sometimes happens that twins are born at different dates; the *Sporting Magazine*, or 'Monthly Calendar of the Transactions of the Turf, the Chase, and every other Diversion interesting to the Man of Pleasure, Enterprise and Spirit', for August 1794 reports one such example in England.

In the season of ninety-three, Bergem, who keeps a house, known by the sign of the Wrestlers, on Aldenham Common, Herts, had a poney-mare covered by a horse of Ricketts Johnson, Esq. of Bushey, named Sceptre... A little while previous to the time he expected she would foal, he removed her for the convenience of pasture, &c. from the common, to a close adjoining his home, where she shortly after dropped a foetus (if I may use the expression) in the form of a foal, from the smallness of which, it was apparent, she had not gone her full time, although more than eleven months were elapsed since she was covered by Sceptre; it was also so extremely weak and feeble, as not to give any hopes of its even attaining maturity, and so frightfully ill-formed, that Bergem was inclined and universally advised to destroy it. He, however, permitted it to continue with the mare, who, after an interval of fourteen days, to the astonishment of every one, produced a colt-foal of the most lively and promising appearance, which, with the foetus, still sucks the dam.

During pregnancy, the mare should continue to work normally; feeding and general treatment are also unchanged. But the mare becomes increasingly sensitive to the effect of hard blows on the abdominal wall, such as the impact of shafts when roads are rough, to reversing when working with a team or being ridden, jumping, pulling heavy loads, sudden acceleration, and to slipping on wet or icy roads, or falling. Abortions resulting from mechanical causes of this kind have been observed particularly in the third, fifth and eighth month of gestation. Anything that may normally upset a horse is particularly harmful to the pregnant mare, such as tainted or indigestible food, over-exertion, lack of exercise, chills or colic attacks, even rough, unskilled handling.

From about the twenty-fifth week of gestation the movements of the mare become distinctly more ponderous due to the increasing size and weight of the embryo; she is generally more placid and her appetite increases. From about the twenty-sixth week the independent movements of the embryo can be felt and seen at the right lower flank, particularly after the mare stands up or drinks.

During the last weeks before foaling, the mare should be watched carefully. She must be moved in good time into a box appropriate to her size, where there is a liberal supply of bedding. An orderly stable is essential; in particular, strangers, children and dogs have no place there.

It is a wise precaution to remove the mare's shoes before the birth, but long enough beforehand for the mare to be able to maintain her balance easily while it is done. Preparations should be made for difficulties that may arise: water, adequate lighting, two each of traction ropes and tethers with cross-pieces, disinfectant, equipment for heating water for washing, soap and towel, oil, scissors and ligature bandage (both sterile), wide-necked jar of iodine or antiseptic tincture for treating the umbilicus, information about the vet's 'on call' arrangements.

A foal is born

In general it can be said that if the mare carries for eleven months or more, the foal will be fully developed at birth. If the birth occurs substantially before the eleventh month, the foetus has not reached adequate maturity; if, nevertheless, it lives and the dam does not feed it particularly well, such a foal will fail to make up in body weight and body size for its poor start.

Symptoms indicating the imminence of a normal birth include the following:

- Two to eight days beforehand the mare will 'show wax'—resin-like beads consisting of dried colostrum will form on the teats of the udder; milk may also be secreted. Two to six days beforehand the milk veins on the abdominal wall and the udder become swollen; the udder itself becomes increasingly sensitive to touch.
- Four to five days beforehand the vagina becomes swollen and inflamed and secretes more mucus.

- The abdominal wall sinks lower; in addition, one or two days beforehand, the flanks deepen, the pelvic ligaments relax (known as 'slackening') so that the mare's croup and hips stand out more clearly; the foetus enters the birth canal.
- Half an hour to five hours before parturition the preliminary contractions become perceptible. The mare is restless, lies down and gets up quickly, lies with forelegs extended in front of her, excretes dung and urine or attempts to do so, begins to sweat, breaks off abruptly from eating, groans and strains. In the course of the premonitory contractions the foetus is moved into the final position. The cervix opens and becomes dilated—usually a painful process.

Before and during the birth, cleanliness and calm are essential. Immediately beforehand the mare's anus, vulva, udder, legs and feet should be washed. Since the distended belly and udder may be very sensitive, this should be done with care, so that subsequent difficulties do

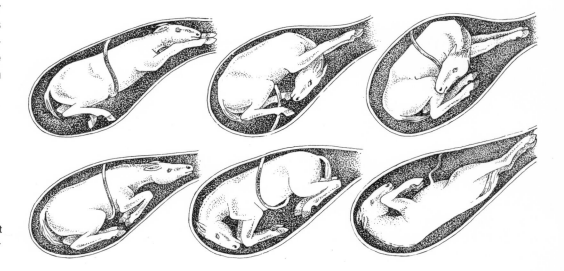

Normal foetal positions for the horse
The most common position is (a); the birth is without complications. Any other position may cause varying degrees of difficulty

not arise when the foal first searches for milk.

Most domesticated mares give birth lying down, rarely while standing. The birth itself is initiated by powerful contractions. First to appear is the 'water sack', the outer foetal envelope or chorion, that has assisted in the dilation of the birth canal and the expulsion of the foetus. It bursts as it passes through the vagina. Usually the foal is born with head presentation, so its front feet, with the head lying on them, appear first, enclosed in a second sac, the amnion. All other positions can make the birth very difficult, so possible complications must be anticipated and veterinary help made available at short notice.

Once the foal is expelled, the foetal membrane (amnion) containing the amniotic fluid has to be broken open by the foal's own exertions. If this does not happen, it must be split open immediately or the foal will suffocate. If possible, the foal should be placed on fresh bedding.

When the mare gets to her feet after the birth, or as a result of the foal's struggling,

Parturition
a The foetus alters its position, period of dilation, first stage of labour
b The foetus moves into the upper position
c Expulsion begins

the umbilical cord usually ruptures without intervention at its weakest point, close to the foal's abdominal wall. If it does not do so, it must be broken at that point by twisting, while supporting it from beneath. Only if tearing is not possible (smooth-edged wounds close up less readily), is the umbilical cord to be cut through with disinfected scissors. But this action should be delayed as long as possible, at least until the supply of blood through it to the foal ceases. In every case the stump of the cord should be straightened out and dipped into a jar of iodine or antiseptic tincture prepared for this purpose, and this treatment should be repeated after a few days.

To avoid risk of infection and behavioural disturbances, no particular assistance should be given if the birth is proceeding normally. Nevertheless, events must be monitored carefully because if obstetric complications arise, only immediate and expert help can prevent the lives of mare and foal being threatened.

Since the newborn foal is extremely susceptible to infection, all assistance and intervention, even after foaling, should be restricted or carried out with strict attention to hygiene. In particular, the navel, nose and mouth cavity should be protected from infection.

The birth, including the second, expulsive stage, lasts about twenty to thirty minutes. Parts of the afterbirth are expelled together with the foal, the rest is discharged within the next half hour. It should be removed, together with the soiled bedding, and burned. If the afterbirth is retained for longer than two or three hours, the vet should be consulted. Under no circumstances should the afterbirth be removed forcibly.

A start in life

After foaling, both mare and foal are equally in need of care and attention, particularly in the first few days. The mare should be towelled dry immediately after she has given birth, and protected from draughts. During the first and possibly the second week, she should be given easily digested feedstuff, rich in nutrients and minerals and low in bulk, that does not overburden the digestive organs. But there should not be any fundamental change in the mare's diet. All the commonly accepted rules for correct feeding should be followed with particular care at this time. Immediately after the birth, and for several days, food should be given frequently and in small quantities; many

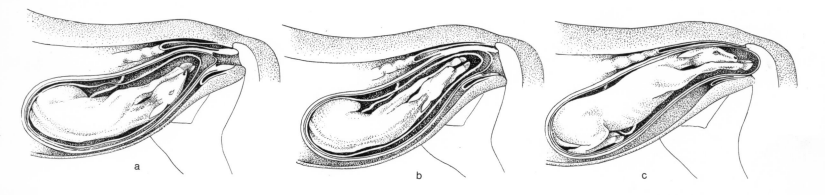

mares eat relatively little soon after the strenuous exertions of giving birth, but on recovery from their exhaustion, and possibly as a result of a new feeling of 'emptiness' in the stomach, they are particularly hungry and may easily overeat.

Five hours after the birth at the latest, the foal should take the first milk, the colostrum, popularly known as 'beestings'. Sometimes if the foal has been licked by the dam and pushed towards the udder, it is necessary to put it to the udder straight away. This should be done carefully because the udder and the area round about are often swollen and taut, and so very sensitive. Mares with their first foal can be particularly difficult here and offer considerable resistance; they kick out at the foal (and the person putting the foal to the teat). If necessary, the udder should be relieved by carefully drawing off milk before letting the foal suck. But it may equally well be that the mare is ticklish and for that reason prevents the foal from sucking or even touching the udder. The only remedy is to be patient and ensure adequate protection from the mare's kicking for the stable-worker and foal.

Not only is the colostrum very rich in energy and easily digestible but it also contains specially effective minerals, vitamins and proteins, as well as antibodies which protect the foal from infectious diseases to which it is particularly susceptible. At the same time, it assists discharge of meconium (the first faeces) that has accumulated in the foal's system during embryonic development and which in the horse, compared with other mammals, is extremely dense and voluminous. It is discharged primarily on the second day. For these reasons, it is a mistake to milk off the colostrum. It is equally disadvantageous if this valuable first milk is given off by the mare before the birth and so lost to the foal. In this case, veterinary help may be required to remove the meconium. Retention of meconium, which manifests itself in the foal in increasing abdominal pain and unwillingness to feed, is a critically dangerous condition and requires immediate veterinary attention.

Duration of the colostrum period varies between individual mares and between breeds. It can be assumed that the transition to normal lactation (true milk) can take place after only eighteen hours, but it may sometimes be as long as forty-eight hours. In any case, every hour that the foal can devote to sucking during the first and second day of life is precious, particularly since frequency of sucking and total duration of milk intake should be especially high in newborn foals because they provide the essential foundation for the start of growth.

After a week or two, the mare and foal should be allowed out to pasture or for exercise for an hour or two at a time in mild, windless weather; after another three or four weeks, the mare may be put back to work for an hour or two. But during the first two months the foal should be given an opportunity to take milk at least every two hours. Later on, intervals between feeds of four to five hours are adequate but, in the interests of the foal's optimal growth, they are better kept short. It is useful if the foal can run with the mare during longer periods of work. Of course, good preparation and, particularly at the beginning, adequate vigilance are essential. In this way, the foal is able to adapt successfully to its new environment, it learns patterns of movement—important for the future sporting horse—and its entire organic structure is trained.

The mare's feeding should be in accordance with the requirements of lactation and of her work; it must be determined individually in each case, so that she is able to feed her foal well without excessive demands on her own physical reserves, but on the other hand is not overfed.

Insufficient milk in the mare can to some extent be made good by feeding diluted cow's milk to the foal. The milk should be diluted with a third of its volume of lukewarm boiled water to which 20 g sugar per litre (approximately $\frac{1}{2}$oz per pint) has been added. When given, it should be at a temperature of about 28 °C (82 °F). The water can be replaced gradually by skimmed milk.

The Great Age of Horse Breeding— the Ancient Orient

Two-wheeled war chariots first appeared in the region of Assyria-Babylonia some time after 1800 BC; but it was the Sumerians who were reputed to be the inventors of the heavy, single-axled war chariots with disc wheels which were quite primitive in their coarse construction and were still drawn by Asiatic wild asses (onagers). The first to use more mobile chariots of lighter construction, equipped with spoked wheels and drawn by four stallions, were the Churittes, who from about 1700 BC spread across Europe as far as Sweden and Norway, to Crete and North Africa and as far as the coast of China. In Britain, by the middle of the second millennium BC, it is thought that chariot races were possibly being held in association with funeral ceremonials on a 2,700-m (2,950-yd) track near the Bronze Age site of Stonehenge on Salisbury Plain. From about the eighteenth century BC, this development was accompanied by the breeding of heavier but also faster and larger horses of at least 14.3 hands, so that from this time onwards at the latest, small and large horses, primitive horses and highly-bred pack horses, saddle and chariot horses existed side by side.

The knowledge necessary for systematic breeding by selection probably came from the Churittes and was passed on by them after about 1700 BC to the other peoples of the Near East. Three hundred years later, their empire of Mitanni in the upper regions of the Euphrates was conquered by the Hittites, who themselves already had considerable experience in the field of breeding, rearing and training horses. They kept horses primarily for military purposes and for hunting, but also bred pack horses for hauling heavy baggage carts.

The Assyrians who lived in the region of the lower Euphrates and Tigris and who had practised agriculture, horticulture and stockbreeding, and engaged extensively in trade since the second millennium BC, also used heavy horses to pull the plough in the thirteenth and fourteenth centuries BC.

To the Hittites—and certainly not to them alone—the horse was one of the most valuable of possessions. For example:

1 sheep cost 1 half shekel (4 g silver)
1 ox cost 12 half shekels (48 g silver)
1 blue wollen garment cost 20 half shekels (80 g silver)
1 fine set of clothing cost 30 half shekels (120 g silver)

According to paragraph 65 of the relevant Book of Hittite Laws, the price of a horse, depending upon age and potential use, was as follows:

If it is a draught horse, the price is 20 half shekels [80 g silver];
For a horse, 14 half shekels of silver [56 g] is the price;
For a yearling stallion the price is 10 half shekels of silver [40 g];
For a yearling pack mare the price is 15 half shekels [60 g silver].

Hybrids bred for domestic use by crossing horse and ass, probably mainly mules, were particularly expensive, costing more than the initial species of ass or horse, for 'the price of a mule is a mina' (120 half shekels = 480 g silver).

Some of the native Anatolian breeds still existing today, such as the Cukurova horse, can be regarded as descendants of Hittite horses.

The army of the Hittites included both foot soldiers and charioteers. The war chariots were manned by a team of three (in Egypt, only two): the driver of the chariot, his shield bearer and the chariot-warrior armed with spear and arrows. Following the invention of the swivelling front axle in Asia Minor or northern Syria, two-axled horse-drawn chariots were favoured by the Hittites from about the fourteenth/thirteenth century BC, and in the course of the first millennium BC, their use spread to Assyria, Elam, eastern and south-eastern Europe.

Among European cultic chariots, there were multi-axled vehicles from as early as the Bronze Age. Between 1300 and 1200 BC, for instance, there was the sun chariot from Trundholm (Denmark), about 1200 BC the three-wheeled chariot from Dupljaja (Yugoslavia) and the four-wheeled urn carriages from Peckatel

and Milavec, all of which had rigid axles and were therefore not associated structurally with the four-wheeled vehicles that were being used in the Ancient Orient at about the same time. These links did not show themselves in practical carriage construction in Europe until the end of the Bronze Age (eighth to fifth century BC).

The instructions for the 'Acclimatisation and Training of Chariot Horses', written by Kikkuli in the thirteenth century BC in the Hittite language on cuneiform writing tablets that were found in Boghaz-köi, include the following:

> When the horses
> have eaten, you will remove oil and urine;
> three times you will work through with each of them
> half of the full extent of training;
> then once again you will pour out barley for them;
> they will eat;
> with covers, they will walk;
> then you will free them, besprinkle them with water, allow oil
> to drip on to them, give them water to drink;
> for each of them you will shake out by hand two measures of
> barley;
> they will eat;
> by hand you will give each one and a half measures of roasted
> corn, each one half measure of barley; they will eat;
> at daybreak they will feed on fresh herbs;
> when daylight comes, you will harness them, release them,
> give them water to drink . . .

The methods employed in caring for, breeding and working horses in the Ancient Orient became widespread in India (about 1800 BC), Egypt (about 1700 BC), Libya (about 1400 BC) and in northern Arabia (about 1300 BC). Until the first millennium BC, horses were principally used as draught and haulage animals; apparently stirrups and stirrup leathers were unknown, although snaffle bits made of strong curved wire were already in use in the period of the Maikop civilisation (third millennium BC) and in about 1700 BC, the Huksos were using bridles with snaffles.

At about the same time as the use of copper and bronze was spreading across the Sahara to the south and south-west in the thirteenth and twelfth centuries BC, this region, then still savannah-like and partially inhabited, was being crossed by single-axled carts. The 'chariot route' began on the coast of Cyrenaica and ended in the upper regions of the Niger on a level with Gao and Timbuktu. As a result, the domestic horse made its way into territories that, as far as we know, it had not occupied in its wild state, such as the coast of the Gulf of Guinea in the south of West Africa. The Togo pony living there today is still reminiscent of this early domestic horse in outward appearance. The 'chariot peoples' of the Sahara probably drew their harness horses to a large extent from the Cretan-Mycenaean cultures of the fourteenth and thirteenth centuries BC. Brentjes wrote that the influence of Crete and Mycenae was 'discernible in representations of horses well into the Sahara and as far as the great curve of the Niger.'

On the trade routes between Fezzan and Gao or Timbuktu and on the 'chariot route', horse-drawn vehicles were common for some hundreds of years. As the Sahara became increasingly inhospitable during the first millennium BC, developing into a desert almost impossible to cross, the links between northern and central Africa were completely severed. In addition to the serious social and cultural consequences for the people of the African continent, one result was the complete isolation of horse breeding in western and central Africa.

In Egypt, Babylon and Israel, horse management and knowledge of horse breeding stood at a particularly high level. Horses of many different breeds were used for hunting and transport. Among the earliest written documents, such as stud books, rules and directions for training, and receipts, is a letter from King Aplahanda of Karkemish to King Zimrilim of Mari (about 1700 BC), referring to the Harsamna stud in northern Syria:

> Concerning the white horses, I have spoken [ie, to himself] and answered: white horses for the two-wheeled war chariot are not on hand. I will send word and from there, where they are on hand, white horses will be dispatched hither. Until that time, I shall have red-brown horses brought from Harsamna . . .

As early as 1800 BC, there were studs in the Near East with vast stocks of horses, in which particular colours were deliberately established and maintained. The stud belonging to the Governor of Babylon in the fifth century BC is said by Herodotus to have included 800 stallions and 16,000 mares.

Kassitic texts from the fourteenth century BC contain information on the sex, colour, lineage and ownership of horses. In detailing genealogy, the mare was ignored and only the sire was named. Where its name was not known, the term *sumaktar*, normally denoting the children of a slave woman, was used. The same source contains a list of ten chosen stallions under the heading 'Horses that have been released for covering'.

Noble, fast horses with good staying power certainly existed in Egypt from the middle of the second century BC. The inscription on the great Sphinx stele tells us about the Pharaoh Amenophis (1526–05 BC): 'He reared horses, and there were none to equal them. They did not tire when he held the reins, they did not sweat even at a very fast run . . .' In about 1300 BC, the following love song of an Egyptian maiden was 'made by the scribe Sobek', and is a further indication of the exceptional characteristics and high quality of the Egyptian horse of that time:

Oh, wouldst thou but come—
Like a horse of the king,
Chosen out of a thousand stud farms;
The best in the stable;
Given preference in feeding
By its master,
Who knows [the performance of] its feet;
If it hears the sound of the whip
It cannot go slowly,
The best Asiatic charioteer
Cannot outstrip it!
How strongly does the heart of the sister feel
That her brother is no longer far away.

Evidence suggests that the shoeing of horses was known in Egypt in about 1500 BC, and at the time of the Pharaoh Tutank-

The Trundholm sun chariot. Bronze, about 1200 BC, Copenhagen Museum

hamun (approximately 1346–36 BC), eye-blinkers were being used. The Ancient Indian Vedas (written between 1300 and 600 BC) and classical Sanskrit literature deal in considerable detail with the horse, which extended its range across India from the north in the early part of the second millennium BC. Initially harnessed to chariots, horses were later used also for transporting loads and possibly to draw the plough, and from the first millennium onwards they were ridden.

According to an Ancient Indian religious belief, mankind is descended from a mare. The horse was deified and revered as the image of the sun. The practice of Aśvamedha (Sanskrit: horse sacrifice) originated in the eleventh century BC. A particularly valuable stallion was selected a year in advance and in the company of 100 mares and 400 warriors was allowed to roam the land freely until, on the day of sacrifice, it was strangled. The queen then performed the ritual act of procreation with it, so that the power of the horse might be transmitted to the royal couple and their descendants.

In the Rig-Veda (about 1200 BC), this belief is expressed in a variety of ways. Sūryā, the radiant daughter of the sun god Savitr, is courted and won by the celestial suitors, in particular by the twin sons of heaven, Aśvin (he who is equipped with horses) and Násatya (the nostril bearer), who move across the heavens in their chariot drawn by winged horses. The Indians considered them to be generous helpers in time of need and skilful physicians, a belief that recurs in Greek mythology in the form of the Dioscuri—Castor and Pollux, twin sons of Zeus—who were begotten of a mare, and in Christian mythology as the saints Cosmas and Damian.

In the Rig-Veda, Dirghatamas sings:

When first you whinnied, at your creation,
Arising from the dark waters
With the wings of the falcon,
With the haunches of the stag,
Great praises were sung to you, O Arwan.
Yama gave it, Vrta harnessed it,
Indra was the first to mount it,
Ganghara caught hold of its bridle;
From the sun, you bright-shining gods,
You have made the horse.

The great Ancient Indian epic Mahābhārata, composed between 1000 and 800 BC, which throws light on almost every aspect of In-

dian life, includes a detailed account of the general theory of the horse and the treatment of its diseases. It provides information on horse breeding, on the kinds and varieties of horses and their special characteristics. At about the time when the Greek historian and essayist Xenophon wrote his lastingly important works, we find in the Indian *Arthaśāstra* (first century BC), written by Kautaly, the chancellor to King Tschandragupta Maurya, detailed information on the training, stabling, management and grooming of the horse, and its veterinary care. Many essays still exist on the subject of the medical treatment of horses, written in the earliest Indian period. This is not only because the Old Indian rulers held a monopoly in the trade of horses, but also because the possession of horses—and elephants—was, and continued to be throughout the following two millennia, the prerogative of the rich, whose power was based to a large extent on the horse as the only rapid means of communication, transport and movement from place to place. So it is understandable that all Old Indian writings on hippology and hippiatry should express the idea that the most beautiful and faultless horse symbolises the prosperity of its master, and that the most meticulous care and attention must be bestowed upon the horse.

In the region of Palestine, the horse had been known since about 1400 BC but, because of the Law of Moses, the keeping of horses was looked down upon by the Jews. If they captured a horse, they would cut its tendons and kill it. In the Bible, Joshua 11, in the context of the direction that the tribes of Canaan were to be slain, we find the following text:

And the LORD said unto Joshua, 'Be not afraid because of them; for tomorrow about this time will I deliver them up all slain before Israel; thou shalt hough [hamstring] their horses, and burn their chariots with fire.

So Joshua came, and all people of war with him, against them by the waters of Meron suddenly; and they fell upon them.

And the LORD delivered them into the hand of Israel, who smote them, and chased them unto great Zidon, and unto Misrephothmaim, and unto the valley of Mizpeh eastward; and they smote them, until they left them none remaining.

And Joshua did unto them as the LORD bade him: he houghed their horses, and burnt their chariots with fire . . .

David, King of Israel, who lived in the first half of the tenth century BC, was probably the first to disregard the law concerning the keeping of horses. During the reign of his son Solomon, stables for large numbers of horses were developed. Excavations in Megiddo, Egdon, Hazar and Thaalnach have brought to light stable complexes each with 450 horse boxes and accommodation for 150 chariots, with servicing alleys, rough-cast paving, fodder cribs and a water supply. According to tradition, the horses came there first from Egypt and the Hittite Mitanni kingdom and, after the destruction of Mitanni, from Cilicia, particularly from the fertile plains of Koa.

The Iranians living in central Asia in about the year 1000 BC, were farmers and stock breeders. They bred noble horses of great renown that were used for riding and driving. In the Ancient Orient, the Bactrian horse was considered for many centuries the epitome of the ideal horse. The pre-Iranian tribes yielded in the face of pressure from the East brought about by the unification of China. The eastern tribes, such as the Parthians (the term *Pahlave* denoting the Parthian rulers can be translated as 'Bactrians') and the Choresmians, moved south-westwards; the western tribes, such as the Medes and Persians, spread as far as the Persian Gulf by the end of the eighth century BC; and the northern tribes, such as the Sarmatians and Scythians, moved to the steppe regions of the Caucasus and, later on, also to those of southern Russia. In about the tenth to ninth centuries BC, the Scythians crossed the Ural river westwards, remaining at first to the north of the Caucasus.

Detail from 'Chigikanne': riders, horse-drawn chariot and hunters with dogs, about 630 BC, Museo di Villi Giuba, Rome

Between the eighth and sixth centuries BC, and particularly among those peoples in the Eurasian steppes between the Don and the Far East, there was a transition to herd-based nomadism, with horse breeding playing a dominant role. It is known as horse nomadism. Agriculture was discontinued, permanent settlements were gradually abandoned or reduced in size until all that remained were some *kurgans*, burial chambers covered with great mounds of earth. They have provided a rich source of information on the horses of that time, their equipment, harnessing, saddling and bridling, and on the manners and customs of horse management.

When the pre-Iranian tribes migrated into the mountain ranges and high plateaux of present-day Iran (the land of Arya), they turned increasingly to the extremely lucrative trades of horse breeding and horse management, and also to the discipline of military equestrianism. The difficulty of the terrain here meant that they could not use chariots successfully, so they developed the skill of riding in all its technical and tactical variations, and also the necessary breeds for this purpose. The Caspian pony, discovered as recently as 1965 in the fairly inaccessible fringes of the Caspian Sea (northern Iran), can be seen as the descendant of this ancient horse population. We find such horses in the second millennium BC in Iraq on terracotta ornamental plaques, increasingly more frequently from the eighth century BC onwards on Assyrian seals, reliefs and statues, and from the sixth century BC on Iranian ones.

As a result of wars, in payment of tribute and in the course of trade, horses of this type were moved into neighbouring regions and other countries. The nucleus of the small herd of Caspian ponies that was discovered in our time was taken to the Norouzabat experimental field station near Teheran where, since then, the ponies have been bred systematically.

The small size of the Caspian pony—it stands at only 10 to 12 hands—is undoubtedly less than that of the Old Iranian (Old Persian) horse, and may be the result of a long period of isolation. The most striking of its morphological features are precisely those that were depicted in the Old Iranian period: the broadly developed forehead, the concave facial profile, small ears, basically wedge-shaped head narrowing sharply to a small mouth, the specific form of neck, back and croup and the oval shape of the hoof, which in its extreme sturdiness is more reminiscent of that of the onager than of the horse. If one ignores the overall scale, this breed's similarity to the Arab is striking and also relates to Oriental horses of all groups.

In the year 612 BC, the Medes and Chaldeans destroyed the city of Nineveh, at that time the hub of the Ancient Orient, and so conquered the kingdom of the Assyrians. They had developed equestrianism to a very high level, on a basis of large stud farms with vast areas of pasture. There was a variety of grass particularly valuable in the rearing of horses that was imported into Italy by the Greeks and Romans in about AD 100 under the name of *medicae poe*, which later developed into the generic name *medicago*. In the fifteenth century, this plant came via Spain to France and Belgium; it is known in English as lucerne (and popularly as purple *medick*). The Medes' wide experience in the sphere of horse breeding and management was reflected particularly in the Nicaean breed of horse. Oppian (300 BC) writes:

The horses of Nicaea are the most beautiful, worthy of only powerful rulers, they are magnificent, move with speed under their rider, obey the bridle willingly, they carry their arched muzzle high and proud, their golden mane streams out splendidly.

Obviously, selective breeding for the feature of a Roman nose (ram-headedness) was in accord with the aesthetic criteria of that time. The same reason can be given for the outward appearance of the Old Indian Chandella horse. This breed features in temple reliefs in the district of Khajuraho (northern Madhya-Pradesh, central India) dating from the tenth and ninth centuries BC, which depict horses with a distinctly convex nose line, very curving neck, straight back and round croup. Similar representations of horses can be seen in mural paintings in the Old Indian cave temples of Ajanta (Dekhan) dating from the period 700 to 400 BC, and in reliefs on the great stupa (Buddhist shrine) in Sanoi from the first century BC. Ram-headed horses are still found today in Kathiawar, which was ruled by Khajuraho at the time of the Chandella dynasty. In early times, there were also ram-headed horses in China, Gaul, Britain and Spain which have genealogical links with today's Kladruber horse in Czechoslovakia. Ram-headedness must be seen as a fashion trend, but one that was not particularly widespread.

The horses of the Parthians living to the east of Nicaea are described in old manuscripts as noble horses, gleaming in magnificent colours and fearing no danger. Under Cyrus the Great (559–29 BC), the Medes were defeated by the Persians in 549 BC. The latter fought with great arrays of war chariots. When they took control of Bactria, they also adopted Bactrian ideas on horse breeding and riding, which they developed and extended. Chari-

ots were still used under Darius III (336—30 BC), but were finally superseded by mounted troops.

With the expansion of the Persian kingdom under Cyrus the Great, eastwards to the Amudarja and Indus, westwards to the Sea of Marmara, and under his son who succeeded him, Cambyses II, as far as Egypt, this style of horse management, breeding and utilisation, including the use of the horse for transport and the development and deployment of cavalry, extended across virtually the whole of the Ancient Orient.

In order to rid their horses of timidity, the Persians accustom them to noise and the clash of arms, and make a great din, so that in battle, they shall not fear the clanking of arms and the thunder of swords against shields. They throw effigies of corpses made from straw-filled sacks in front of their horses' hooves, so that they become accustomed to trampling on the dead in battle, and do not shy away in fear, making themselves unserviceable for the craft of war . . . [Aelianus, about 200 BC]

Horse Nomads and Their Heritage

The horse nomads were able to obtain a good many of the essentials of life from the horse: milk and the cheese they made from it, as well as meat and fat; the horse served as a beast of burden and a mount for riding. Like certain sedentary peoples of Asia, they developed a fairly complicated cult based on the horse, which was taken over by some European tribes such as the Magyars, Slavs and Teutons. For example, sacred horses, already familiar in the shape of Kantakha, the horse of Buddha, and the Oracle Horse of Rügen, and also found in the Svantevit cult, were usually white.

Other traditions included the adornment of sacrificial horses and the selection of a white horse for sacrifice. There was also the practice of cult racing and competition riding among the Avars, Slavs and Teutons. The Scythians living in south-eastern Europe in the sixth to fourth centuries BC would inter as many as forty horses in the burial tombs of princes; there was a similar practice at approximately the same time in China. In the fourteenth century AD, horses were still sacrificed and placed in the burial chamber of a dead Mongol ruler. Among Turkic peoples, this custom, unchanged in its basic elements, was still practised as late as the nineteenth century. The Chuvashes, for example, would slaughter a white horse in the open air to mark public ceremonial occasions, and for family celebrations, a foal. The funeral feast always included horsemeat. Federov and Davydov, writing in the nineteenth century, tell how every Chuvash must sacrifice a horse or foal to the *Keremet* (sacred shrine) to avoid a poor harvest and a severe winter.

From the Rig-Veda it can be inferred that the practice of horse sacrifice is as old as that of horse domestication itself. Among the Germanic peoples, the worship of the horse was particularly marked and horses occur even in the realm of the Norse gods. Almost all the Germanic gods, the Aesir, are mounted. In addition to the sun horses and summer horses, there are also night and winter horses, as well as cloud horses, from whose appearance prophecies can be made. There is also the concept of water horses, thunder and lightning horses. Included here are the *alfs*, *alps* or *albs* (equivalent to English elves), which live as incubi or evil spirits under the horse's stable; if a horse is restless or sick, it is because an *alf* is pressing down upon it; from this comes the German name for a bad dream, *Alptraum*. Equivalent to the *alf* is the Old Norse *mara*, from which derives the word 'nightmare'. Wotan (Wuotan, Odin) riding the white horse Sleipnir, as father of the gods, rules supreme over life and death, and thus is the Prince of the Dead. The concept of 'death mounted on horseback' (which also appears in the Apocalypse in the Bible), as represented by Dürer and others, has its roots here.

Arabian stallion Haleb, foaled in 1901. After a drawing by H. Davenport, showing the purchase of the horse

Bolt-lock fetters, used by nomadic Bedouin tribes to fetter their horses

An Arabian saddle horse is fettered (Photo: Stein)

Veneration of the horse is also reflected in Christian belief in, for example, the horsemen saints such as Saint George, who, mounted on a white horse, slew the dragon with his spear and became patron saint of horsemen; and Saint Martin, a Hungarian, who gave his cloak to a beggar he met near Amiens and saved him from freezing to death. Saint Eustachius was successor to Diana, Roman goddess of the hunt, and is represented in the company of a hind with golden antlers, since he was once regarded as patron saint of the hunt. This characteristic was transferred to Saint Hubert in about AD 700. The anniversary of his death on 3 November is, in Europe, the occasion for huntsmen and horsemen to celebrate his memory in the Hubert's Day Hunt, which in its original form had a high moral purpose: the rejection of indiscriminate hunting, protection of game animals and of hunting, and the love and care of animals.

According to our present-day views on sportsmanship, the hunting of wild animals in all its varieties, particularly as practised in the European feudal courts of the Middle Ages, was extraordinarily cruel and violent. The real patron saint of horses is Saint Eligius, the substitute as it were for the Celtic horse goddess, Epona. He provides protection from vicious horses and so is also the patron saint of farriers.

Until well into the sixteenth century, across the entire range of territory between China and south-west Asia and eastern Europe inhabited by horse nomads, there were regularly recurring nomadic raids which, every three to four hundred years, virtually laid waste the areas that were overrun, destroyed those regions where farmers had settled and the towns, reduced cultivated land, often supplied with irrigation systems, to vast pastures or to desert, and exterminated the population of whole tracts of land. Among them were the invasions of the Huns and Mongols which in part extended deep into Europe.

The path along which the nomadic riders moved westwards from that time onwards, in order to feed their herds and to acquire wealth by plunder, led along the Black Sea and the Mediterranean. They moved either along the northern route between the Urals and the Caspian Sea into eastern and central Europe, or to the south of the Caspian Sea and the Mediterranean across North Africa and the Strait of Gibraltar to western Europe. In both cases they were accompanied by their lightweight, tough, untiring saddle horses. On the eastern borders of Poland and Hungary they met with the ponderous style of riding and driving that originally came from Roman antiquity, and at the same time with correspondingly heavier, less mobile horses.

Growth and Early Management

The term 'growth', applied to mammals, is taken to mean the general increase in body mass that begins with cell division and proceeds as cell multiplication and differentiation. In the case of prenatal growth at the embryonic stage, the simple increase in body mass as an isolated factor may have a significance secondary to the development of new organs and new body parts, but is nevertheless always present. In postnatal growth there is a continuous increase in mass. The process of growth continues as long as the construction of organic material (anabolism) exceeds its breakdown (catabolism); it is the consequence of the overall metabolic process. The capacity for growth in the mammal, that is, its constitutional predisposition to a quite specific course of growth, to a particular ultimate size and to the termination of growth at a particular point, is a genetically-determined characteristic of the species, eg the 'horse', and also of the breed, eg the 'heavy draught horse'. It depends upon numerous interrelated factors within the living animal, such as hormones and enzymes, the state of cell differentiation, the state of water absorption (ie, alterations during growth in the content of water relative to that of dry substances), upon the process of ageing and on the relationship between the animal and its environment, which includes diet, vitamin and mineral supply, climatic factors, and active movement (early training).

Development within the womb

Particularly in the first few months of gestation, the placenta and embryo enjoy high priority in the mare's metabolism. Yet the metabolic rate of the embryo and placenta decreases during development; that of the placenta ceases completely at a very early stage. Placenta and embryo develop at the expense of the mare, and growth of the embryo is largely independent of the mare's environmental conditions, even, for example, of her diet. This can mean that under unfavourable conditions—such as too early covering, or twin embryos—the mare's constitution can be harmed by the pregnancy, to the detriment of the foal's development. The possibility of damage to the mare is, however, kept within a particular safety margin: the size and weight of the foetus and also of the newborn foal develop approximately in proportion to the size or weight of the mare. This parallelism in development continues until the foal's growth is concluded: for instance, foals with a relatively light weight at birth remain as a rule relatively smaller and lighter at the conclusion of growth. This influence exerted by the dam is also to be observed in other mammals, and illustrates the basic principles that govern prenatal growth.

Whereas growth in length is approximately constant in the horse embryo, increase in body mass is periodic, depending upon processes of differentiation, and occurs principally in the first four to five months, and again in the course of the eighth and ninth months. At birth, the total weight of foetus, foetal membrane including the amniotic fluid, and placenta is some 13 to 15 per cent of the weight of the dam; the weight of the foal alone is 8 to 11 per cent of her weight.

The foal begins to grow

Postnatal processes of growth in all mammals are also subject to certain laws, knowledge of which makes it possible to draw valuable conclusions that affect the rearing of foals. Intensity of growth depends upon weight. By absolute growth intensity we mean growth within a unit of time (eg length, breadth, weight), by relative growth intensity the increase relative to the initial (birth) weight or final weight (termination of growth). The limitation of the intensity of growth is characterised by the fact that the build-up of the body substance is proportional to the body surface.

As the body grows, its mass (body weight) increases approximately to the power of 3, but its surface only to the power of 2. At first, the foal takes in more food than it uses up in maintaining itself and in exercise, and so has a surplus available for its growth. In the course of growth, this surplus becomes progressively smaller,

Previous page:
33 Taking an interest in the camera. But curiosity and restraint are finely balanced in this foal

34 Foals 'grow by playing'. For their proper development, particularly as sporting horses, they should have adequate space and opportunity to exercise freely throughout the day

35 Foals together

36 The horse, more than almost any other mammal, needs adequate exercise in order to develop and perfect foot and leg technique

37 Still too immature to mate—not to mention the inadequate mastery of 'technique'. But when they are about a year old, the sexes must be separated. Early pregnancies are damaging to the development of young mares

38 The overall format of the new-born foal is upright and rectangular; most highly developed are the head and legs, some 65 per cent of the total increase in breadth and depth is still to come

39 Irritating scurf is cleared from the skin by nibbling

40 Horses are able to scratch many parts of their bodies themselves; but here, the foal must take care not to lose its balance

41 The younger the horse, the more unfavourably situated is its centre of gravity. As a result, foals stand with the forelegs straddled in the first few weeks of life; this also enables them to reach the ground more easily to graze or sniff

42 In the gallop there is only a short period of foot-ground contact and a flight phase making up some 70 per cent of the total movement. To perfect the necessary foot technique, the foal must practise until it is adult; for this, it requires frequent exercise and plenty of space

43 Mares with foals; while grazing, they keep a keen eye on their surroundings

44 It is advantageous if at least two foals can be reared together so that there is always a companion for play

45 Piebald and skewbald markings are more often seen in ponies than in horses. They are born with this colouring. Dappling of this kind consists of the alternation of light-coloured patches of skin and hair with dark of various colours. Fetlocks and hooves are also marked in this way

46 In an adult horse, enforced crossing of the legs can reduce a tendency to rearing and control a superiority complex in stallions. But this foal is having difficulty in standing and still has to learn to 'sort out' its legs

47 The mare constantly checks the anal region of her foal to establish its identity, even though it is already three months old

48 The only way a horse can groom its own hock is by lying down

49 The mare cannot immediately recognise her foal and raises a hind leg ready to ward it off. She will very quickly establish its identity by naso-anal contact

50 Resting in the shade of its dam

51 Parts of the body inaccessible to
the horse are rubbed against any
available object

52 When its skin itches and no
partner is available for 'social grooming', the foal obtains relief by rolling
on the ground

53 When the top of its head itches, the horse has to look for something to rub it against

54 Among the less accessible parts of the body that the horse nibbles at is the croup region

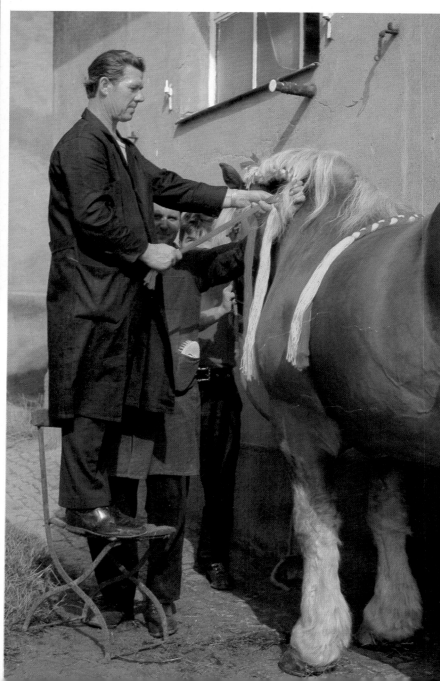

56 Preparation of a horse for a show includes the plaiting of its mane. But is it advisable to stand on a wobbly garden chair to do so . . .?

55 Every horseshoe must be specially made to fit the hoof. So the farrier must be highly skilled and must tackle each piece of work individually.

A good farrier makes a vital contribution to the development of a good action in a foal and to the maintenance of mobility in a horse, thus also prolonging its life. No horse owner should forget this

57 The long hair of a heavy draught horse requires particular attention. Mane and tail are 'pulled' and groomed by hand and brush

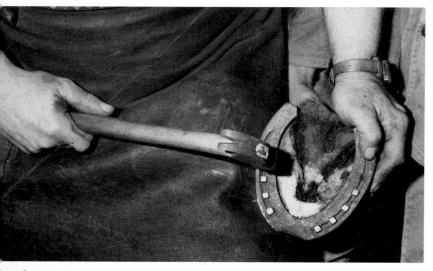

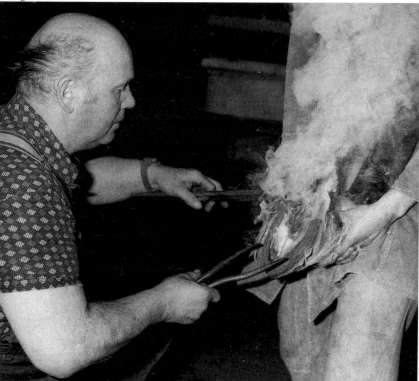

58   The horseshoe attached to the hoof by nails has been known in Europe since the ninth or tenth century. Preparation of shoe and hoof and the fitting of the shoe must be carried out with careful attention to the posture of leg and hoof, the quality of the hoof and the kind of work the horse will be doing

59   The correct presentation of horses requires a good deal of practice. It is a very important element in assessing a horse, particularly its action (Photo: W. Ernst)

60   The earliest examples of horse-collars date from the ninth to tenth centuries AD. With the collar, the draught capacity of the horse was three to four times greater than with the double neck-yoke formerly used. This type of harnessing has been retained for heavy draught work to this day, in so far as horses still carry out such tasks

Following page:
61   Regular rest breaks are necessary in very heavy work such as hauling timber. The equine stomach holds only 10 to 15 litres, so the horse must be fed regularly, if possible five times a day

intensity of growth diminishes and finally a state of balance is reached in which food intake just covers the requirements of physical maintenance, movement and activity. At this point, the build-up of the bodily substance is concluded and the termination of growth achieved.

The process of growth can be expressed mathematically and is subject to fixed laws. Growth in size and length can be represented as a linear graph-curve which gradually flattens out. The line of the curve reflects the cycles of growth, eg weaning from the dam, sexual maturity (earlier in fillies than in colts) and working requirements. Increase in weight, on the other hand, appears as a curve with a tendency to an S-shape, gradually flattening out. Body size (height at withers and rump) and thickness of bone (circum-ference of cannon bone) reach their final values first, markedly ahead of body length which comes a short distance after the termination of growth in breadth and depth, particularly of the barrel of the chest. With normal feeding, growth in bone length comes to an end before growth in bone thickness; therefore a very underfed foal has long, thin bones.

The external form of the developing animal is the result of particular processes of growth. It is characteristic that in every instance of growth that alters form, the relative speed of growth of the individual parts of the body is different. It is a feature of all mammals that the relative speed of growth of a particular part of the body remains in a particular constant ratio over a quite long period of time to that of another part or else to the body as a whole. This principle is defined as allometric growth or allometry. It affects both morphological (body size, weight etc) and physiological (heart size, respiratory volume, metabolism etc) features as well as biophysical and biochemical characteristics and statistics. A striking example of alteration in form in the course of growth is the change in the proportions of the body between the newborn foal with its distinctly high, upright-rectangular overall shape to the elongated-rectangular format of the adult horse.

The foal achieves its final body weight only at the end of its total development. Correct care and feeding of the foal during the period of growth are therefore vitally important for subsequent performance. This means that youngstock management must allow not only for changes in bodily measurements but also ensure that, in parallel, the internal organs can achieve optimal development. Important criteria are the conditions of

Embryonic development of the horse

age of embryo in weeks	stage of overall development of embryo	weight in kg	length in cm
4	all internal organs begin to develop	0.002	1.0
6–8	extremities show typical equine articulation, sex is apparent	0.020	6.5
10–12	development of hooves begins	0.100	12.0
14–16	placenta fully formed	1.600	23.0
20	external sexual organs developed (apart from scrotum). Hairs on lip, edges of ears, mane and tail present	4.000	30.0
24		5.000	42.0
28		6.000	55.0
32		12.000	70.0
36	hair on back and mane fully developed, entire body covered with short hair	19.000	80.0
40	frontal zone of head still protruding	35.000	90.0
46–48	central milk incisors present, three milk premolars begin to erupt, scrotum and prepuce clearly visible, foetus has reached maturity	52.000	103.0

stabling, a programme of compulsory exercise, extensive grazing periods and training in particular patterns of behaviour.

It should be borne in mind that the horse's final size and weight are breed-specific, and the speed of growth does not depend upon age but on the body weight at any particular time. Both in the wild horse and in the wild forms of other domesticated mammals, it is well known that the animal's capacity for growth does not as a rule diminish, or scarcely does so, until the genetically-determined final values have been reached. In the domestic horse, on the other hand, because of the deliberate development, to an extent far in excess of the natural measure, of highly efficient, specialised organs of respiration and digestion, of a resilient cardiac-circulatory system and a perfect locomotory system for an outstandingly high level of performance (speed, jumping), the best possible standard of feeding and care in quality and quantity during growth is an essential prerequisite if the aims of breeding and utilisation are to be fulfilled. If the level of feeding and general care is too low, and as a result the development of the foal is inhibited, particularly in the early stages of rearing, it is impossible to make up later for lost ground; and even if subsequently the animal is given larger quantities of more nutritious food, it cannot achieve the high quality of features that are genetically programmed. It remains to some extent in a state of undernourishment or underdevelopment. Later, foals of this kind can develop into runts, in contrast to the rare, 'genuine' runts that are born stunted.

It is important that statistics on breed-specific development that have been established by experience should be known and taken into consideration, to enable a constant check to be kept on the course of growth and, as a result of correct feeding and management, to direct it along the most favourable lines to produce a horse that is valuable for breeding and economically useful.

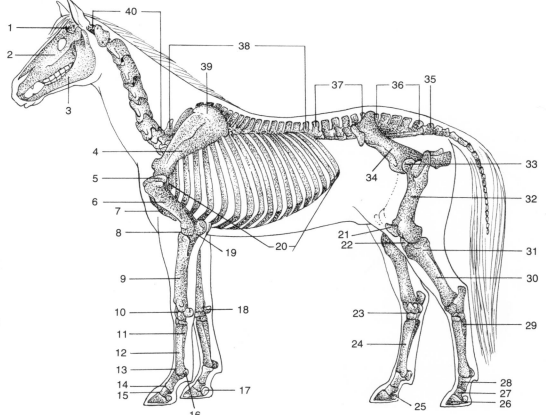

Skeleton of the horse
1 neurocranium or cerebral cranium 2 facial skeleton 3 mandible 4 scapula 5 shoulder joint 6 humerus 7 sternum 8 elbow joint 9 radius 10 carpus 11 splint bone 12 large metacarpal 13 fetlock joint 14 pastern joint 15 coffin joint 16 sesamoid bone 17 lateral cartilage of hoof 18 os pisiforme 19 oleocranon 20 17 ribs (18) 21 patella 22 knee joint 23 hock (corresponds to ankle joint in man) 24 metatarsal 25 pedal bone 26 coffin bone 27 coronal bone 28 long pastern bone 29 splint bone 30 tibia 31 fibula 32 femur 33 hip joint 34 pelvis 35 caudal vertebrae (18–20) 36 sacral vertebrae (5) 37 lumbar vertebrae (6) 38 dorsal vertebrae 39 scapular cartilage 40 cervical vertebrae (7)

Mother's milk is the best foundation

As soon as possible after the birth, the foal should drink the first milk, the colostrum. In the interests of optimum growth, a regular and adequate milk intake by the foal must be ensured, particularly in the first weeks of life. After birth, the foal has a good appetite and a very strong sucking power, which from the start stimulates the milk supply of its dam. As the foal gets older, its sucking power and the length of time spent each day in sucking diminish, as does the mare's milk supply. Nevertheless, the quantity and quality of the milk remain high, and provide the founda-

tion vital to successful rearing in the first five or six months. The quantity of milk produced depends on the weight of the mare and the ratio of body weight to body surface; this explains the relatively very high milk yield of small mares and the mares of dwarf breeds. The foal's increase in weight in the first week of life is considerable. The time required for doubling the birth weight depends again on the character of early or late maturity (termination of growth) in the particular breed: the 'warmblood' breed of horse requires some 20 per cent longer than the early-maturing heavy 'coldblood' breed, because its increase in weight per unit of time is lower.

To ensure a favourable start, the foal should be fed supplementary concentrates while it is still being suckled, and given regular exercise and periods of grazing alongside its dam. For future saddle horses and racehorses, the activity that this involves is an important and effective preparation for later training.

With an average suckling period of five months as the minimum for a horse that is bred for endurance and speed, an approximately twenty-four-hour rhythm for the foal can be made up as follows: 50 per cent rest and sleep, 30 per cent grazing and exercise, 10 per cent in the stable, 6 per cent suckling by the dam, 4 per cent feeding on concentrates.

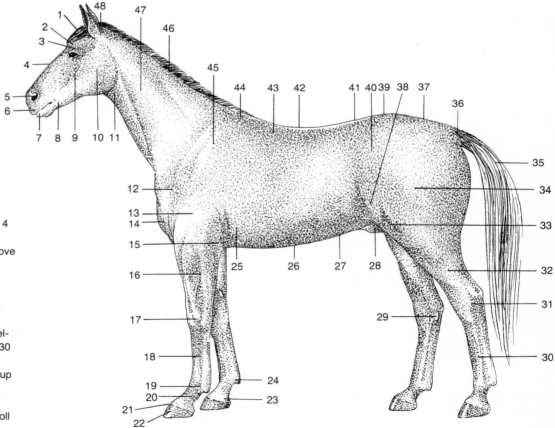

The points of the horse
1 forelock 2 forehead 3 superciliary arch 4 bridge of nose 5 nostril 6 upper lip of muzzle 7 lower lip 8 cheeks 9 zygomatic groove (edge of cheek bone) 10 jowl 11 throat latch 12 point of shoulder 13 forearm 14 chest 15 olecranon process 16 lower arm 17 carpus 18 cannon bone 19 fetlock joint 20 pastern 21 coronet 22 hoof 23 bulb 24 fetlock hair 25 region of the heart 26 belly 27 abdomen 28 sheath 29 chestnut 30 shank 31 hock 32 gaskin 33 knee 34 thigh 35 tail 36 dock or root of tail 37 croup or rump 38 flank 39 sacrum 40 hip 41 loin 42 back 43 saddle position 44 withers 45 shoulder 46 crest 47 neck 48 poll

The foal should be weaned as late as possible. Foals of early-maturing breeds can be separated from the mare after four months, those of late maturing breeds should not be less than five months when they are weaned. The mare's milk yield in the fifth month is still usually so high that it also makes good economic sense to extend the period of suckling into the sixth month. To safeguard the healthy condition of the mare's udder, weaning should be a gradual process carried out over a period of about a week.

Rate of weight gain in horses of different breeds with early or late maturity

Breed	as multiple of birth weight at end of		
	1st year	2nd year	3rd year
Arab	5.8	7.4	9.0
Warmblood	6.0	8.4	9.6
Coldblood	7.2	9.5	11.5
Haflinger	6.2	8.5	10.3
Shetland pony	5.3	6.5	9.0

Correct feeding for optimal growth

The newborn foal is a long-legged, narrow, short-bodied animal with a relatively long, narrow head and short muzzle.

Feeding, then, must provide primarily for the development of extra breadth and

Important body measurements
1 length of trunk   2 depth of breast   3 height
4 girth   5 circumference of cannon bone

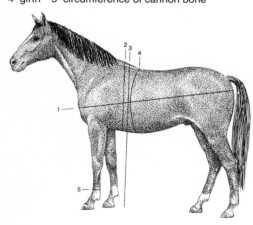

depth, length of barrel, breadth of forehead and length of nose. The genetically-fixed potential total increase in height at withers and croup, and cannon bone circumference is, in comparison, of much less importance. Growth in the initial stage is particularly intensive, irrespective of the breed of the foal. By the end of the first year of life, the measurements of height and circumference of the cannon bone—indicative of skeletal thickness—reach 80 to 90 per cent of the potential final value, whereas at the same age the development of breadth and depth (chest and hip), barrel length, width of forehead and length of nose have reached only 60 to 70 per cent of the final values. The feeding programme must take these facts into consideration. The greatest problem is achieving the necessary height, particularly in sporting horses (about 16.1 hands) as well as a correctly proportioned development of depth and breadth in the growing horse.

The process of total growth in the horse is terminated between the fifth and sixth

years, or even later in certain breeds such as the Arab and other Eastern breeds. Height and cannon bone circumference measurements usually reach their final value during the horse's fifth year; barrel length, breadth and depth measurement in the course of the fifth or sixth year. Since the continuous increase in weight is the product of the growth rates of the individual parts of the body, the final weight is to be expected only after total growth is concluded, that is, not before the sixth year. Differences between breeds of horses show up particularly clearly in the pattern of weight increase. Conclusions can be drawn that are important for the correct morphological and physiological development of the foal. Using scales, the breeder can easily carry out a practical check and, on the basis of his findings, vary feeding and care so that they influence the growth of the foal in the best possible way. The greatest chances of realising a horse's genetically-programmed potential lie within the period of rearing.

In about 800 BC the Scythians living in the region between the Don and Danube held a leading position in horse breeding and horse management. They used the horse both as a saddle animal, particularly for their warriors, and also to draw single-axled and double-axled chariots. They passed on their extensive knowledge and experience in this field to other peoples; especially close links existed with the Greek colonies along the coast of the Black Sea and beyond to Greece, which took over many ideas from the Scythians, particularly concerning the use of the horse for military purposes. A typical practice, as among the nomadic peoples of this period, was their consumption of mare's milk and its products; this habit continues today, especially in central Asia. On this subject, Herodotus remarks:

> The Scythians blind all their slaves, on account of the mare's milk, on which they live. When milking, they proceed as follows: they take a reed pipe which they insert into the mare's vagina and blow into it with their mouth, and while one blows, the other milks. Apparently they do this because it causes the mare's veins to swell up and the udder to stand out. Once the milk is drawn off, it is poured into wooden tubs and shaken by the blind slaves who are made to stand round the vats. The part that rises to the top is skimmed off and is held to be the best, but the liquid below to be less good. Therefore the Scythians blind their slaves; they practice no agriculture, but live as nomads . . .

The Thracians, who four thousand years ago colonised the area that today is Bulgaria, had equally close links with the Greeks. They were renowned for their horse breeding and for their chariot horses. In the *Iliad*, Homer extols their country, Thrace, as the mother of sheep and home of fast horses; referring to the army that the Thracian king, Rhesos, brought to support the troops confined within the fortress of Troy, he writes: 'Rhesos, whose horses are the finest and largest that I have ever seen, whiter than dazzling snow and fleet as the wind . . .' And when Nestor is speaking to Odysseus about the Thracian horses captured by the Greeks, Homer lets him say:

> How have you come to possess these horses?
> Did you force your way into camp
> or did a god present them to you, when you met?
> Their lustrous gleam is wonderfully like the rays of the sun!
> . . . yet never have I seen horses like these
> or heard report of them . . .

As a result of the very strong bonds with Greece, particularly from the middle of the fourth century BC onwards, Greek influences fused with the ancient Thracian traditions. During this period, the export of fine horses to Greece played a particular role. This is probably why the regions of Boeotia and Thessaly can be considered as the cradles of Greek horse breeding. And undoubtedly horse breeding in the motherland was influenced in fundamental and lasting ways by the Greek colony in present-day Cyrenaica. In 630 BC the Greeks founded the city of Cyrene, which had direct trade links along the Silk Route between Alexandria and the Far East with central Asia and so also with Bactria, and this may well have included the import of Bactrian 'noble horses' that then found their way from Cyrene to Greece. The inhabitants of the Greek colony of Cyrenaica took over many ideas on chariot driving and chariot battle strategy from the Libyans who had been breeding horses since the first millennium BC. In the Olympic Games of that time chariot teams from Cyrenaica often took a first or leading place.

Horses were probably also transported from Asia Minor to Greece. But the highest honours in horse breeding went to Sicily, which at that time was Greek. On Roman race courses, as well as in the Greek motherland, Sicilian horses were considered formidable opponents; according to Pindar (about 520–445 BC), the best mules were also to be found here. Towns such as Agrigento had large stocks of valuable horses. This town received its victorious

Olympic champion, Exanetos, with a ceremonial escort of 300 two-axled, decorated chariots drawn by white horses. The main breeding area of Sicily was the countryside round Syracuse. Here there were large stud farms, of which those on the island of Ortygia were the most valuable. According to Strabo (about 63 BC to AD 19), their horses were descended from the Heneter breed that was among the most important in classical antiquity.

From the seventh century BC, use of the war chariot also gradually declined in Greece as mounted troops were increasingly employed, which was undoubtedly one reason for the introduction of racing into the Olympic Games in 648 BC. At the battle near Marathon (490 BC), there was as yet no Hellenistic cavalry, but in the Peloponnesian War (431–404 BC), some thousand mounted warriors were deployed. Because of the high cost of maintaining such an army, the horsemen were usually selected from wealthy families; each had to provide two horses and a groom. We have reports on this written by Xenophon (about 430–354 BC), the only ancient writer whose work has been preserved in its entirety. Because of the simplicity, clarity and faithfulness of his descriptions and the wide range of his writings, his contemporaries called him the 'Attic Bee'. In addition to numerous writings on questions of history, politics, economics and military affairs, he achieved recognition primarily with his *Anabasis*, in which he describes in detail the 'retreat of the ten thousand' Greek mercenaries under his leadership

from the battlefield of Cunaxa near Babylon to the Black Sea in the year 401 BC. Among the ten thousand mercenaries there were small groups of mounted soldiers, and Xenophon himself covered the 3,420-mile route on horseback. For him, as the son of a well-to-do Athenian family, who had begun to ride at an early age and had later taken part in mounted military expeditions, these experiences may well have provided the incentive for his two didactic hippological works *Hipparchikos* ('The Colonel of Cavalry') and *Peri Hippikes* ('On the Art of Riding'). In both works, Xenophon refers to earlier hippological instructions written by Simon, which unfortunately have not been preserved, and which he expands considerably. Because of the quality of the two writings, Xenophon is recognised as the founder of the science of hippology. A good deal of what he says is still valid today in dealing with the horse, training it and developing it as a multi-purpose riding horse. Particularly in 'On the Art of Riding', he shows the importance of mutual trust between man and horse as the prerequisite of excellent performance, and gives logical, systematic and scientifically objective directions for achieving it. The renowned Greek sculptor Phidias (about 500–438 BC) illustrates the teachings of Xenophon in the friezes of the Parthenon at Athens: the riders are mounted on Thessalonian horses.

Certain beliefs and traditional sayings in connection with quite specific events make it clear that, in practical horse management, ignorance and superstition existed alongside scientifically-based knowledge. For example, the somewhat rare occurrence of the hippomane at a birth gave rise to various interpretations. This is a solid, brownish to olive-green body consisting of solidified uterine milk, which can sometimes be found attached to a newborn foal. An account written by Aelianus (about AD 22), shows what curious ideas were attached to unusual biological phenomena, the causes of which were not properly understood. It reads so well, that the following extract is included to illustrate the tradition of superstitious beliefs that still exists today among some horse breeders (similar to that concerning sex determination).

Chariot-racing in circus arena. Clay relief, British Museum, London

When a Mare gives birth, some say that a small piece of flesh is attached to the foal's forehead, others say to its loin, others again to its genitals. This piece the Mare bites off and destroys; and it is called 'Mare's frenzy'. It is because Nature has pity and compassion on horses that this occurs, for had this continued to be attached always to the foal, both horses and mares would be inflamed with a passion for uncontrolled mating. This may, if you like, be a gift bestowed by Poseidon or Athena, the god and

the goddess of horses, upon these animals to ensure that their race is perpetuated and does not perish through an insane indulgence. Now those who tend horses are fully aware of this and if they chance to need the aforesaid piece of flesh with the design of kindling the fires of Love in some person, they watch a pregnant Mare . . . Any man who as a result of some plot tastes of that piece of flesh becomes possessed and consumed by an incontinent desire and cries aloud, and cannot be controlled from going after even the ugliest boys and grown women of repellent aspect. And he proclaims his affliction and tells those whom he meets how he is being driven mad. And his body pines and wastes away and his mind is agitated by erotic frenzy.

I have heard also this story of the bronze mare at Olympia: horses fall madly in love with it and long to mount it, and at the sight of it neigh amorously. Hidden away in the charmed bronze it contains the treacherous Mare's frenzy, and through some secret contrivance of the artist the bronze works against living animals. For it could not possibly be so true to life that horses with their eyes open should be deceived and inflamed to that extent. It may be that those who relate the story are speaking the truth, or it may be that they are not: I have only reported what I have heard.

Of the Greek painter Apelles (fourth century BC) it is said that he painted mares so lifelike that stallions were taken in by them. He was a representative of four-colour painting technique (yellow, red, black, white and mixtures), and court-painter to Alexander the Great. The latter had taken over from his father, Philip II of Macedonia, a strictly-organised army with a cavalry capable of effective attacking action. With it, he shattered the Persian Empire and spread the influence of Hellenism across the Near East as far as the Indus, to Egypt, to the Oasis of Sova and to Libya. He recognised early on the great strategic importance of a cavalry army for his campaigns of conquest. The Greek horsemen went into battle wearing light bronze armour and carrying lances over 6 m (20 ft) long, which proved to be fearsome and superior weapons. Most of Alexander's troops rode thoroughbred Oriental horses, of which he himself was particularly fond, giving active encouragement to their breeding. His favourite horse, Bucephalus ('Bull-headed'), died in the battle on the Hydaspes (northern Pakistan) in 326 BC. Arrianos (about AD 95–150) referring in his *Anabasis* to the foundation of the town of Bucephala on the western bank of the river, writes:

. . . he founded it in memory of his horse Bucephalus that died here, not from wounds inflicted at the hand of man, but from over-exertion and old age. For at nearly thirty years of age, this Bucephalus was completely exhausted, after having undergone very many hardships and dangers . . . He was of imposing size, full of noble courage and marked out by a bull's head [broad brow, large eyes and concave nose profile] from which his name derives; but according to other information, it was because although completely black in colour, he had a white mark on his forehead that resembled a bull's head . . .

An exceptional feature of the horse Bucephalus was said to be the presence on his legs of pendant residual fifth toes instead of the usual chestnuts. Even many centuries later, his name might still be heard in areas such as present-day Pakistan and Afghanistan, where he was remembered as the founder of valuable strains of horses. Marco Polo, for example, wrote of his journey through Asia in 1298:

The horses born here—Badakshan, mountainous country in Afghanistan—are of an excellent breed and run very fast. Their

Mounted warrior. Bronze, about 550 BC, British Museum, London

hooves are so hard that they do not need to be shod. The inhabitants are able to gallop them up the steepest mountain side where no cattle would dare to run. They assert that it is not long since horses lived in this land that were descended from Alexander's famous Bucephalus, and all of them had come into the world with a mark on the brow. The entire breed was owned by one of the king's uncles, who had been executed, because he would not yield them to his nephew, upon which his widow, in a passion of despair, had all the horses strangled; so this breed was lost to the world.

In contrast to those in Greece, horses on the Italian peninsula served primarily the practical purposes of communication, transport and military affairs, while the true art of riding was not developed. A military cavalry came into being relatively late, since its importance was not recognised until the time of the Punic Wars (third and second centuries BC), when the Romans came up against the extremely well-trained Punic (Tunisian) horsemen. In general, the Romans left the practice of fighting on horseback to their foreign allies, such as the Numidians, with whose help they conquered Carthage. Moreover, like the Greeks, they were familiar with neither saddle nor stirrup.

It was only during the early centuries AD that horse breeding became more systematic and intensive in the Roman territories. By way of the Iberian peninsula (the Roman province Hispania), the Numidian horse gained considerable influence, and contributed to the recruitment of the Roman cavalry. As the centuries passed, several groups of breeds could be distinguished, and in the early years of the Christian era, the situation was approximately as follows:

Materies generosa (horses 'of noble blood', known today as full-blooded, whole-blooded or thoroughbred horses): they included horses for the racecourses and circus, which were reared primarily in Apulia and Thessaly and were descended from breeds from the Iberian peninsula, Sicily and Persia. There were accurate genealogical trees, names for breeding animals, documentary evidence of performance and brand marks.

Materies mularis ('half-blood', half-bred horses): they were closely associated with the *Materies generosa* and were used for military purposes. Tradition suggests that they were of Burgundian, Hunnish, Phrygian and Epeirian descent. The swift, noble carriage horse came mainly from Cappadocia and was also used to draw the triumphal chariots.

Materies vulgaris (heavy horses, roughly equivalent to our heavy draught horses, coldbloods): this category included all working horses used in agriculture and in the transport of heavy goods. The horses bred by the Celts, Britons and Teutons were fairly small and slow but, as a result of appropriate selection, larger, heavier animals gradually became available. Stallions not required for breeding were castrated.

From this short account it is clear that, until the beginning of the Christian era, the Romans practised horse breeding only to a limited extent and, instead, imported their pedigree horses and certainly horses for general use. So almost all the breeds of antiquity

Equestrian statue of Marcus Aurelius, second century AD, Rome (Photo: Anderson)

were to be found in the Roman mother country. This is confirmed in contemporary accounts. One interesting fact is that, even at this time, horses from Spain were especially renowned for their ambling pace. They were called 'Thieledones'. Pliny the Elder (AD 23–79) wrote: 'In moving, they have not the normal stride but a gentle amble, in which they advance both feet on one side alternately with those on the other, for which reason the other horses are taught artificially to walk at an amble . . .'

On the subjects of breeding and training, there were clearly defined teachings which have been represented fairly extensively in Roman literature. The required standards for breeding-horses, particularly stallions, were clearly laid down, not unlike the requirements in today's system of inspection for licensing, and they were published, by, for example, Palladius (fourth century AD), Columella (first century AD), Horace and Virgil (first century BC). Important works of equestrian art date from this time, such as the statue of Emperor Marcus Aurelius or the four bronze horses that were taken from Rome to Constantinople in the fourth century and from there brought as spoils of victory by the Doge E. Dondolo to Venice in 1204, where they adorned the archway above the main portal of St Mark's Cathedral until the mid-1970s. To avoid environmental damage, they have now been replaced by copies.

Horse races were very popular with the Romans, less from purely sporting motives than from a desire for sensation and spectacle. The horses were ridden or driven, usually as a team of four, a *quadriga*, or else as a team of three, a *triga*. To red, green, white and blue that were the usual racing colours of that time, yellow (or gold) and purple (or crimson) were added under Emperor Domitianus.

In about 100 BC, horses used for racing and for military purposes were 'shod' with bast or leather sandals. Emperor Augustus encouraged horse traffic on the streets and had post-stations built along the 46,000-mile-long road network of the Roman Empire, the *cursum publicus*. The couriers were changed every 15 miles. The milestones placed at the edge of the road made mounting easier.

The question of determining the sex of a foal at the time of conception was one that also occupied horse breeders in the Roman realm. Two methods in particular that were handed down by Columella and Pliny the Elder were given general credence. One consisted in binding either the right or left testicle of the stallion, depending upon whether a colt or filly was required, the other in observing whether the stallion dismounted from the mare after covering to the right (colt foal) or left (filly foal). 'Testing' or 'teas-

Bronze horses on the front of St Mark's Cathedral in Venice
(Photo: Lala Aufsberg)

ing' stallions also existed as early as this; they were usually taken from the stock of the *Materies vulgaris*.

It is reported that the mares were covered on the seventh day after foaling, since they were most likely to conceive then. Stallion and mare were given special preparation for the period of covering. It is interesting that the mares were kept short of food while the stallions' diet was intended to slow down the pace of mating, in both cases with the aim of ensuring fertilisation. The 'sedative feed' was given to the stallions at the start of the covering period in the form of barley and vetch (known as *erve*). Virgil gives an account of this practice and its immediate consequences in some particularly charming passages.

In western and central Europe until the fourth century BC, horses were almost without exception quite small. Even up to the La Tène period, they apparently served mainly as pack animals. The Celtic horse of the third to first centuries BC has been shown to have had an average height of 12 hands; only under favourable

dietary conditions did it become a hand taller. Information from Roman sources covering the Germanic horse show a similar situation; it was a draught horse and usually small. In the Gallic Wars (first century BC), Germans rode horses that in comparison with those of the Roman warriors were small, but which had great stamina and were suitable for mounted combat. Tacitus, writing for his contemporaries in his *Germania*, says of the Germans: 'Horsemanship is the pastime of the children, the emulation of the youth and the habit of old age.' The height of their horses was between about 12 and 13.1 hands. Gravestones depicting Roman legionaries mounted on Gallic and Germanic horses also show animals of this kind. It seems that as a result of the conditions of feeding at that time, and of deliberate selection for breeding, more of the typical draught-horse type of animals were developed, characterised by a larger rib cage, sturdier bones, large hooves and a thick, wavy tail. Such were the horses that the Britons used when they fought against the Romans in AD 54—5. An increase in the size of horses in central and western Europe came about only between the first and fourth centuries. It resulted from the adoption of practical nobility, and the provision of more suitable conditions of care and feeding.

At the same time, the horses became suitable for riding. The history of equitation in England goes back to the time of the Roman occupation in the first century AD. Until then, the principal means of conveyance and vehicle of war for the Celts in Britain had been the horse-drawn chariot.

When they invaded Britain, the Romans were mounted on horses that came from their province of Hispania, and these also left their mark upon horse breeding there. The Celts, who as nomads extended from Britain (sixth century BC) as far as Asia Minor (fourth century BC—Galatia) and were called Gauls by the Romans, naturally came in contact with the Greek, early Roman and Etruscan cultures. From here they took the models for the minting of their coins—equestrian figures, four-horse teams—and they fought in the army of Alexander the Great (356—323 BC) and in the Roman legions. This also explains why, even before the occupation of Gaul (second and first centuries BC), they had adopted the Roman goddess of fertility, Epona, as their tutelary goddess of horses. Epona was usually represented carrying a bowl of fruit or a cornucopia, mounted side-saddle on a horse or standing between two horses. Inside Celtic stables, an altar was consecrated to her; coins and tomb ornamentation celebrated her memory. As the 'horse goddess', Epona later 'spread back', as it were, into other parts of the Roman Empire as well, but her original significance as goddess of fertility either declined or was lost.

Women in the Saddle

In Europe, the first representations of women riders in works of art appeared in the tenth century, initially merely as symbols of virtues or vices, but later as genuine representations of the horsewomen at the courts of feudal lords, princes and kings. In keeping with ancient Greek ideas of the Amazon, they are seen mounted astride. According to Greek legend, the Amazons were a nation of women warriors in north-eastern Asia Minor, known and feared as horse breeders and horsewomen. They invaded Greek territory several times. On a frieze at the Parthenon, the marble temple of the goddess Athene on the Acropolis, there is a representation of the Battle of the Amazons; here too, in the fifth century BC, it was normal for horsewomen to ride astride. After the conflict, the Greek hero Theseus took their queen Hippolyte, also known as Antiope, to Athens as his wife. She bore him a son, Hippolytus, who was later killed by his own horses which took fright and bolted, dragging him along behind, at the sudden appearance of a bull sent by the god Poseidon. The story is told in detail in the *Hippolytus* of Euripides.

Among the Asiatic tribes of herdsmen, women used the horse very little, occasionally on migrations, mainly for herding cattle. They rode astride as the men did. It was difficult to envisage fighting and hunting on horseback in any other way. Chinese and Persian art almost always shows women mounted astride as they play polo and other competitive games, as well as hunt. In the Middle Ages, the women still accompanied the men in this way when they went hawking or to jousting tournaments, and they used the horse as a means of transport unless they preferred a carriage. This, of course, was after the introduction of the saddle—at first only an animal skin or a blanket—and the stirrup.

The side-seat for women has been known for more than 2,500 years; the rider sits with both legs on the near side of the horse. As far as is known, it was used almost exclusively in the Celtic-Gallic area and in the area of later Roman occupation in Europe. Epona, revered by the Celts as the tutelary goddess of horses, is shown in this position in pre-Roman times; she is however seated on the off side on a small Celtic horse without a back cover. From about the middle of the first millennium BC, women were conveyed seated sideways on seats with a foot support, probably exclusively on ambling horses. This undoubtedly played a role in the development of the side-saddle for women much later on.

With the end of the Age of Chivalry, the typical knights' horses, which were only medium-sized, heavy and thickset, disappeared

Louis Tuaillon: statue of an Amazon

in Europe, gradually making way for larger, more elegant horses for representational and military purposes. Until the sixteenth century, when there was a transition to the sideways seated position, many women still rode astride in the so-called man's position, but the fact that the type of horse was a different one meant

Miniature from a Persian courtly epic. Oriental Department of Staatsbibliothek Preussischer Kulturbesitz, West Berlin

that the need for safety in the saddle played a greater role. Because women differ anatomically from men—the inner surfaces of the upper thighs are rounder, the pelvis broader, deeper and inclined backwards—they have a tendency to an 'open', outward-turned knee position with insufficient knee and calf grip, making it more difficult to maintain a firm seat and so to keep control of the horse when riding astride. This does not affect the sideways position in a side-saddle, but comes into effect particularly strongly when riding astride a narrow-backed thoroughbred horse which cannot be gripped flatly and closely by the legs. In an age when neither equestrian sport nor competitive horse jumping existed, the disadvantages of the side-seat in connection with them, such as restriction on the rider's ability to enter into the movement of the horse in jumping, can scarcely have played a part. Indeed, it had the positive advantage that the horsewoman's seated position was almost independent of the rein action, so that rein handling could be particularly gentle, encouraging a reliable responsiveness in the horse and its absolute obedience. The greatest risk in riding to the hunt as practised by the ruling classes of the time—slipping or falling when landing after a jump—was very much reduced for horsewomen side-saddle. The disadvantages of this saddle were not purely concerned with equitation. One was that an individual saddle had to be made for each horse. In addition, it required particularly careful training of the 'lady's riding horse' by specially qualified riding teachers, and could lead to excessive strain in the horse's two nearside legs and to pressure bruises and chafing on the horse's back.

In general, however, until the time of the Renaissance in Europe in the thirteenth and fourteenth centuries, ladies of high rank travelled by coach. *Luciliburg's Chronicle* (1434) describes the journey made by Saint Elisabeth of Thuringia through her native land of Hungary to her father King Andreas II in 1225, and mentions that she travelled in a coach, while her husband, the Margrave Ludwig of Thuringia 'came riding on a horse according to the custom for men'.

The side-saddle for women introduced in the Middle Ages requires the rider to sit on the near side and to be lifted into the saddle, and at first came into general use only in Europe—and in China and Japan not until the seventeenth or eighteenth century. In the course of the sixteenth century it was approved at court and therefore generally accepted. Its final form with a horn at the front and the stirrup on the near side is attributed to an idea of Marie de Medici, wife of the French king Henri IV; it makes mounting easier and ensures stability. But there were also earlier models: Mary of

Burgundy, wife of Emperor Maximilian I, is represented on a sixteenth-century seal riding side-saddle. In parallel with this development there was general denunciation of the astride position for women which was designated as the 'male' position by the noble and princely courts.

There is little specialised literature of this period dealing with the side-saddle and its use, and the training of horses and horsewomen. The earliest discussion is probably that found in a book written by the Dutch writer Van Oebschelwitz and published in Leipzig in 1766/8 under the title *Horseriding for Women*, which deals with the subject in considerable detail.

In the nineteenth century the use of the side-saddle and the rejection of the 'Amazon' reached a peak. Views were so conservative that, for example, on the plinth of the equestrian statue commemorating the national hero and revolutionary, Giuseppe Garibaldi, the Italian artist Gallori depicted the horsewoman charging with him to attack the occupying forces of the French as riding side-saddle. But ideas changed rapidly with the arrival of competitive sport and the emancipation of women at the beginning of this century. There were, however, a few horsewomen who, even during the 300-year-long period of supremacy of the side-saddle, continued the old tradition of riding astride, in spite of considerable social opposition; these intrepid females included the niece of Frederick II, Sophia Wilhelmina and the Spanish Queen Maria Louisa, who was painted riding astride by Francisco Goya in 1789.

Under modern conditions of horse breeding and equestrian sport, the factors that led to these developments in the history of equitation no longer exist. In this field too, men and women have equality of opportunity for reaching the highest levels of athletic achievement.

Hester Stanhope, an Englishwoman, known as the 'Princess of the Lebanon', lived in Dycum castle where she maintained a small stud farm

Care of the Horse

The principal aim of horse management is to compensate as far as possible for those deviations from the horse's natural way of life that arise from its being kept in a stable and used in the service of man. In this way, damage resulting from stabling, decline or fluctuation in performance, premature deterioration, parasitic or infectious diseases and, perhaps most important of all, disturbance in patterns of behaviour can be restricted or avoided altogether.

Care of the horse is closely linked to its training, which requires a good knowledge of the horse's behavioural patterns and a calm and patient approach. Accustoming horses to handling at an early age makes day-to-day care more effective, simplifies training later on and prevents accidents in dealing with them. Timid, sensitive and highly-strung horses should be tended only by experienced professionals and require particularly gentle handling.

During feeding times, all other measures of care must be suspended; otherwise, as a result of being disturbed, horses are inclined to bolt their feed, scatter it about or take up fragments of dirt and dust with it, and make the work of the handler difficult. In addition, the risk of an accident is increased by the horse's powerful urge to eat, associated with possessiveness towards its food and its lack of concentration on the person in charge.

Together with the provision of accommodation and food, grooming also plays a decisive role in the well-being and level of performance of the horse, and in establishing a positive relationship between man and horse.

Grooming

For the horse, the skin is not only an organ of protection against impact, injury, bacterial and fungal infections and animal parasites, but it also helps to regulate processes of metabolism. The skin is the vehicle for important physiological interaction between horse and environment. Therefore particular importance must be attached to maintaining it in a healthy condition by means of appropriate measures of care.

A horse that spends much time in a stable is denied the natural means of cleaning the body such as rolling on the ground, scraping and rubbing, and mutual nibbling. Moreover, when the horse is used for sport, its skin is frequently subjected to strain far in excess of the normal, both mechanically—particularly the saddle position and girth region—and physiologically when the work puts a greater strain on the overall metabolism, resulting in higher demands on the regulatory processes of the skin. In this respect the horse relies entirely on human assistance. This is particularly true of working horses which may spend only very few hours of the day in the open air.

The skin is an intricate system of interwoven fibres, glands, blood vessels, nerves and muscles. Any injury within this system necessarily leads to a disturbance of its functional efficiency and to damage to the entire process of metabolism. Particularly in thoroughbred and warmblood breeds, the epidermis is very fine and thin and therefore very sensitive to contact and pressure; this must be taken into consideration when carrying out all grooming procedures, as well as when fitting the bridle, saddle or harness, so that the horse does not become nervous and acquire the habit of resisting.

Grooming must be carried out regularly, usually in the morning. As far as possible, cleaning down should be carried out in the open air, so that the air inside the stable is not polluted by dust. If a horse returns from work dirty, sweaty or wet, grooming must be repeated accordingly. Every time the horse has been used, the feet must be picked out.

If horses are worked exclusively in the afternoons and evenings, the main grooming can be postponed until the evening, so that the animals can spend the night—biologically intended as the principal period of rest—in the stable clean and free from dust and dried sweat that can irritate the skin. In this case, the morning programme of care is restricted to a simple rub down, the coat is brushed smooth, the mane and tail brushed through and the eyes, nostrils, mouth, anus and genital organs wiped clean.

Only horses that are thoroughly dry can be groomed properly. So horses that have been washed must first be rubbed dry.

Thorough cleaning should be carried out rapidly, since any unnecessary extension of grooming makes the skin more sensitive and accelerates the intensity of skin activity, resulting in an increased production of scurf. In addition, the horse is kept longer than necessary in a state of tension, making it restless and nervous. A horse is clean when no scales of scurf can be found at the roots of the hair, when a finger can be run through the coat

a After washing, excess moisture is removed with a scraper
b The horse is dried with a hay wisp
c A hose pipe is used to clean the legs; the horse is held on a long rein attached to the snaffle

against the direction of hair-growth without picking up any dirt or, in the case of a dark-coloured horse, when no dusty streaks are visible on the coat.

Grooming equipment includes a dandy (coarse-bristled) brush for cleaning dirt-encrusted parts of the coat; a water brush, used damp for removing stains; a body brush; a curry comb (the best are oval-shaped) to clean the body brush; a hay wisp (a roll of hay, straw or even bast that has been knotted several times and beaten firm against a wall) to dry off a wet or sweaty horse and also to massage and stimulate the skin; two sponges, one to clean the eyes, nostrils and mouth and the other for wiping the dock and genital areas; a comb for trimming the mane and tail; a stable rubber, or soft cloth, for removing flecks of dust left on the coat and for giving a final polish; a stiff brush for removing mud and dirt from the feet; a hoof pick.

Anyone entering the stall or box should first speak to the horse, forewarning it so that it is not startled. The groom starts on the horse's near (left) side, facing the tail,

holding the body brush in the left hand, and the curry comb to clean off the brush in the right; the opposite hands are used when grooming the off (right) side of the horse. Basically, grooming is carried out in the direction of hair-growth, from the front, starting with the neck, to the rear. The body brush is wielded with sweeping movements of the arm which carry it smoothly and evenly across the coat with a degree of pressure adapted to the individual sensitivity of the horse. Pressure should be reduced on those parts of the body where there is only a thin covering of muscle over the bone. Where there is a great deal of encrusted dirt, this can be dislodged with the dandy brush, but care must be taken on sensitive areas and when grooming particularly thin-skinned animals. In recent times, vacuum cleaning equipment has come into use to which horses readily become accustomed. It can, of course, remove only loose dirt. Horses that are very dirty should, if possible, be washed before grooming—perhaps by hosing down—at least on the worst affected parts, and afterwards they

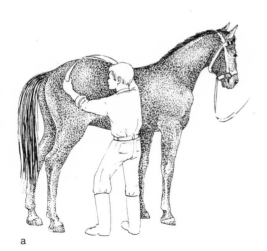

During grooming, the curry comb can be used on 'well upholstered' parts of the body. The halter should be raised so that no parts of the body are neglected

should be rubbed dry with straw or hay. It is neither necessary nor correct to use a metal curry comb for cleaning the horse, but a plastic or rubber one may be so used.

The horse's very sensitive head is cleaned gently with the body brush and eyes, nostrils and mouth are wiped, using a cloth or sponge. A different sponge is used to clean the anus, genital organs and dock area. Mane and tail hair should be disentangled gently with the fingers, or, if very fine, brushed with the body brush. The hairs of the tail are very slow-growing and should be treated especially carefully. They should be separated from one another by hand and smoothed out. Scales of scurf or dirt flecks along the hairline should be removed with the body brush or dandy brush. In order to thin out a mane that is too heavy or thick, or shorten one that is too long, hairs that are to be removed can be twisted round a finger, a few at a time, and drawn out slowly, but never plucked out sharply or suddenly. Manes that are erect can be brushed flat when they are damp, or plaited.

When horses have sweated profusely, those parts covered by saddle or harness should be rinsed with clear water, or washed with soapy water to get rid of the dirt completely. The use of soap must always be followed by a thorough rinsing, since soap residue can cause inflammation of the skin.

After work, the horse's feet, which have been subjected to considerable strain and fouling, should be cleaned and then massaged with a brush, or in the case of a sensitive horse, with a cloth. After very strenuous exercise, such as cross-country or endurance rides, strenuous show-jumping courses, sessions of intensive training and so on, the legs should be treated with liniment and possibly bandaged. After a few hours of rest in the stable the bandages should be removed to avoid congestion of the blood vessels. A careful check of the horse should be made for this. Daily hosing after exercise, working from below upwards, has proved very effective, provided the horse is accustomed to it gradually. It cleans well, refreshes the horse and helps to stabilise skin processes, the sinews and the general physical condition. Care must be taken to prevent the stream of water from striking the eyes, ears and nostrils, as well as the udder, sheath and scrotum.

Riding or leading horses in a pond, lake, river, stream or artificially-constructed swimming pool is also beneficial. It is necessary to ensure that the bottom surface is free from refuse and broken glass. In the case of rivers and lakes, if accidents are to be avoided, it is essential to check beforehand the depth of water, the nature of currents and the type of ground. Horses that are already heated from exertion must cool off adequately before entering the water. This can be done by riding at walking pace, much as is done to dry off a horse. At temperatures of about 15 °C (59 °F) or below, swimming time should not exceed five to ten minutes.

If a horse sweats easily as a result of an excessively thick or long growth of hair, or is infested with parasites, clipping may be necessary. This should be carried out before the winter coat is fully grown, because otherwise no growth occurs after clipping, the horses are inadequately covered and may easily catch cold.

Care of the feet

The daily grooming routine includes examining the feet for possible foreign bodies or injuries and cleaning them. The frog clefts are cleared of dirt, sand and small stones using a blunt hoof pick, and the sole is then cleaned thoroughly with a coarse brush. The hooves are washed only if necessary, using soap and water. Too frequent washing, constant use of the horse on wet ground or stabling on wet bedding make the hooves soft and spongy. Heels that become wet during washing must be dried especially carefully to prevent skin diseases that easily develop there. Oil can be applied to the hooves only when they have dried out completely; in this way the retention of moisture and resulting damage to the horn of the hoof is avoided.

Foot care and possible corrective treatment is based on: stimulation of horn growth and improvement in its condition; maintenance and encouragement of a functional hoof shape appropriate to the foot posture of the horse; maintenance of hard, strong horn.

Stimulation of horn growth and improvement of the condition of the horn is achieved primarily by walking the horse unshod on soft ground. The consequent activation of the hoof mechanism leads to increased growth of the hoof and improves the quality of the horn. In unshod horses the horny wall surface grows some 25 per cent more quickly than that of shod horses. To obtain a shape of hoof that is functionally correct and at the same time corresponds to the leg stance of the horse, it must be borne in mind that unshod horses wear down their hooves in an irregular pattern, particularly if they are carrying a load. In working horses the toe is worn down most rapidly and the heels become excessively high; though in correctly schooled dressage and jumping horses there is more loading of the heels (particularly at the landing phase in a jump, the heels act as shock absorbers) so that they experience greater wear.

With a faulty leg action, there is always uneven abrasion of the two halves of the hoof, which in turn has a detrimental effect on an already incorrect limb posture. This is often underestimated. The result can be the development of sharp edges on the hoof wall, which then chips, or, even worse, the unwelcome occurrence of sand cracks, which are vertical splits appearing just below the coronet. At the same time the sides of the frog come to lie across the lateral lacunae, closing them so that they cannot be cleaned. The frog becomes cracked and brittle, leading to hoof disease and lameness, so that the horse is quite unfit for use.

Unshod horses kept permanently in stables need the attention of a farrier every four or five weeks; if periods of grazing are combined with indoor stabling, the interval can be extended. Treatment consists of working on the hard horn, particularly the sharp crust in the region of the toes. Dead and loosened tissue should be removed from the sole of the hoof and the frog. The frog clefts are opened up by cutting the sides of the frog. This must be done carefully to ensure that the frog is not cut away excessively. For example, too deep paring of the covering supports of the horny wall surface can cause the back part of the wall surface to contract, causing the condition known as contracted heel, which can reduce the performance of the horse, even making it totally unfit for use.

Shaping treatment should restore the natural rounded shape of the hoof and the level ground surface. When foals are being treated in this way, particular attention should be paid to correct limb posture. While at grass, foals generally wear down their hooves constantly, but mostly not sufficiently. If irregularities in hoof wear or hoof formation are not remedied quickly, the effect of uneven pressure on the developing limbs will cause differing intensities of growth. This leads to faulty leg posture and additional strain on tendons and joints. Left too long, damage becomes permanent and the horse useless.

Posture faults include the following deviations from the norm: legs set down too wide apart or too close together; toes

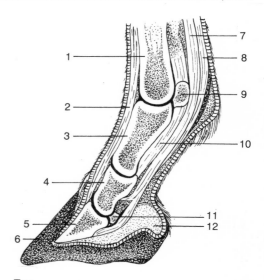

Toe
1 anterior metatarsal bone   2 cannon bone
3 coronal bone   4 coffin bone   5 sesamoid bone   6 pedal bone   7 common extensor tendon   8 deep flexor tendon   9 superficial flexor tendon   10 sesamoidean ligament   11 horny frog   12 pododermic tissues

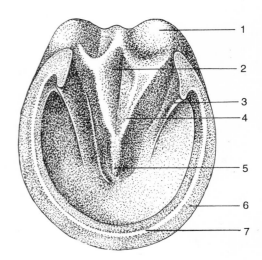

Ground surface of hoof
1 bulbs of heel   2 central cleft of frog   3 bar of hoof   4 lateral lacuna   5 apex of frog   6 crust or wall   7 white line

turned too far out, often associated with a straddling or knock-kneed posture; toes turned in, often with feet too close together and bow-legged posture; alterations in the region of the pastern, eg steeply upright pastern with obtusely-angled hoof (known as club foot), oblique pastern with hoof too obtusely-angled (known as bear's paw), or oblique pastern with excessively acutely-angled hoof.

In foals, it is absolutely essential to carry out a check of the hooves every four to five weeks.

The hardness of the horn depends not only upon its degree of cornification and development, but also upon its condition of health and moisture content.

Constructed as it is of hair-like tubes, the horn absorbs water rapidly but just as quickly gives it off. Horses of the heavy draught type (coldbloods) develop more intercapillary horn but also a thinner cortical layer and a thicker medullary layer of the horn-ducts; the result is softer horn, which inclines to higher water absorption. Warmblooded breeds have denser horn-ducts, less intercapillary horn and consequently harder horn that is less sensitive to the effects of moisture; in this respect, thoroughbreds and all breeds of steppe horses hold the best position and at the same time have the smallest hooves in relation to body size, in contrast to draught breeds which have large hooves.

Clearly then, one of the most important aspects of hoof care is that of ensuring the optimum moisture content of the horn. Long periods of dry weather, warm ground etc can lead to rapid moisture loss; the hoof becomes rough and splits. Damp stables, wet litter, pastures with boggy, constantly damp ground, the use of horses on wet land, cause the horn to become soft, weakened and finally brittle.

Liquid manure in the stable also has a highly corrosive action. By the sensible use of hoof grease and wood tar, an optimum moisture level can be maintained and decay, particularly in the region of the frog and the 'white line', can be avoided.

The breeder can learn from the farrier or by taking a technical course of instruction how to carry out simple work on the hoof such as paring or minor corrective adjustments. All major corrective measures, hoof dressing and treatment of the hooves to remove posture anomalies should be carried out by the farrier. Where necessary, particularly in the case of posture faults and diseases of the hoof, veterinary advice should be sought at any rate.

It is up to the breeder to recognise quickly the need for corrective treatment and to carry it out or have it carried out immediately. The more regularly and frequently corrective measures are carried out, the less radical will they be and the less likely are malformations in the foal.

Shoeing

Correct shoeing is an essential prerequisite for a high level of performance in the horse. Because of the speed at which the horn of the hoof grows, renewal, or at least removal, of the shoes by the farrier is essential every four to six weeks, irrespective of the breed of horse or the nature or intensity of its work.

The purpose of shoeing is: to protect the horn from excessive and uneven wear; to maintain and improve the natural foot and leg posture and the horse's pattern of movement; to prevent or treat diseases of the hoof, tendons and joints which can take the form of lameness.

The shoes must correspond to the shape and size of the hoof and the use to which the horse it put, and should be as light as possible. Usually they are fitted while hot, allowing the best possible adaptation to the hoof. 'Cold' shoeing should be carried out only in an emergency; it does not produce a smooth supporting surface so that as a result, dirt and small stones become wedged between the wall, sole and shoe, and bruises (causing lameness and inflammation of the hoof), splits and cracks can develop.

To ensure that hoof dressing is in keeping with limb posture, the horse must be examined both standing still and in movement before shoeing or hoof paring. Attention must also be paid to the type of wear shown by the old shoe.

The old shoe must not be torn off, but the rivets of the shoe nails should be loosened carefully with a rivet-blade, and after that, the nails drawn out one by one. This is the only way to prevent damage to the horny wall. The hoof should be shortened only with a paring knife and farrier's rasp, care being taken not to damage the varnish-like horn covering, the periople.

The ends of the shoe branches should lie broadly beneath the bulbs of the heels, extending beyond them on the outside by 2–3 mm ($\frac{1}{12}$ – $\frac{1}{8}$ in) but cut at the back precisely at the end of the heels. The heels of the hind hooves must be left as long as possible in order to protect the tendons, particularly in the case of show jumpers (because of the ability to absorb shock in the landing phase). If the branches are too long on the front shoes, the horse 'forges' (ie strikes its hind feet against the fore) and tears the shoes off; if they are too short, pressure is not spread across the entire available surface and the toes carry too much weight. In horses that tend to stumble, the toe of the shoe should be rounded off upwards.

The shoe is nailed on with six to eight nails which extend 1.5–2.5 cm ($\frac{1}{2}$–1 in) above the crust of the hoof wall. This means that the front nails lie higher than the back ones (parallel to the coronet). Broad clips increase durability and the stability of the sit of the shoe. They are fitted to the toes and sometimes the outer quarters of the shoes of the forefeet; as a protection against 'forging', the clips of the hind shoes are placed on the front inner side and back outer side.

Stud holes are drilled in pairs about 1.5 cm ($\frac{1}{2}$ in) from the end of the branch of the shoe. They make it possible to use screw-studs which help to prevent slipping when jumping, turning, making an abrupt halt or sudden movement on heavy or slippery ground, moving sideways and so on. They must be applied with great care so that the horses do not injure themselves or become lame which, otherwise, is likely to happen.

Permanently fixed studs, that is, those that cannot be screwed out, are not recommended because particularly in the stable or during transport, but also while at grass, the horse can inflict severe injuries not only upon itself, but also upon horses in its vicinity and even upon those persons in charge of it.

Cavalry Storms and Equestrian Contests

The Huns who stormed westwards in the fourth and fifth centuries, bringing about the migration of the peoples and the end of the Roman Empire, were mounted on small horses. Their relationship to the horse is spoken of in many contemporary accounts and they are summed up by Vaczy in this way:

Nature cannot weld the centaur more firmly to his trunk than the Hun is seated on his horse. While the children of the Huns are still scarcely able to stand, they are already used to riding. Other peoples sit on the horse; the Hun lives on it. The Huns do not dismount even to satisfy the call of nature. Mounted on horseback, they carry on trade, eat, drink and sleep bent over the horse's neck; they even hold important discussions on horseback. They are perfect bowmen and strike their target with sure aim, even from a galloping horse.

The Huns were followed by the Avars in about 570, again a nomadic race of horsemen that had its origin in the region that is today the Mongolian People's Republic. They rode with stirrups which at that time they had probably already known for some seven hundred years, but which were not used by European horsemen until about the year 1000, in defensive combat against the Magyars. The Avars disappeared in the eighth century; numerous graves of horsemen bear witness today to their existence in eastern regions of Europe.

At the time of the Magyar's occupation of the low-lying lands between the Danube and Theiss in about 896, their horses were about 13 hands high and those of the Finns, who about a hundred years earlier had crossed northern Russia and the Baltic regions to reach their present homeland, were roughly the same size. Both nations belong to the Finno-Ugrian tribe which came as nomads from the Ural into the region of Lebedyan between the Don and the Dniester, but were pushed further westwards by the Turkish Pechnegs. With their horses, that were now up to 14.3 hands high, the Magyars or Hungarians (the Slavs called them

'Ungri', introducing a nasal sound into the name 'Ugri') arrived in droves, creating insecurity throughout Europe. By the middle of the tenth century, they had reached northern France, northern Spain, southern Italy, Greece and Bulgaria, laying waste broad tracts of land along the whole of the Elbe and Danube. They were finally defeated at the battle on the Lechfeld in 955 by King Otto I, later Holy Roman Emperor. As were the Avars three hundred years before, the Magyar warriors were accompanied by their reserve horses which, following a leading mare, provided sustenance and allowed for frequent changes of horse and therefore a rapid advance.

The Byzantine Emperor Leo the Wise described them thus: 'They are followed by a great troop of horses, both stallions and mares, partly because the horsemen drink the mare's milk, partly to give the impression of larger numbers.' Although the Magyars carried sword and javelin, their principal weapon was the arrow, which they shot from the bow on a galloping horse with great accuracy.

Analyses of horse skeletons from the time of the migrations of the peoples (fifth and sixth centuries) found in the tombs of Avarian, Slavo-Avarian (seventh to ninth centuries) and Old Magyar (tenth century) horsemen show heights of between 12 and 15 hands, while the main body of horse stocks fell into the range between 13 and 14.2 hands. At this period in the second half of the first century, the custom was widespread in eastern and southeastern Europe, including the eastern parts of central Europe, of placing a horse and riding equipment into the tomb with the dead horseman. These saddle horses were usually stallions, which, because they worked as riding horses, were unlikely to have been used for breeding purposes. And since it was the larger animals that were chosen, they were the ones that were excluded from breeding. It was probably for this reason that for many centuries, across the large territory of eastern Europe and parts of southern and central Europe, horses did not become any larger and no deliberate, purposeful horse breeding could be carried out.

It is true to say that until well into the nineteenth century farm horses in most of the countries of Europe remained small and ungainly, in contrast to the saddle and carriage horses that were bred and used for representational and military purposes.

The Arabs, who were first mentioned as a tribe in the ninth century BC, were not at first horse breeders but semi-nomads, for whom the camel was the principal mount and beast of burden. The military value of the horse was probably first fully recognised by Muhammad, when his camelry was beaten by his enemy's cavalry at the battle of Mount Othod in AD 625. From that time on, he vigorously encouraged the development of horse breeding among the nomadic tribes of his native country. In his sayings, written down in the Koran, he incorporates the horse firmly into the religious and social mind of the Bedouin. The horse is mentioned in several of the suras, for example, in the third: 'Seemly unto men is a life of lusts, of women, and children, and hoarded talents [unit of credit equivalent to 26.2 kg silver] of gold and silver, and of horses well-bred, and cattle, and tilth; that is the provision for the life of this world; but Allah, with Him is the best resort.' The hundredth sura, 'The Chapter of the Chargers', invokes horses as witnesses.

A wealth of maxims on the subject of the horse dates from this period and recurs constantly in Arabian and later also in European literature. Although horse breeding and the use of mounted troops were developed rapidly by the Arabs, the fact that the horse was originally alien to them revealed itself for a long time in clothing and weaponry; for example, they had not yet adopted trousers or the sabre, and still used the javelin rather than the bow. In the thirteenth century, riding and carriage driving, fighting on horseback and equestrian sport were, on the whole, still at the level of Roman antiquity. Whereas in Europe the stirrup was in general use in the tenth century, in the Arabian countries, even in the thirteenth century, it was still the prerogative of the Turkish upper classes.

Since the keeping of horses in the climatic conditions of central Arabia and of parts of its border areas presents many difficulties, arising in particular from the large amounts of water required daily, horse breeding and horse management still remain today restricted to a small circle of wealthy Bedouin. In contrast to the nomadic horsemen of central Asia, none of the nomadic Arabian peoples made use in historical times or make use today either of the milk or flesh of the horse as food. Until the present century, the horse has been used only for riding, carrying out raids and in military conflicts. In the Battle of Bekr in 634, for example, only 100

Talisman belonging to an Arabian mare; such ornaments are still used on special occasions in Jordan today (Photo: Flade)

horses were used together with 700 camels. When, under Caliph Omar, animals were driven into special pasture lands for the purpose of increasing the numbers of riding and pack animals for the army, they included 30,000 camels but only 300 horses.

The conquest of Persia with its rich store of horses first provided the right conditions for the Arabs to build up large mounted military units and led to unparalleled military triumphs under the green flag of the Prophet. By 628, southern Arabia belonged to the territory of the caliphate; at the beginning of the eighth century, half of the known world had been conquered; and in the ninth century, the Arab-Islamic Empire had been set up, stretching from the Atlantic to the Indus, from the Caucasus to the southern Sahara. At the same time, Arabian scientific knowledge and culture were spread across the conquered territories and were enriched by contributions from the subject peoples. Such knowl-

edge included the theories and methods of horse breeding and horse management. Between 785 and the fifteenth century, no less than eighty-six books on the anatomy, physiology and behaviour of the horse and on equitation were produced in Arabia, containing a good deal of information that is still valid today. They include the *Book of Kabus*, of particular interest to the specialist, written by King Kjekjawus Unsur II Mali of Mazanderan in 1080 for his son Ghilan Schah, and which Goethe used in preparing his *Westöstliche Divan*. The chapter on the horse trade interested him so greatly that he wrote in the copy belonging to him:

How to move with care upon the earth,
Whether uphill or down from the throne,
And how to handle people, as well as horses,
All that, the king teaches to his son.
We know it now through you, who presented it to us . . .

Such works as the Baisonqur Manuscript (about 1420) provide detailed information on every aspect of the horse at that time. In 1286 there is mention in the literature of a case of artificial insemination. A Bedouin successfully impregnated his mare with the sperm of an Arab stallion. The latter's owner had refused to allow him to use the stallion for natural mating. A tuft of hair was used to transmit the sperm.

At the same time, the influence of Arab horse breeding increased in the occupied and in neighbouring territories. As a consequence of being bred for several thousands of years in this region with partial steppe or desert climate and the associated frugal conditions of care, the noble Oriental horse, that existed at that time in numerous varieties and breeds, exhibited here the characteristic 'dry type'. As a result of the prevailing natural conditions, particularly in central Arabia—predominantly in the Nejd uplands—and by selection for physical constitution and the use of particular methods of breeding, the true 'desert type' of Arabian horse developed. From the Oriental horse, a process of the very strictest selection produced the pure-bred Arabian. And so one of the oldest, most influential breeds which are existing today came into being.

As early as the ninth century, Arab horses had made their way via Spain and southern France to western and central Europe, while in the eleventh century, contacts began with south-eastern and eastern Europe. In Egypt, north-west Africa and Spain, new Arab-like breeds of horses developed, based on indigenous, very old breeds of domestic horses. Among the most important were the Berber horse, the Spanish Andalusian, and later, by way of the latter, the Neapolitan, Frederiksborg and the European medieval knight's horse. The Kladruber and Lipizzaner were influenced by the Andalusian, and all these breeds left their mark on the entire range of horse breeding in Europe, which in its turn influenced that of other continents as well. In the course of the 500 years of Arab rule, the Arabian horse made its permanent mark upon the breeds of Iran, India, Turkestan and areas further afield. In India, Iran, southern Russia, Hungary, Poland and in districts of the caliphate as it existed from the seventh to ninth centuries, there were, as there are still today to some extent, constant introductions of Arabian blood, so that there Arab half-blood breeds developed, the genetic standard of which is maintained by Arabian pure-line breeding and imports of Arabian stallions. The influence of Oriental breeds, in particular of the pure-bred Arab on the subsequent development of the English thoroughbred will be considered later.

It is interesting that the game of polo, which was first widespread throughout central Asia, was also played in the caliphate on Arabian horses. Polo was probably played in Persia from the seventh century BC and had been developed by the Persians from the game called *chaugan* (or *chaugana*). They called it *tschougàn* or *cōgān* (polo stick), the Sassanides of the third century AD, *chûvîgân*.

A variation is still in existence today in the Transcaucasian Republics of the USSR as the national equestrian game known as *tschowgan*. The Greeks adopted it as *tzykanion*; the Frankish knights brought it from Constantinople to France under the name of *chicane*. From Persia, the game spread to China in about the seventh century (*ta-ch'iu*—balled wool, woollen ball) and to Japan in the eighth century (*da-kyu*). The Empress Yang (wife of Tu-Tsung) wrote:

Ta-ch'iu is not a game purely for pleasure,
The deeper significance of the art of riding is not forgotten.
Skilfully, while riding with new agility
The player strikes the ball behind his back
So that it flies like a star.

In about the tenth century the Afghans (who called it *cavgan*) and Mongols also took over the game of polo from the Persians. In Persia itself, polo had its heyday from the fourteenth to sixteenth centuries. In the *Divan* written by the Persian poet Hafis (1325—90) there are, for example, numerous references to polo:

Sacrifice a thousand souls to him
whose head, in the game of love,
fell like the ball
into the hook of his stick.

or

Love cannot be called a game.
Heart, there is a head to risk:
for with the stick of desire,
the ball of love will not let itself be struck.

Caliph Jassid I introduced it under the Arabic name of *sawled-schân* (also *soldschan*) to Damascus, at that time capital of his Empire, and Caliph Harun Al-Raschid took it later to Baghdad. This perhaps most typical but at the same time most dangerous of equestrian games also gained a foothold in Arabian Egypt. Achmed Ibn-Tulun had the first polo ground laid out close to Fustat, today's Old Cairo. In spite of many, often serious accidents that befell a number of ruling sovereigns, the game remained for several hundreds of years an important means of education and equestrian training, with a marked representational function in the princely courts of the East and for a particularly long time in Persia (Isfahan). But from the nineteenth century onwards, no mention is made of it there.

As a result of close links with Persia, polo was known in India from the seventh century, but particularly in the fifteenth and sixteenth centuries it was played by the ruling houses, as, for example, under Emperor Akbar, who recruited polo ponies from his breeding stocks—12,000 of 'the most noble stallions'—and cavalry—200,000 horses; but it persisted only until the seventeenth century. It remained indigenous for another 200 years only in the region of Manipur, and was then 'exported' to Calcutta, and from there it again spread across India.

Only in Tibet was polo a truly national game of the common people from about 1600 onwards. Probably the name 'polo' comes originally from the Tibetan language. *Pu-lu*, *bo-bo* or *po-lo* was the name for the willow root from which the ball was made.

The English took over the game from Manipur in the middle of the nineteenth century—India at that time was a British colony—and in 1859 founded the first Polo Club; in 1869 the 'new' sport reached Britain where, in 1871, the first public polo competition was held. The old Persian name was unknown, and the game received its name 'polo' from the Tibetan *po-lo*, under which it is played in many countries of the world today.

Equestrian stone from Hornhausen. Seventh century, Museum für Vorgeschichte, Halle (Photo: Bieler)

At the time of the first victory of the Reconquista over the Arabian 'Moors' in Spain and the liberation of Valencia by the Spanish national hero, El Cid, in 1094, orders of knights were founded to liberate the Holy Land from the domination of Islam and to protect the Christian faith. After a number of crusades to Asia Minor, which in the end proved fruitless (1187), the Teutonic Order of Knights (founded 1190) directed its expeditions of conquest to the east and north-east and consolidated its dominion there.

There are many representations of the horses belonging to the knights of medieval Europe. The weight of the knight in his heavy armour called for a powerfully-built horse which was therefore in itself heavier and which, in contrast to the smaller, lighter horses that had been used until then, was necessarily also less mobile.

A game of polo. Indian miniature, around 1800. Oriental Department of Staatsbibliothek Preussischer Kulturbesitz, West Berlin

The armour, weapons and clothing of a knight weighed about 130 kg (290 lb). The added weight of the rider himself made a total of some 200 kg (440 lb) that the horse had to carry into battle. And precisely in southern France there were horses with a strong Oriental influence in their breeding, which had come by way of the formerly 'Moorish' Spain and from the thoroughbred horses imported by crusading knights, and these had left their mark in the breeding of the heavy horses that were now required (in the sense of coldblood breeds). These were seen particularly impressively in the Percherons, whose descendants, in spite of their large conformation and weight, betray the Oriental influence in, for example, head and croup shape.

In addition to the Ardennes horse already indigenous to France, experience of the newly-developed 'coldblood' breed was carried to the remaining princely houses of Europe and to their military commanders by the Order of Knights. In contrast to the horse bred for speed and for enduring long marches (*Palefridus*), or the ambler often used for journeys, the less hardy, slower and at the same time more massive war horse (*Dextrarius*) was evolved, into which a greater aggression and eagerness to fight had been instilled; this made it more difficult to look after but a more efficient fighter.

But with these horses, western and central Europe could do little against the attacks by Mongolian horsemen in the thirteenth century. Under Genghis Khan, vast hordes of horsemen had moved westwards—as well as eastwards and south-eastwards —from the area settled by the Mongols, riding their small horses that were clearly very similar to Przewalski's horse. Then in 1240, under his successor Ogotai Khan, they reached the Carpathians and laid waste central western Asia, eastern Europe and the Balkans. The losses they inflicted were terrible. During the winter of 1220/1 alone, more than six million people died in central Asia. In countries that were overrun, development was held back for centuries and traces of the chaos still exist in some of them today.

Irreplaceable cultural treasures were lost, including the flourishing stud farms in Turkmenia, Turkestan and Bactria; the Turanian horse was virtually exterminated in its original home; its traces petered out in the Oriental breeds of horses in Asia Minor and North Africa, apart from small groups including the Akhal-Teké. The terrorism of Genghis Khan was exceeded by that of his nephew Tamerlane in the second Mongolian invasion. As the Magyars had been, the Mongolian mounted warriors were also followed by a fairly large group of horses; contemporary reports suggest twenty to thirty, including several riders whom the horses

'ran after like dogs'; in this way, horses were always available and the high speed of advance could be maintained. As a typical example, the mounted vanguard of the Mongolian troops invading Hungary in 1241 covered the 300 miles between the Vereche border pass and Pest in only three days.

Genghis Khan had, of course, a particular interest in looking after the horses in his army. A thirteenth-century 'Secret Chronicle' contains an order of the day on this subject to the commanders of his troops, from which the following is an extract:

Take good care of the leading horses of your troupe, before they grow thin . . . Once the horses have become emaciated, you can treat them with as much care as you will, but it is no longer effective . . . On the way, you will come across many game animals. Do not allow the men to hunt them for pleasure as they feel inclined . . . Do not permit hunting equipment to be strapped to the saddle. During the march, no snaffle bit may be used; the horse's mouth must remain free . . . When *you* have once given an order, those who contravene it must be arrested and punished by the stick. Of those who contravene *our* orders, send those who deserve attention to us. Let all the rest, that is, the insignificant ones, be beheaded on the spot . . .

The 'Secret Chronicle' also mentions the wild horse that can be hunted on horseback like other game. During one such hunt Genghis Khan fell from his horse; the animal threw itself onto its back in fright when startled by the sudden appearance of a herd of wild horses, and the Khan was fatally injured (1227).

In 1268, Thomas von Spalato reported that the Mongols rode 'peasant-fashion' on their small, hardy horses that had the distinct appearance of the *taki* (Przewalski's horse) in contrast to the larger, longer-legged and more noble 'western' horses. He noted that their horses, also known as Tatar horses, were extremely frugal and were ridden at a fast gallop over hard, stony ground.

During the Mongolian domination of the Yüan dynasty (1271–1368), Marco Polo visited China (1292). According to the report that he published in 1298, the Khan owned very large royal stables in Xandu, the present-day Shang-tu, 30 miles north-west of Tolun (to the north of Peking), housing some ten thousand stallions and mares that were 'white as snow'. The milk from these mares could be drunk only by members of the 'family descended from Genghis Khan'. And further on he reported that every year, 'on the 28th lunar day in August, the milk of these mares was scattered to the wind. The esteem in which these horses are held is so high that no one dares to place himself in front of them or to hinder them in their movements when they are grazing on the Imperial pastures.'

Horse breeding in China at that time, particularly in the south, was of a high standard. In the province of Karazan, today's Yunnan, Marco Polo saw very large horses that were sold to India while still young. 'It is usual to cut off their tail so that they do not toss it back and forth.'

Concerning the courier postal system set up by Genghis Khan in the territory under his rule and continued by his successors, it is reported that it had at its disposal some two hundred thousand horses and ten thousand buildings. There were about four hundred horses at every post station, of which at any one time, half were being rested at pasture. A postal messenger covered 30 to 40 *parasangs* per day (about 125 miles). Express post could achieve 60 *parasangs* (about 210 miles) in a day. The average speed of the post horses, which were changed en route, was between 7 and 11 mph.

The Behaviour of the Horse

Large numbers of people, particularly the young, are actively engaged in equestrian sport; many stables and stud farms take a special interest in breeding and training good quality, all-round horses, and every year many thousands of holiday-makers spend their vacation with horses.

Lack of experience in handling such a large domestic animal—a riding horse weighs between 500 and 650 kg (10 and 13 cwt)—sometimes leads to serious accidents, the standard of performance of the horse remains low and, particularly in highly-talented horses, the capacity for improvement slows down prematurely.

In dealing with a horse, the handler must take the behavioural patterns of the horse as the starting point, and not human ways of thinking or human reactions. This requires a knowledge of the normal relationships between horses themselves (there are some fifty known means of communication between horses), of their patterns of behaviour and of the functioning of the sensory organs. It is a common mistake to apply human standards to the handling of a horse and to assume that the horse understands man. But because, in comparison with man, the intellectual capacity of the horse is minimal, this is simply not possible. Most of the great writers on equitation, starting from Xenophon, have pointed this out emphatically, with advice on the consequences.

The predisposition to particular patterns of behaviour is largely hereditary and can therefore be a component in selection for breeding.

Innate behaviour patterns are supplemented or replaced by experiences that the horse undergoes during its development as a foal and in its training. Undesirable innate behavioural patterns are eradicated, desirable ones consolidated. This process can be accomplished successfully only by consistent treatment, systematic and correct influencing, the proper use of the fundamental principles of animal training combined with a great deal of intuitive empathy, patience and kindness, together with a sound expert knowledge of the subject. The distinctive individuality and extreme sensitivity of the horse must be given meticulous consideration; from the very start, these two factors rule out a routine approach to rearing and training a horse with a high standard of performance. Modern animal training—and this also covers the training of the horse—rejects the use of force but not of firmness; fondling and rewards play a vital role, but disobedience must always be punished. Xenophon wrote:

What a horse does when compelled by force, it does not retain and performs badly, like a dancer trained by lashes of the whip or by cruel jibes . . .
Never to approach the horse in anger is an essential principle and an excellent habit for anyone who has to deal with one. The entire art of riding rests on a system of reward and punishment . . .

Johann Wolfgang von Goethe:

You must learn to read the thoughts of the noble horse that you want to ride. You must not make unwise demands or demand anything injudicious from it . . .

J. Fillis:

. . . Fondling and endearments, such as you will learn to give, are devices that should not be neglected. Alternating with punishment, they lay the foundation of the horse's training. Punishment should follow the fault as rapidly as a caress follows obedience.

The earlier the trainer can begin to exercise influence over the horse, the more certain will be the success of the schooling process which is a decisively important part of training.

Many of the problems in training a horse lie in the fact that its expressions of well-being or refusal can be recognised by a handler only with difficulty and after long individual experience. Cats purr, dogs wag their tails to express a sense of well-being; they are signs that can be recognised easily and acted upon by the person in charge. But it is much more difficult to recognise indications of general tranquillity in a horse, the freedom from tension as an indication of well-being. The essential pre-requisite for achieving lasting success in the training of a horse is the ability to interpret correctly and react immediately, and in a way appropriate to the level of understanding of the horse, to patterns of behaviour as diverse, but for the work of the horse breeder and equestrian sportsman as important, as 'reservedness to boisterousness', 'inhibition, anxiety to boldness, obstinacy' or 'affection, trust, obedience'.

Since Xenophon, other great writers on equitation have considered the psychological and emotional life of the horse. A general description including his own extensive experience of the behaviour of horses is given by Captain Thomas Brown, who wrote in the year 1831:

> The senses of the horse are acute and delicate; his intellectual character is marked by a quick perception, an excellent memory, and a benevolent disposition. It is very rarely, indeed, that a horse will tread on a human being, if left to his own will.
>
> Such is the disposition of the horse, although endowed with vast strength and great activity, that he rarely exerts either to his master's prejudice; on the contrary, he will endure fatigues, or even death, for his benefit. Providence seems to have implanted in him a benevolent disposition, and a fear of the human race, with a certain consciousness of the services man can render him.
>
> Though the horse is naturally bold and intrepid, he does not allow himself to be hurried on by a furious ardour. On proper occasions, he represses his movements, and knows how to check the natural fire of his temper. He not only yields to the hand, but seems to consult the inclinations of his rider . . .
>
> The affections of the horse are not confined to man, for he, in general, extends his attachment to other animals who are associated with him . . .
>
> The horse certainly reasons on consequences, for he at all times shews the greatest caution. If walking over boggy ground, it is next to an impossibility to urge him forward with speed, for every step betrays his fear of sinking; and if on rocky or uneven ground, where the stones are moveable, he will also pick his steps with much caution, feeling with his foot before he puts it down. It is well known that horses have a great dislike to cross muddy streams with which they are unacquainted. 'I have often remarked', says Professor Henninges, 'that when I have wanted to ride through clear water, where the bottom could be seen, the horse went through without hesitation, but when the water was muddy, he shrunk back, tried the bottom with one foot, and, in case he found it firm, advanced the other after it; but if, at the second step he took, he found the depth to increase considerably, he went back. Why did he act in this manner? Certainly for no other reason than because he supposed the depth would increase still further, and be attended with danger . . . That horses proceed very cautiously over elastic turf, or marshy ground, is known to every one who has travelled on horseback over ground of that description. Pontoppidan says, that the Norwegian horses, in going up or down the steep paths among the rocks, feel their way very cautiously before them, to ascertain whether the stones upon which they are about to step are firm . . .'

The innate behaviour patterns of the horse, and also those acquired by experience, must always be seen in the context of the specific efficiency of its sensory organs, and therefore they differ from horse to horse, and are to be considered and classified individually.

The horse's behaviour is based on a system of fear and self-protection, and its natural reaction is flight. Conforming with this system are its innate programmes of behaviour that come into play automatically when they are triggered off by a particular stimulus.

Curiosity— the instinct of flight

Among innate patterns of equine behaviour is a constant readiness to take flight. The principal reason for this is that, compared with its natural enemies, the horse is a relatively slow animal, with a speed of about 35 mph (wild horse), while the leopard, cheetah and other large beasts of prey can achieve 60 mph or more. Therefore, in the wild, it was necessary to be able to recognise danger early and evade it. Instant flight in the face of any unfamiliar situation was vital for survival of the wild horse. Fear provides a stimulus and the horse automatically reacts with the reflex action of 'self-protection'. For this reason, the horse seems to us to be timid and easily alarmed; but not so much fearful as inquisitive. This curiosity arises from caution and is reflected in exploratory behaviour carried out hesitantly with an eye to potential dangers.

The horse's visual faculty has developed a specifically protective function, which comes into effect extremely rapidly. If the horse senses that it is in danger, it relies first on its eyes and immediately takes evasive action. It does this by jumping aside or forwards, at the same time accelerating rapidly. Its extremely acute sense of smell interprets the situation more thoroughly but much more slowly, allowing a detailed check of an object to be carried out. In order to prevent anxiety or inhibition of the horse's protective function, it should always be given an opportunity to sniff at anything that might alarm it. When horses are left to themselves, they can be observed to move against the direction of the wind in order to be able to draw rapid and clear conclusions from any scents they discern.

It is necessary to provide the horse with experiences which eliminate the effect of fear and anxiety as triggers for the reaction of flight. Trust of human beings and obedience must take its place. Nevertheless, the rider should try to note any object that is potentially alarming before the horse discovers it, so that the horse can be reassured in good time by the voice and a patient attitude that no danger exists.

When a flight reaction is triggered off, but flight is impossible, the horse defends itself effectively by kicking, biting, rearing, pushing, or striking out. So before anyone touches a horse, enters its stall or box, starts to harness it or approaches it from behind, it is essential to talk to the horse. If a horse is startled and cannot escape forwards, it defends itself immediately, usually by kicking. And horses will also defend their territory against members of their own species or animals of other species, even against humans. Such behaviour is particularly likely when space is too restricted; serious accidents are caused by the horse's pushing, kicking, biting and rearing because the handler fails to make allowances for the territorial behaviour and natural 'claustrophobic' reactions of the horse, and overlooks the fact that though the horse's defensive actions are meant for its fellow species (usually causing little damage), for the human victim they can have extremely serious consequences.

In the sphere of fear and self-protection, one can perhaps also include the fact that in nature horses rarely jump. In contrast to beasts of prey, their physical structure does not favour this action, and the necessity for altering the course of movement at the take-off to a jump places them at a particular disadvantage. Their high centre of gravity and restricted capacity for stretching cause additional difficulties. In nature, the horse will walk round an obstacle behind which it cannot see, since danger may lurk on the other side. Horses are afraid of water; they only jump over it if there is no other way out of a dangerous situation (and then only a distance of about twice their body length). Important consequences follow from this for show jumping and cross-country training. Training horses successfully to absolute obedience and unswerving reliability for cross-country and show jumping work implies eliminating their fear of the unknown. To this end, the horse's sense of smell can be used (let it sniff at objects and take its time), and by frequent repetition innate behaviour patterns can be eliminated in favour of the desired ones. Training in technique and training in behaviour must form a single unity. In training the horse a number of special features must be taken into consideration.

The hunger drive

One behavioural pattern in the horse that operates particularly forcibly is its pronounced hunger drive. So strong is it, that it frequently overcomes inhibitions, fear and anxiety. It should therefore be exploited in order to transform innate reflexes into those desired by the trainer. This is a well-known tactic also used successfully in training other species of animals. One possibility is to offer a handful of oats, a sugar lump or other titbit as a reward after a difficult—because unnatural—action has been demanded of the horse. Overcoming inhibition or hesitation by simply showing or actually giving the horse some favourite titbit is one of the methods by which the horse can be persuaded effectively and without conflict to fulfil difficult tasks. A perfectly satisfactory way to establish and maintain contact between handler and horse can be 'through the stomach'; here, feeding plays an important part and, for this reason, it is advisable to give the task of feeding the horse to the person who has most to do with it, and to urge the rider always to have something edible for 'his' horse in his pocket as a reward after a difficult, strenuous performance.

Because of the intensity of the hunger drive, care must be taken that rivalry does not develop among horses. Length of the manger, the area of pasture land, watering facilities and so on must be properly measured and adequately provided. When feeding takes place in the stable, attention must be given to order of precedence. It is pointless to keep a pushing, jostling and therefore high-ranking horse waiting for its feed with the intention of teaching it to wait, or the idea that its turn should come later. Jostling and pushing are usual among horses being fed and watered. The degree of aggressiveness and force used is adapted to members of the same species and is therefore considerable. For a stableman to get in among horses that are displaying possessiveness towards food can be extremely dangerous. Because the horse has a very marked sense of time, which is linked to particular experiences such as feeding, returning to the stable, being taken out to and brought in from pasture, starting and finishing work etc, its perception of feeding times is accompanied by the appropriate physiological consequences (saliva flow, start of digestive action). Therefore regularity of feeding, stable work and training and the maintenance of a well-ordered routine is essential. Lack of organisation and muddle cause unrest in the stable or among a group of horses, and are a source of losses arising from injuries (that reduce the animal's value), decline in performance, disturbance of growth, and the effects of abnormal stress.

The nervous habit of crib biting, in which the horse nibbles continually at hard food, paddock fencing, wood, or stable equipment, can be seen as part of the hunger drive, and perhaps also as a manifestation of the horse's strong play instinct.

The feeding behaviour of the horse fundamentally directs it forwards (in any case, it is very difficult for a horse to move backwards and it is not a natural movement). This must be remembered when tying up a horse: it may entangle itself round a tree or post and be unable to extricate itself again.

Learning capacity

In man, behaviour is directed largely by his own processes of thought (conscious action), in animals by innate programmes and those learned by experience (imprinted), and these in turn, if they are properly supplied and utilised by the rider, make it possible for the horse to be used as a sporting animal.

The horse's ability to learn, in comparison with that of other mammals such as dogs, dolphins, and primates, is only moderate. However, the predisposition to learn varies individually from horse to horse, as it does from breed to breed, and this is to be taken into account in schooling and training, indeed in dealing with horses in general. It demands a detailed consideration of the special features of the individual animal. It should be borne in mind that to achieve a certain level of performance (eg specialised tests in dressage), the horse must possess a high constitutional inclination to learning. Because of the great diversity in learning capacity, there are undoubtedly some horses that are simply not intelligent enough to be trained to top-rank performance.

Bearing in mind the potential degree of understanding that the horse is able to develop from its primitive pattern of behaviour, the following principles of learning should be applied: the eradication of undesirable modes of behaviour from the innate behaviour pattern and the consolidation of desirable modes of behaviour in the horse's innate behaviour pattern; the instilling of desirable modes of behaviour by means of experiences that the horse undergoes in the course of its relationship with humans and with its environment. This last point includes carrying out par-

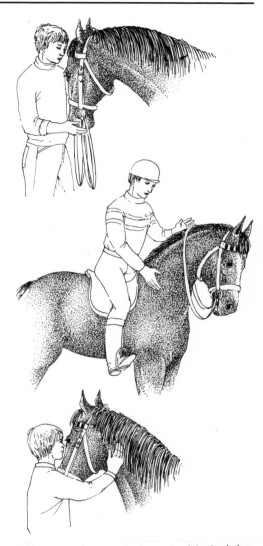

Stroking or patting particular parts of the body has a soothing effect on the horse and helps to establish contact between rider and horse

ticular movements and lessons (dressage exercises, jumping courses), and teaching safe behaviour in traffic and in the technological environment of today.

Because the faculty of memory is differentiated and specialised in the horse, practice experience, particularly in the techniques of equestrian sport, must be repeated constantly and at quite short intervals. The quality of the experience must remain constant, for example, in the use of aids (that is, methods by which the rider conveys instructions to the horse) and the application of such aids to particular parts of the body (always the same place). This is why so much importance is attached to the quality of the rider's use of natural aids such as seat, hands, legs, voice, and to the general professional ability of people who handle horses, care for and train them.

The capacity of memory in a horse can be equated with the ability of its brain to store particular information for a specific duration, which is highly individual. It is directly linked with the ability to learn. Like other vertebrates, the horse has a good memory for what it has learned, retaining it sometimes for several years. After a year without training, it can still carry out nineteen out of twenty visual tasks. The following are some of the aspects of the equine memory:

Visual-motor memory   The horse has a very good power of recollection in a place where earlier some specific event occurred; for example, the horse will show fear on revisiting the site of an earlier alarm.

Temporal memory   Times for feeding, beginning and end of work, or rest periods in the stable are well remembered. It is necessary for stable and work schedules to be followed scrupulously and planned methodically.

Memory for places   This is the basis of the horse's ability to find its way about in familiar surroundings, also of its pronounced ability to find its way home unguided.

Acoustic memory   The horse will instantly recognise the voice of some one well known to it, even after a long period of time; it recognises commands and responds to its own name (preferably a two-syllabled word), the latter, however, only with frequent repetition.

Olfactory memory   Even after a long interval, the horse recognises someone it knows well by that person's specific body smell (note that a change of clothes can have an effect), as well as particular objects such as the stable or loose box; blind horses easily find their own stall in the stable by sniffing it out.

The following facts must also be remembered. Like most mammals, the horse has a very restricted short-term memory, probably at most five to ten seconds. It serves to trigger off particular rapid reactions. For this reason, praise and blame for particular actions must be handed out immediately, since the horse is able to recollect the context—cause and effect—only for a few seconds. Mistakes made here by the trainer can lead to serious training faults, are cruel to the animal and can prevent the horse from reaching a high standard.

The horse has a very poor isolated visual memory. This includes its 'recollection' of people it has seen before. It recognises a person only as a whole figure, not from individual parts of the body, so it cannot perceive facial difference, for example, as a distinguishing characteristic.

The horse's ability to learn and its faculty of memory play a special role in the 'mother-child' relationship and in the 'imprinting' of the foal on its dam, which takes effect from the first hour of life. The hormonally-directed (innate) phase of care-giving behaviour lasts some three to six days; from the seventh to tenth day of life, the hormonal phase declines and the readiness of the mare to provide care gradually reaches a stage where it is maintained only by constantly repeated contact with the foal. During the transition from the 'hormonal' to the 'contact-related' care phase, care-giving behaviour is particularly sensitive to stress: the mare displays rejection towards other members of the herd, towards animals of other species, often towards a familiar handler, even towards 'harmless' foals belonging to neighbouring mares, driving them off by kicking and biting. She pushes herself between the handler and her foal, and between the sun and the foal. In this way, she is protecting the foal from any disturbance of the imprinting bond during the critical period.

A foal that is raised in the absence of its dam will imprint upon a 'substitute mother', the person who feeds it from a bottle, for example. It is a particularly difficult problem if the mare dies during the critical period after the imprinting bond has already come into effect. In such cases the substitute mother is usually not accepted, and the foal can be kept alive, if at all, only with a good deal of effort, and never achieves the growth norm.

Mother-child contact is established initially by the mare's olfactory memory, later by acoustic and visual means. Only from about the twelfth day is individual recognition necessary, since before that time, the foal remains close to its dam. Nevertheless, the mare invariably checks the foal by sniffing even when she has perceived it visually. Foals up to seven weeks of age which have lost sight of their dams are unable to recognise them visually at a distance of more than 20 m; they produce a distress call which is answered by the dam, and then run in the direction of this acoustical signal. From the second week of life, a foal invariably answers the call of its dam; it is thus also acoustically imprinted on her.

The imprinting effect declines very quickly after the foal is weaned or in the case of a new pregnancy. But until that time, the mare-foal bond remains strong, even when they are separated for a particular length of time such as the daily working period of the mare. The same is true of the substitute mother.

Concerning the learning ability of the horse, it will generally be found that, because of the relatively slight storage capacity of the equine brain for information of every kind, excessive input blocks further absorption. Particularly in intensive training, work should be planned systematically with the aim of deliberately avoiding any overtaxing of the horse's brain.

Group-related behaviour

Group-related behaviour in a horse can bring about joint action by contagious impulses. If, for example, an individual animal takes fright, a whole team of horses may bolt; if one horse in a herd or in a column of riders is startled, the entire group 'explodes'. It is also this transmission of mood that causes the whole group to lie down, turn round or neigh simultaneously. It can even happen that the remaining members of a group, while still in the stable, will take over the genuine mating behaviour of an individual, even when the physiological condition is absent, that is, they are not themselves in oestrus. Stable vices such as wind-sucking (swallowing air), weaving (swaying movements, shifting the weight from one foreleg to the other) and chain rattling can be transferred from horse to horse.

One effect of group-related behaviour is to include among the horse's innate patterns of behaviour the compulsion to create a hierarchy within the group. Its structure is based primarily on body mass (weight) and the age of the horse as a member of its group. In this, body mass represents increased physical power, age correspondingly greater experience. Age is clearly a more significant factor in deciding precedence than size, which is also true in the case of cattle and pigs.

An existing hierarchy in horses remains in effect for a long time. As a member of the group, the individual animal remembers its position for several months, even when there are interruptions, and acts in accordance. Female animals exhibit this characteristic particularly strongly. It affects principally feeding, sexual behaviour and selection of eating place and resting place in loose housing. The highest ranking animal is the first to eat, and in the case of a stallion, the first to cover.

During the period in which an order of precedence is being established or when it is disturbed by the arrival of new horses, the animals are most likely to be quarrelsome, and this is when the risk of injury or accident is at its greatest. Over a long period of time, the top and bottom positions of a table of ranking order are the most stable.

Particularly among foals, alterations and extensions of existing groups should be avoided. If new additions are unavoidable, the horses must conform with the group in age and state of development.

While it is feeding in the stable, the horse usually defends its eating place only while it is taking up food. Once it has its mouth full, it allows itself to be pushed aside from the manger or water bucket by animals of lower rank (even by the handler, but with care). Once its mouth is empty, there will be trouble again. Therefore it is necessary to ensure that all members of the group can obtain food and water with ease and without crowding. This is the only way to provide for individual rates of growth and feeding requirements and to exclude injuries and accidents.

In training saddle horses, there are certain further considerations. Horses of high social status do not like to walk at the back of a column; but since this behaviour pattern is innate, it can be changed only by systematic work and not by force. At the moment of punishment, horses that are being corrected feel themselves to be lower in rank than the person punishing them, therefore they push backwards, run away or defend themselves, if flight is impossible, by rearing, kicking, or pushing. It is as well to be aware in advance of these probable consequences.

Social patterns— instinctive gregariousness

Instinctive gregariousness, the herd instinct, is a very strong drive, since it represents a crucial protective function for the individual animal in the herd. In addition, the group makes it necessary for each member to have a particular place within it (order of precedence) and gives each individual horse a feeling of security.

Within the framework of the herd, the dam provides her foal with essential experience during its first few weeks of life and in this way secures for it a place within the herd. In contrast to the bull, the stallion does not participate in this process, and the mutual tolerance displayed between mares is less than that between cows, for example. Antipathy towards particular 'alien' foals, especially young ones, can be very dangerous, as can that towards certain members of the same or different species, often leading to open hostility.

The herd provides repose for the individual animal, but at the same time, supplies social contact which shows itself in mutual grooming, active play (activity encourages growth and food intake, the foal 'plays its way into adulthood'), communal food-seeking (it eats and drinks better in company). Quite often, the horse's herd instinct can be satisfied by a 'group' consisting of only two horses. Such 'friendships' between two horses should, where possible, be recognised as beneficial and treated with consideration.

The herd instinct also explains the horse's attachment to various other living creatures that it accepts into its own pattern of living, treating them as conspecifics, and especially so if its relations with its own species are restricted or non-existent. Horses develop social relationships with these creatures that can lead to permanent bonds. They especially favour goats, sheep, dogs and cats. Destruction of these bonds can have a serious effect upon the horse. A vital factor in a relationship between man and horse is that the horse accepts the man on its own initiative and seeks to enter a relationship of trust with him. The horse's urge to establish contact with members of its own species or with other creatures finds expression in the following ways:

- attempting to establish physical contact with a familiar animal, including

gripping the skin with its teeth as a gesture of friendship, also soft whinnying to express affection;
- running to a familiar creature (or even object) in anxiety or danger, eg a horse's attempts to re-enter a burning stable can be prevented only by force (in such cases, keep a close watch on exercise areas and paddocks);
- readiness to approach objects that appear dangerous in the company of the familiar person or animal;
- following along behind or frisking round the familiar person or animal (beware of high-spirited gambolling).

Action of this kind is, of course, only the working out of the horse's innate behaviour patterns and experience gained in contact with man; it is not deliberate, conscious action on the part of the horse. The horse has a conception of man as an animal (zoomorphism), with all the consequences this entails, applying standards of animal behaviour to its treatment of man, which can therefore be dangerous. Anyone who seeks to establish a good relationship with a horse in order to train it effectively and safely must base his thinking on the mental processes and mental capacity of the horse and act accordingly. This includes particularly the use of physical contact as a means of communication, calling into play the horse's extremely acute and receptive sense of smell and touch, and establishing contact as frequently as possible in the course of everyday care. It is always wrong to impute human characteristics and capacities to the horse.

Regularly recurring behaviour patterns (periodicity)

In all mammals, particular patterns of behaviour occur regularly each day, and can be classified as a twenty-four hour rhythm. They are species-characteristic, and therefore differ from species to species. Within the animal species, in for example, the horse, one can distinguish between:

- species-characteristic type of rhythm that is typically normal (TN);
- species-characteristic type of rhythm that comes into effect when the animal is in an abnormal state, for example, as a result of alterations in the hormonal level during oestrus and lactation (TAN);
- atypical behaviour as a result of abnormal stress, characterised by displacement of periodicity and alterations in the duration of its phases (AT).

The horse reacts to nervous strain and related alterations in status in a variety of ways, but generally with extreme sensitivity. Therefore conditions of stimulation almost always cause alterations to the typically normal behaviour patterns. This susceptibility to stress varies from individual to individual and is related to age and social status. Particularly affected are the periodicity of feeding and sleep.

Typically, the principal maximum food intake is very stable and occurs at about two hours before sunset, with a total activity of twelve hours (roughly midday to midnight). This has implications for feeding arrangements that should be taken into consideration. Subsidiary maxima vary between individuals, but are generally

Previous page:
62 These young stallions play. In a serious fight between rivals the fighters bite at the neck of the opponent

63 Attentive and actively interested, the stallion sizes up all that happens on the edge of its exercise area

64/65 Inquisitive but at the same time ready to attack, the Haflinger stallion watches the photographer's movements

66 When getting to its feet, a horse almost invariably raises its forequarters first and then its hindquarters

67 To lie down, a horse first bends its forelegs inwards, then lowers its hindquarters to one side. Any other sequence of movements is rare

68 A horse rolls on the ground to reinforce scent-markings, but also as a means of skin-care and grooming

69 Neck-to-neck combat and going down on the forelegs can be the fourth stage in a fight between rival males after threat (1), striking out with the forelegs (2), and biting at the neck and forequarters (3). In the case of these foals, it is still play and learning

70 A mock fight between rivals has begun. Both horses are about to rear. The foal on the right has already raised its forelegs from the ground

72   Whinnying, consisting of a series of separate sounds, is used to mark out territory. A rhythmic sequence of sounds is part of the sexual behaviour of the stallion. Horses also use calls on other occasions, for example, to indicate well-being or affection, and also pain or extreme fear

73　Cowering attitude. This mare is
extremely mistrustful and is guarding
her foal jealously

74　I have to do it and it is an effort!

75　Typical attitude of a mare while
'staling'. Stallions and geldings do
not straddle the legs

76 Typical position for covering, including mimicry

77 These two are becoming acquainted; the young Lipizzaner stallion displays *flehmen*, baring the upper teeth and 'sniff-tasting', the better to investigate the finer points of a scent

78 A horse rolls on the ground to
scratch its rump, back and neck

79 Thirst and hunger are particularly strong instinctive drives in the horse, even supplanting caution and restraint. These horses are trying to force each other away from the bucket. Aggression is the usual result

80 Mutual nibbling between horses is a natural inclination and the basis of 'social grooming' which is an important aspect of skin health. The closer the partners are in the social hierarchy, the more frequent is nibbling contact; the practice is less frequent between horses of widely differing rank than between co-ranking individuals

81 Sitting sideways on its belly —one of the various positions in which a foal will rest. As it grows, it abandons certain of these positions entirely

82 A horse rarely yawns. When it does so, the cause is usually an excess of carbon dioxide that affects the bloodstream and respiratory centre. But, as in humans, yawning can be 'contagious'

83 From time to time, the dam makes nasal contact with her foal to be sure of recognising it and remembering it as her own

Following page:
84 Caution, not fear, is an instinctive characteristic in a horse

concentrated in the period between about 5 pm to 9 pm.

The effects of stress on adult horses can entirely disrupt this periodicity and should be considered as unfavourable (AT). Where alterations in schedule are necessary (changes in work programme, changes in clock time), quite long periods, at least three weeks, are necessary for adaptation.

Typically, the principal maximum period for rest and sleep (standing or lying) occurs about four hours before sunrise. The sleep pattern of the individual animal is group-related and probably follows that of the horse of highest rank. There are individual small subsidiary maxima occurring within the hours of daylight between 8 am and 8 pm, but they are insignificant. In this context, sleep should not be confused with rest.

The effects of stress lead to an atypical pattern of the phases of sleep, reduce the principal maximum and, if repeated, can lead to the disturbance of all bodily functions. The causes can be interference in stable routine, constant disturbance of horses in the stable and paddock, or failure to maintain training and work schedules. When the horse is in transit, on treks lasting several days or on visits to shows and events, it is essential that the animal's accustomed sleep rhythm is maintained. It is significant that the presence of the highest-ranking horse has the effect of reducing stress in the rest of the members of the group. In order to turn this phenomenon to practical use, the handler must, of course, be able to recognise which horse is the highest in rank.

Rest and sleep

For adult horses, the necessary duration of rest is some seven hours a day, although it may be less. In horses of the highest rank, there is an observable reduction in the duration of the rest and sleep period.

As the horse gets older and consequently higher in the ranking order, there is a clear reduction of the sleep phase (principal maximum) in favour of other activities such as exercise, feeding and particular social interactions.

The handler in charge should note that the action of seeking out the sleeping place introduces the psychological state of rest. The sleeping place is a suitable part of the loose box or paddock selected by the horse, to which it always returns when it wants to sleep (corresponding to appetitive behaviour).

There are various positions that a horse is likely to adopt for its necessary periods of sleep and rest, such as curled up in a prone position, lying on the side of the belly, crouching position usually with muzzle supported, extended side position, standing with back legs taking weight alternately.

The horse's rest positions reflect to a considerable extent its phylogenetic development. As in the embryonic state, the principal position of rest and sleep for horses of all ages is with bent limbs. Up to one or one and a half years, the rolled-up position or side-belly position is characteristic as the infantile position of rest. It is scarcely ever observed in adult animals. The crouching or extended sideways positions together with the standing position are used throughout the lifetime of the horse. Very rarely, a horse will rest in a seated position.

It is interesting that, like other ungulates, a horse preparing to lie down will first make preparatory pawing and turning movements, then simultaneously start to bend its limbs and direct its head downwards towards its couch, will lower the front part of its body first, with alternate bending of the forelegs and let itself drop to the ground. Perhaps the action of revolving and pawing the ground can be interpreted as the preparation of a hollow in the ground as a sleeping place. In general, standing up follows the same process in reverse. Older and hard-worked horses clearly find it quite painful to lower themselves to the ground and a considerable effort to stand up again, so they prefer a standing position for sleep and rest. It is necessary for horse handlers to be familiar with the details of the lying and standing processes, so that in the case of illness, accident, a fall or inability to get up, they will be able to provide the correct measures of help.

Self-grooming

In the horse, as in all other equids, many actions can be observed that contribute to the care of the body. Such actions can be in response to internal stimuli such as itching of the skin, loss of hair, change of coat, wounds that are healing or smarting, and the presence of foreign bodies, or external agents such as insects or ectoparasites. The horse deals with the first group by cleaning activity, with the second by defensive measures. It is possible to distinguish a series of such grooming activities undertaken by the horse itself, such as movements of the skin (twitching), shaking, pushing and rubbing against objects, stamping, scratching, rolling on the ground, nibbling at itself.

These grooming activities also include 'social skin care' in the form of mutual nibbling, mainly on those parts of the body that the horse itself cannot reach. Priority is given to the region of the mane (more than 50 per cent), withers (about 15 per cent) and back (about 10 per cent). The inclinations to nibble and to be nibbled at are equally strong and therefore the principal element in social skin care. The closer two horses are in the ranking order, the more frequent is nibbling contact likely to be, that is, there is less nibbling between a horse of high rank and one of low than between two horses of approximately equal status.

It is important to provide the horse with opportunities for skin care (cleanliness, avoidance of disturbance and stress) and to support it by active assistance (grooming), especially during protracted periods of stabling, when there is excessive sweating or when the seasonal change of coat takes place.

Bodily excretions

Even in the domestic horse, bodily excretions are associated with particular signalling functions and trigger off typical patterns of behaviour. The aim of such behaviour is to keep urine and dung away from the horse's own body; the places where the horse sleeps, feeds and grazes are to remain clean. In the pasture, dung is usually dropped at places where grazing is poor, for example, where there is much long, stalky grass, producing areas of rank growth which the horse avoids until the dung is completely humified. This innate 'hygienic' behaviour should be borne in mind when the horse is stabled, in the interest of the animal's welfare and to avoid infestation by parasites (worms) and putridity. Putrefactive agents harm the animal by producing putrescent gases, ammonia, hydrogen sulphide and carbon dioxide. These gases are insect attractants and encourage large common houseflies and stable flies to breed in excessive numbers. Air in the stable that is contaminated by putrescent gases attacks the respiratory organs; it reduces performance and has a damaging effect particularly on saddle horses and racehorses. Rest and sleep are disturbed, since the ground layers especially contain a high concentration of ammonia and hydrogen sulphide, and give off the smell of the horse's own (species-characteristic) excreta most strongly. Horses have a particular aversion to this and try to avoid it. So it is essential that the bedding is constantly kept fresh and clean and that there is good ventilation.

A horse's micturition behaviour (urination) involves seeking out a particular place, exploratory sniffing, pawing the ground, taking up a stretched position with the legs straddled and tail lifted, at the same time holding the ears in a characteristic position, all the while maintaining a particular rhythm. Micturition is a means of transmitting information (time, place, dam-foal relationship, sexual partner relationship); sexual status is conveyed by accessory glands with a special signalling function (hormone secretions).

Much the same is true of defecation (excretion of dung). Because faeces take a considerable time to break down, a certain optical component comes into play in addition to the effect of smell, although only in a subsidiary role. As in micturition, there is a signalling function, giving information on the status of the sexual partner by means of olfactory examination. This gives rise to marking behaviour. The stallion inspects the dung of a mare then walks over the area and marks it with its own dung.

Feelings of pleasure and fear encourage autonomic urination and dunging, for example, riding in to dressage or show-jumping competitions. Binding the eyes, which causes anxiety, leads to increased bowel activity and can dispel colic due to constipation. Fresh bedding induces increased urination.

Feeding

Because of the horse's compulsive urge to eat and nibble, it also chews or ingests hard organic materials that are not part of the normal range of feeding stuffs, for example, wood (stable fittings, fences, gates), particularly when it is fresh (trees), so it is necessary to take precautionary measures. Trees and shrubs in paddocks should certainly be fenced off. Horses are also especially fond of nibbling leather such as the tack of a neighbouring horse or its stable halter.

The anticipation of food is frequently associated with the horse pawing the ground with its forelegs. In contrast to other herbivorous mammals such as cattle, one leg is placed well forward during grazing, enabling the head to reach the food more easily. With jerky movements of its head, the horse plucks off the food with its incisors, chews and swallows it. Lips and tongue gather up loose parts of plants, chaff, grains of corn, and in the course of this collecting-up action the horse is able to sort out any foreign bodies that might be present. This technique of selecting is based on the horse's sense of smell and is undoubtedly highly competent. Frequent snorts remove dust and other loose pieces of food from the horse's nostrils (although not from the manger).

In addition to a preference for sweet or salty foods, it is noticeable that while at pasture in the afternoon the horse eats a higher percentage of acidic plants. The causes are undoubtedly physiological and dietary in nature, linked to the horse's metabolism. Dew-covered grass is universally grazed. But there are certain distinctions here. On the one hand, the evening hours before dew falls are used for grazing, on the other, it is claimed that grazing horses actually prefer dewy grass. It may be that there are climatic or other factors here, or even acquired habits that have brought about the different behaviour patterns.

An important factor in feeding is ranking order. The feeding place is defended if an 'attack' is anticipated. This requires separation of the horses within the stable between barriers, stalls, or loose boxes, which also provide a measure of protection for the handler. A horse will continue to eat only when it does not need to be on the defensive.

In a grazing meadow, it is usual, and indeed necessary in view of the low concentration of foodstuff, for a horse to feed continually and, as a result, to be left with little time for other activities. The horse in a stable, on the other hand, with relatively few feeds (being fed three to five times each day at most) and with a highly-concentrated diet, has a good deal of time during which it can develop bad habits, usually as a result of boredom. If its urge for activity is not fully satisfied by means of exercise, a horse can easily develop stable vices such as weaving, sucking wind, crib-biting, chewing at the halter of a neighbouring horse and so on. It is always well to consider how far the time spent by the horse in the stable can reasonably be reduced and replaced by grazing or exercise.

Reproductive behaviour

The general reproductive behaviour of the horse is based on the complicated interaction of many internal and external factors, a few of which are considered below. The more highly developed the brain of a species of mammal, the greater is its participation in and influence on the reproductive behaviour. This higher level of development of the nervous system is associated with the sensitivity of the animal to influences that affect the nervous system. Abnormal stress leads to severe, degenerative physical and psychological disturbances; stress situations affect directly the endocrinal system and therefore also the hormonal system. Since the horse is one of the higher mammals, it can be expected to exhibit high susceptibility to stimulation in this respect. Quantitative differences in the intensity of reproductive behaviour are largely inherited. Mating behaviour is not learned but represents a stage in the maturing process. With increasing age and experience, the stallion's covering technique improves. It is for this reason that experienced stallions are used as trial stallions in stud farms and breeding establishments. It is also well known that the intensity of mating behaviour (sexual drive) decreases with the increasing degree of inbreeding.

Normal sexual behaviour presupposes contact with animals of the same species.

And here, ranking order can be seen as a further regulatory element.

Stallions have extremely intensive reproductive behaviour. They are guided by the sexual smell of the mare (the region of the sexual organs, dung and urine), from which they infer her current physiological status (the time of ovulation) and so the most favourable time for mating. The horse will display signs of *flehmen*, a fleering facial posture that serves to intensify the olfactory investigation. Fights between rival males represent one aspect of the stallion's mating behaviour. They are 'rehearsed' even between female foals (bisexual characteristic in the horse). In the wild, they can lead to serious injuries or to death. Even domesticated stallions are usually quarrelsome when together. This characteristic is, however, partly dependent upon training and breed, partly upon climate (in warm zones there is greater tolerance). A handler who attempts to separate fighting stallions is risking his life. Young stallions that have not yet covered can come to tolerate one another. But breeding stallions must be kept apart although, if possible, allowed to see and sniff at one another through boxes with latticed partitions. When riders are in groups, care must be taken to maintain adequate distances between horses, including sideways. When stallions are harnessed as a team, there must be an assistant driver to see that the stallions do not become quarrelsome when making a halt.

A fight between rival males, making allowance for transitional situations, takes basically the following course, though not all, or additional, actions may be performed: threat (head low, ears laid back, slow circling of opponents, or galloping towards one another with bucking); rearing, striking out with forelegs, clasping (fighting with blows); bites to the neck, shoulder, forelegs, withers, if the opponent retreats or attacks from behind, also to flanks, croup, and hind legs; striking out with hind legs; retreat or gestures of submission. During all phases, grunting and whinnying can be heard, as well as squeals and a soft, deep wheezing from the defeated horse.

With a violence and intensity typical of the fights between rival males, but unique among mammals, the stallion carries out the mating preludes and the mating act itself. Mare and stallion are equally involved in the foreplay which creates a readiness for mating and directly affects physiological processes that are dependent upon the sexual stimulation of the partner and which determine fertilisation.

The stimulation of a psychological response in the mare should be given careful encouragement. It is worth pointing out that orgasm should be achieved in order to bring about the best possible psychological reactions in the mare and a greater likelihood of fertilisation. Evidence of fertilisation is the fact that as a result of mating the duration of oestrus is reduced. As the final stage approaches the mare's oxytocin reserves drop. When it ceases, the mating drive is fulfilled.

In a herd, the stallion drives the mare, and when she is in oestrus she follows the stallion and pushes against him. Then there is cautious contact between the two, gentle gripping of the skin with the teeth, nibbling and muzzle contact (naso-nasal) or muzzle to sexual zone contact (naso-anal), while the stallion gradually takes over the more active role, thereby preparing himself to mount.

The mare indicates readiness to mate when she turns her croup to the stallion and lowers it, lifting her tail to one side and straddling the hind legs, and sometimes also the front legs.

An indication that the mare is in season is that she seeks out other horses, sniffs at them and touches them intensively, uttering squealing sounds. If the belly and particularly the flanks and the area of the pelvic ligaments of the croup are touched, she lifts her tail and a reflex comes into play that inhibits her movement—for this reason, mares in season that are ridden can be moved forward only with difficulty—the hind legs are straddled, she lowers her croup and bends her back, mucus is secreted rhythmically from the swollen and reddened vagina, with eversion of the vulval lips known as 'winking'.

The sexual stimulation of the mare depends to a large extent upon that of the stallion. Even in a state of considerable sexual excitement in the mare, other vital functions, eg food intake, are suppressed scarcely at all. On the other hand, it is hardly possible for the state to be inhibited by external influences, in contrast to the stallion. The behavioural programmes for 'fear and self-protection' and for 'reproduction' may overlap, and possibly an acquired complex blocks the mating behaviour of a mare and releases flight behaviour instead. This means that mares of this kind refuse to stand still, even when fully in season. It is also worth knowing that, in certain mares, oestral rigidity does not start when the stallion mounts but only when intromission of the penis is effected.

Mares that are not in oestrus ward off the stallion by striking out and biting. This can also happen with maiden mares or those that have a foal at foot and miss their foal. Physiological oestrus may also occur without exhibiting the usual outward signs (silent heat), so that the important period for coitus may be missed.

Before the first covering, it is essential that breeding maturity has been achieved. Premature mating can not only cause disturbances of growth in the mare and possible malformation in the foal, but can also cause the mare to exhibit unwillingness to mate throughout her life as a result of having been covered at a time when the sexual (sensory and sensomotory) mechanisms had not yet developed.

The covering behaviour of the stallion is extremely selective. Particular mares are preferred or rejected, factors including: colouring, probably also colour-linked specific odour, the particular aroma exuded by the partner, the preliminary behaviour of the mare, and the use of methods that the stallion is unfamiliar with and rejects. There are numerous examples of this. Of the Arab stallion Bahyran, a grey, foaled in 1787 and employed from 1795 onwards in the Neustadt (Dosse) stud in East Germany, for example, Helmbrecht and Neumann (1798) report:

Fighting between rival stallions

a

... that during the months of March and April that are often still cold, it is very unwilling to serve mares and goes to work very slowly; it also has a greater eagerness for grey mares than for chestnuts or browns; therefore a grey mare is generally shown to it to increase its inclination to cover a non-grey.

The sexual stimulation of the stallion, in contrast to that of the mare, is easily inhibited by external influences, but overcomes other natural characteristics such as vigilance. In this phase, the horse is very exacting as to the particular aroma exuded by the mare, but not at all demanding as to the form of the mare. The sexual excitability of a stallion that is restricted to one and the same mare becomes blunted.

The act of mating, including pelvic thrusts, orgasm and ejaculation, lasts about sixty seconds. The stallion mounts directly behind the mare in an action that can be so violent that the mare's hind legs buckle when the stallion's hind feet momentarily lose contact with the ground. The mare is gripped as far forward as possible between shoulders and rib cage, or else between back ribs and hip. The stallion may sink its teeth into the crest of the mane or withers (a habit that is predictable, so in such cases, lay a blanket over the mare's withers), but often rests the head or else only the muzzle on the mare's shoulder (usually the left). In mares particularly strongly in oestrus, the normal inhibition of movement can be intensified into an active bracing of her weight against the mounting stallion. The associated lowering of the croup provides the stallion with an especially favourable covering position. The same is true of the slow drawing forward of the mare; left to her own devices, she arches her back and lowers her head well down. As a result, the stallion is stimulated into increased activity with powerful thrusting of the pelvis.

During coition, maiden mares in particular exhibit typical indications of submission; the ears are laid sideways with the orifice pointing downwards, the mouth is slightly open, sometimes there are masticatory movements which possibly indicate orgasm.

After covering, mare and stallion usually stand together for a while. Often there is post-mating play, which, depending upon the activity of the stallion and the length of the refractory phase, can develop once again into mating foreplay.

In very excitable stallions, for example, in herds of young stallions, it is not unknown for a stallion of lower ranking order to mount or attempt to mount stallion foals or even representatives of other animal species. Recent scientific investigations show quite clearly that differences in the intensity of the mating drive are probably inherited.

b   c   d

Medieval Tournaments in Europe

From an old form of mounted combat known as the *buhurt*, the medieval tournament developed in Europe in the eleventh century as a contest of skill between riders using blunted weapons. The term 'tournament' (French *tourner*—to turn, revolve) was first used in France where jousting combats were keenly cultivated. It is for this reason that many of the technical terms still used today, in, for example, the sphere of dressage or of *haute école* (advanced horsemanship), both classical and circensian, come from the French language. As far as is known, it was Geoffrey de Preuilly who in 1066 was the first to summarise the rules of this courtly and highly formalised combat, that had its first flowering in the twelfth century. Various customs and practices associated with it became established, such as the formulation of the Seven Virtues and the Seven Deadly Sins, the custom of recognising the title 'knight', until the fourteenth century in the conferring of a sword as a symbol of acceptance into the knighthood, and after that in the granting of the accolade of knighthood by the symbolic touch of a sword.

But the Church turned against these practices which were becoming increasingly frequent and were strengthening temporal power at the expense of ecclesiastical. They succeeded in banning tournaments several times, in, for example, the Council of Clermont in 1130 and the Lateran Councils of 1139, 1179 and 1193. But their efforts were in vain. After 1487, under Emperor Maximilian I, jousting tourneys flourished again, particularly in Germany and Flanders. It is interesting that the reward for victory in a courtly tournament consisted of prizes presented in the form of valuable weapons, chains, rings or as garlands. Technical mastery of the weapon and brave, chivalrous, fiery conduct were also honoured and rewarded. Prizes differed from 'favours' such as scarves, ribbons, or locks of hair. The winning of such prizes could be acknowledged by the conferring of family titles. For example, in the Sixth Tournament in Rostock in 1311, some 6,400 knights took part. The knight Schinkel from Zierov won nine victories and so nine prizes. From that time onwards, he and his family

Knight in battle and jousting dress, as worn on ceremonial occasions. Bibliothèque Nationale, Paris

used the name Negendank (*neunmal Dank*—nine prizes), but retained a shank (*Schenkel*) in their coat of arms as a reference to the name Schinkel.

From the middle of the fifteenth century, when the tournaments of the nobility were already declining, there developed in parallel

tournaments among the peasantry and craftsmen, which had a more light-hearted character, including activities such as pole-jousting, mock fights of fishermen held on the river, and goose racing. At about the same time, racing was taken up as a new form of tournament; races had been held for thousands of years, but from now on they were officially given a place within the tournaments, and appropriate rules were drawn up. In place of the dangerous jousting events—at a tournament in Neuss in West Germany (1241), for example, almost a hundred knights were killed—competitive games became established in the sixteenth century which gave the rider an opportunity to display his skill and prowess to its best advantage. There was also much scope for pageantry and so such a ceremonial satisfied all the requirements of courtly entertainment. Until about 1880, there still existed as the last remaining relics from the medieval heyday of the knightly tournament, events such as quintain tilting and the jousting matches known as *carousels* that have often been described in literature and which take their name from the Persian.

In parallel with the 'horse ballet' (*La Fola*—the fairy tale) that had its origin in Italy, and with much mutual interaction, the art of riding was developed in the sense of the classical *haute école* as represented so brilliantly by Ridinger in 1760, and as it is preserved today in its purest form in the Spanish Riding School in Vienna. At the same time, we find it reflected in our 'quadrilles' in a number of variants. Combined with the findings and conclusions of Xenophon, which came into prominence again after a period of three hundred years, the progressive traditions of medieval tournament riding have been accepted into the modern theory of equitation as the criteria for national as well as international sport, for the training of saddle horses and for their presentation in competition.

Among the precursors of the renaissance in horsemanship which came with the rejection of outmoded views on breaking in, training and the use of saddle horses, one must include the Italian Griso, who founded the first Riding Academy in 1532 in Naples, and the German Löhneisen, who wrote his major work in 1588. In about 1626, in his *Manège Royal*, the French writer Pluvinel was the first to describe the modern method of training based on kindness and co-operation, making use of the natural inclinations of the horse, which his countryman Guérinière successfully developed in his *École de Cavalerie* in 1733, helping to achieve the eventual breakthrough of this method. His views and ideas are preserved today in Vienna and, with modifications, also in the French Riding Academy at Saumur. They are the basis of today's art of dressage as first described in theory and carried out in practice by Steinbrecht (1808–85).

Ideas on horses and equitation that were current in the Middle Ages are reflected in numerous artistic representations, including contemporary equestrian statues. Out of many, one might mention here that of the victorious mercenary leader (*condottiere*) Gattamelata (tabby cat) that was erected in front of the church in Padua in 1446/7. Its creator, Donatello (about 1386–1466), took as his models the previously-mentioned memorial to Emperor Marcus Aurelius in Rome, and the bronze horses on St Mark's Cathedral in Venice. Another important work of this period, presently in Venice, is the equestrian statue of the *condottiere* Colleoni, depicting him as he sets out into battle, which was created by Verrocchio in 1479–88. In notes and sketches made by Leonardo da Vinci (1452–1519)—incidentally a pupil of Verrocchio—there are numerous details of horses which are the result of studies he made of particularly handsome horses in his stable in Milan. Particularly impressive are the sketches, housed today in Windsor Castle, which he made for the horses on the Trivulzio monument that was never completed.

The Sensory Capacities of the Horse

The extreme sensitivity of the horse is the result of the intense and rapid reactive capacity of the nervous system and of the specific efficiency of the sensory organs. Here too, there is great individual variation, which must be taken into consideration. Horses sense the start or approach of avalanches, mudflows or earthquakes considerably sooner than humans do, and try to get to safety at all costs. The same is true of an approaching thunderstorm or sandstorm, from which they will seek refuge even before their riders have become aware of danger. Clearly here, all the sensory organs are acting in combination to decisive effect.

Senses of smell and taste

In the horse, the sense of smell and the sense of taste are highly developed. The sense of smell serves to satisfy the horse's instinctive urge to investigate, which in turn has an essentially protective function. Thus it is the most important of the sense organs in establishing and consolidating relationships between man and horse.

The horse is extremely sensitive to smells. It rejects odours that it finds unpleasant, such as its own excreta, the smell of blood, the scent of certain other species of animal, and the odour of human sweat. This characteristic must be taken into account in, for example, maintaining a high standard of cleanliness in the stalls, loose boxes and feeding equipment, in the provision of veterinary care, in keeping the horse in particular areas, and when transporting the animals.

The ability to sniff out water, and to detect particular objects by smell (stable, animals, certain people) can be effective over many miles. The horse can locate underground springs and the burrows made by rodents even in total darkness by means of its sense of smell and will avoid stepping into them (so in terrain of this kind, give the horse a free rein); horses that are completely blind can find their stable by sense of smell alone.

The horse distinguishes between people that handle it by their individual body odour, and in this respect has a very good power of recollection. So contact is best initiated, renewed and consolidated by allowing the horse to sniff thoroughly at, say, an open hand or other part of the body, by gently breathing into the horse's nostrils, and by consistently wearing the same garments. The distinct preference for men or for women that a horse may show (although children are not differentiated in this way) has its foundation in the horse's acute olfactory sensitivity.

Because human body odour changes in accordance with the subject's physiological state of stimulation (particularly in respect of intensity), the horse is able to infer the mood of its handler or rider at a particular time. For the horse, a man wears his heart not on his sleeve but in his sweat glands. This is probably the explanation for the popular belief that a rider's agitation or tension is transferred to the horse.

By quietly investigating alarming objects with its nose, a horse will become convinced of their innocuous nature. Its highly developed senses of smell and taste lead it to refuse bad and potentially harmful food or water and, to a large extent, any toxic substances. It is possible to accustom a horse to certain smells and tastes, such as water from an unfamiliar source, certain feeding stuffs such as silage, carbamide, or straw pellets. However, habituation of this kind is long-lasting and should be undertaken only with care and due consideration of the effects on the horse's digestion.

To investigate unfamiliar smells in detail, the horse displays *flehmen*, a posture in which the nostrils are closed by invagination, with the head stretched forwards and upwards, allowing the odorous substance direct contact by way of lips and tongue with the roof of the mouth and thence with an accessory olfactory zone which is known as Jacobson's organ. Here, olfactory sensitivity, which in human terms is already incredibly keen, is greatly intensified.

Vision

The horse's visual faculty has a valuable protective function based on its versatility and a speed of reaction greater than that of any other of the senses.

Compared with other mammals, the horse has large eyes. The shape of its head and position of its eyes, which vary according to breed, sex and individual structure, permit a field of vision, wide in comparison with that of man or a beast of prey, of some 300 degrees, which by slight sideways movements of the head can be extended to full panoramic visions (360 degrees). Therefore it is always able to perceive objects situated behind it. One result of this that is important for the rider, driver or handler is that a horse or team of horses is likely to run away from objects that appear suddenly behind it, if they are unfamiliar. A horse, then, must be allowed to get used to traffic, for example vehicles overtaking. It can see the knee and leg of its rider, riding crop, sideways movements of the hand or fluttering garments. The same is true of the driving whip and lungeing whip, and of sideways movements from a vehicle that it is pulling.

A horse is not capable of stereoscopic vision, so it has difficulty in estimating distances, for example, in assessing the depth of an obstacle. Because of the shape of the horse's skull, its forward field of vision is restricted and it can extend this zone only by moving its head sideways and to some extent upwards. Therefore this movement should never be restricted by force.

At pasture, in a forest and also in the wild, the horse moves on a zig-zag course since in this way it enjoys an all-round panoramic view without needing to make any special head or body movements.

The equine eye has poor accomodation, that is, it has a restricted capacity for adjusting the lens of the eye to changes of distance. A horse is able to see an object with sufficient sharpness of focus, especially at distances of between 3 and 5 m (10 and 16 ft), only by raising and lowering its head. It is for this reason that in approaching a jump an inexperienced show jumper will lift its head high as it gets progressively closer to the point of take-off. In general, it can be said that a horse's vision works on the principle of the wide-angled lens (the eagle's, on the other hand, on that of the telephoto lens). At distances of less than 5 m (16 ft), however, even apparently very slight alterations are perceived and interpreted, such as in the mimicry of stable companions—angling of the mouth, incipient alterations in the position of the ear, the tensing of muscles before kicking out—and after intensive contact, even, to some extent, the mimicry of humans, including movements no greater than 0.2 mm, demonstrated in circus acts with 'counting' or 'reading' horses. Such performances are based on astigmatism; in this condition, rays are not focused at one point, so appear as lines. Although this impairs sharpness of vision, it means that all movements that occur within the horse's close visual range are perceived with considerably greater intensification. This visual sensitivity to movement also explains certain types of behaviour, such as fear of the ground, sudden jumping aside, hurrying quickly through constrictions in the path (such as entrances to stables), for which the rider should be prepared. But it is possible to accustom the horse to this situation as part of its daily training routine.

The horse's sharpness and strength of vision in the dark is excellent in comparison with other mammals, but here again, the above-mentioned characteristics must be taken into consideration. In this situation, the fluorescent, zinciferous screen in the back of the eye has the function of reflecting incident light rays through the lens of the eye, thus increasing their effect on the visual centre. This enables the horse to find its way very effectively in semi-darkness; in total darkness, however, it relies upon its excellent sense of smell and also its sense of touch.

The horse perceives colours, but its colour spectrum is very much more restricted than that of the human eye in that it sees the colours at the end of the spectrum only very poorly. It can distinguish yellow from the other colours with the greatest reliability, green less well. Correspondingly, visual acuity is slight in the blue-red range, and positively weak in the blue-grey range.

So it is one of the most difficult tasks of training to achieve clear-cut reactions to particular colours. One trainer who managed it was F. Knie senior, with his 'traffic horses', which, in the circus ring, would stop when the light was red and gallop on when it was green.

The horse's direction of vision is linked with an upright position of its ears. In spite of its large eyes, it looks at a person only if at the same time it pricks up its ears. But since, as a result of the structure of the head-neck zone, it is obliged to look forward and downward, it sees only objects in this line of sight, for example, an outstretched hand. Only if one deliberately crouches down or if the horse has a naturally erect stance, is it possible to look a horse straight in the eye, and vice versa.

Every condition of the spirit finds expression in the eye, even in that of a horse, although it is impossible to point to any alteration in its form or composition, or indeed to explain in words wherein this expression lies. It is the innermost condition of the soul, anger, love, joy, hate, which shines forth from the endlessly changing brilliance of the eye into the soul of the observer [v Tennecker, 1827].

It is interesting that when a horse uses its sense of sight to distinguish between different members of the same species, different species of animal or human beings, it is guided by the total form of the creature, ie the silhouette, and not by parts of the body. It can be very startled by animals of unfamiliar overall appearance, but scarcely or not at all by the sight of individual parts of the body.

Sense of hearing

The horse's sense of hearing is also very acute. Horses react very intensively to acoustic stimuli, responding to them with specific patterns of behaviour.

It is therefore always advisable to make use of the voice when handling a horse. At just under normal volume and in a low frequency range, the human voice has a calming, reassuring effect. High frequencies have a stimulating effect and in the long run can be unfavourable. This corresponds to the frequency range used in neighing (high = exciting and excited; low = reassuring and reassured). A horse quickly becomes accustomed to noises and is soon indifferent to traffic noise, the sound of applause, loudspeakers, the crack of a whip and so on.

The horse directs its ears and head towards a source of sound or of interest. If it cannot locate it with certainty, one ear is directed towards the other. If it is not interested, both ears are directed backwards. This is not to be confused with the action of laying back the ears as a sign of extreme uneasiness and of imminent or actual defensive activity. Important as an external indication of a particular pattern of behaviour is the fact that ears and head are turned towards a source of interest even if it emits no noise.

Examples of occasions on which the head is turned with ears pricked include the provision of food or water, or the expectation of them, the approach of stable companions or members of the herd, the establishment of contact with people or animals, when the eyes are fixed upon an obstacle before and during the take-off phase or upon the landing place in the flight or landing phase, and when the eyes are fixed upon an unfamiliar and potentially dangerous object.

When a horse's attention is fully engaged, its interest in its external surroundings is reduced or entirely suppressed. Once this stage has been reached with a dressage or saddle horse, the way is open for optimum performance. It can be recognised externally by the turning back of the ears combined with relaxation of the muscles that maintain the position of the ears. The degree to which the ears are turned back is variable and will depend upon the individual excitability of the horse and the intensity of the stimulus at the time.

A horse also responds to sound stimuli with motor activity in the form of a particular sequence of movements, carried out in time to the rhythm of the sound stimuli; whip-cracking can be used as an aid, but

sparingly, because the horse quickly becomes inured to it. Horses have a distinct fondness for music, preferring certain rhythms that are appropriate to their perception of timing and their capacity for movement, and which can be varied only within this framework. They undoubtedly enjoy them and move with greater precision and verve, while the rider directs the horse with added liveliness. But here, too, the horse's hearing soon becomes blunted; the volume of such accompanying music and the frequency of its use must be adapted to this characteristic. When watching well-managed exhibition and circus orchestras, it is easy to see how much music can contribute to the success of difficult dressage performances. Horses can be drawn along and enticed by music. This has been known from time immemorial. It is clear from individual reactions of horses to noise, that frequency and volume are also decisive factors, and in this respect there are great individual variations.

One of many interesting features is that the horse will turn its head forwards, sideways and backwards towards a source of sound, but only to a very limited extent upwards. Clearly it has no ability to perceive objects in three dimensions, although in enclosed spaces, such as an indoor riding school, its tendency to look upwards and to sniff the air is greater than in open terrain.

The horse is reacting to overhead sources of light, and trying to observe visible objects even when they are above the level of its head. But because of the anatomical structure of its neck region, this is only partially possible. When the situation is uncertain, its first reaction even here is flight, and the rider must be prepared for this.

Tactile sensitivity

The horse's tactile sense is highly effective; the skin, muscles and tactile hairs in the region of the mouth are extremely sensitive to touch, although in this respect there are considerable differences between individuals and also between breeds. Thoroughbreds are especially sensitive, as are other warmblood breeds on which they exert a strong influence; they have a very delicate, thin skin and a fine coat. Heavy draught horses and a number of small horses and ponies can be considered rather more 'thick-skinned'; because of their special tissue structure, their tactile sense is somewhat less delicate. But in every case horses must be handled carefully and considerately. This is particularly true of foals and young horses that have to be accustomed gradually to being groomed regularly, having their feet picked up, and being harnessed and saddled. This is another reason for individual care of foals to be started as soon as possible. Constant stimulation decreases tactile sensitivity. Thus the horse can, to a certain degree, become accustomed to skin stimuli, although there is great variation between individuals. Unlike the sense of hearing, the sense of touch cannot be completely blunted.

In handling horses, the following rules should be observed:

- Care in the use of grooming equipment, particularly on young and highly-bred horses (see Care of the Horse, pp. 82–87).
- Care in carrying out all veterinary and shoeing activities, especially on young and thoroughbred horses. Lifting of the horse's leg should be preceded by downward stroking movements of the hand across the horse's body (do not forget the use of the voice; talk to the horse at the same time); a horse that is grasped suddenly may be startled and defend itself actively by kicking or pushing, seriously endangering the handler.
- Care in tacking up the horse, particularly when putting in the bit and when saddling. Use only tack that lies smoothly against the skin and which is kept in a soft, flexible condition. The horse's withers and back are particularly sensitive.

The use of aids, conveying the rider's wishes to the horse, should be adapted to the horse's tactile sense and be no more than subtly-transmitted indications. This particularly applies to using the leg to urge the horse forward, handling the reins and riding crop, using the driving and lungeing whip. Only in this way can the absolute stimulus threshold be kept low or reduced in order to maintain the horse's sensitivity to details and nuances of directions of this kind that are an essential element in the higher echelons of equestrianism. The action of a rider who 'pummels' his horse with his legs is not to be tolerated.

Just as rough and sudden actions cause the horse to react negatively, so stroking and patting produce a positive, beneficial effect, and in these actions the horse can detect the subtlest of variations. While bearing in mind the horse's individual patterns of behaviour, its tactile sensitivity can be used effectively in day-to-day care and at work.

The Development
of Stud Farms in Europe

With the passing of the age of chivalry, new styles of riding developed that required saddle horses with different features and characteristics: more rapid mobility, high trainability and greater speed in the walk, trot and gallop. These demands were satisfied by the original Spanish horse that over the centuries had retained the characteristics of its ancestor, the swift, obedient and agile Oriental horse. In the sixteenth century, this change of emphasis in breeding became particularly apparent. Emperor Maximilian II set up a number of stud farms, including that in Kladruby in 1572 (where the Kladruber breed was developed)—today in the Republic of Czechoslovakia—in Lipica in 1580 (where the Lipizzaner breed was developed), and in 1572, he founded the Spanish Riding School in Vienna. Henry IV concentrated on the Navarre horse, the Spanish viceroys in Naples on the Aragonese that was strongly influenced by the Neapolitan horse.

In 1858 Engels wrote:

The seventeenth century that had finally done away with the extravagant knightly tradition, increased the strength of numbers of the cavalry to a vast extent. In no army had this particular branch of the service ever taken so high a share. In the Thirty Years' War, two-fifths to almost half of the total numbers in any army were cavalry. In certain cases, there were two horsemen to every foot soldier.

On the whole, the tactics of the cavalry differed hardly at all at first from those of the infantry—the use of small arms, linear fighting, formation etc. Riding itself was neglected. 'It was impossible for movements to be carried out at a rapid pace, but even at a slow pace, there were frequent accidents . . .' At the time of Frederick William I, the Prussian cavalry could still be described as 'heavy soldiers on ungainly horses'. Frederick II reorganised the military completely. A good deal more attention was paid to riding. The ability to fence on horseback was required. As a result, the cavalry became a formidable instrument of attack and pursuit, capable of rapid deployment, and it remained so until the introduction of modern technological weaponry. The consequence of this development was an increasing need for horses that, in comparison with the knight's horse, were faster, more mobile, and 'lighter', but which were as yet available only to a limited extent. Because general agriculture was still largely undeveloped, new breeds of horses could be evolved only in special establishments that were or could be made large enough to provide the quantities required. The original purpose of the large stud farms that were founded in the seventeenth and eighteenth centuries was primarily to provide horses for the armies of the day. Gradually agriculture also became adapted to these requirements, although it had the additional task of breeding heavy horses.

The creation of the state-owned regional stud farm served military ends by providing a stock of suitable breeding stallions, although it would be wrong not to acknowledge the contribution it made to the civilian side of horse breeding and training. It was in the period of the foundation of these establishments at the end of the eighteenth century that Prizelius wrote:

The ultimate aim of such studs is:

1 that the husbandman himself raises his own foals and does not need to let money go out of the region;
2 that he breeds healthy, fine horses and is not fraudulently cheated by the horse dealer;
3 that a sovereign can obtain from this stud horses to mount his cavalry, and that, in time of war, he can obtain all the horses he needs in his own country . . .

And further on he says:

Is not a vast number of horses required for the cavalry of a large army; and is not their use in wartime greatly multiplied by the need to add artillery horses, pack and draught horses? How

many are not lost in battles and skirmishes and by disease? Indescribably many . . . By using fine stallions, he [ie, the breeder] has bred fine horses, which are useful to his master for the cavalry, and which also have power and strength enough to move the heavy loads of guns. He knows that they are healthy and, as a faithful subject, dedicates them only too willingly to the service of his beloved sovereign, particularly since they are used to ensure his safety, protection and defence; for which reason he is also ready to provide them at a modest price. So the prince does not need to pay so much money for the horses he requires, there is no cheating and the money remains within the country, indeed, the master regains a part of it in fiscal dues . . .

Considerable fluctuation in the demand for horses in Europe in recent centuries is the principal reason for the disappearance of many of the important horse breeding centres which relied on the sale of horses for their existence, but were unable to adapt sufficiently rapidly, or indeed at all, to the highly differentiated and rapidly changing demands. Until the middle of the twentieth century, there was the additional factor of serious damage to or even the complete destruction of important breeding establishments as a result of war. Because in horse breeding the succession of generations is a slow process and advances within a unit of time are slight, any loss of valuable breeding stock can be made good only very slowly.

To illustrate this development, four horse-breeding establishments that are representative of many more of their kind are described briefly below.

A thousand years of horse breeding in the Einsiedeln Monastery

Monasteries were among the earliest horse breeding centres. Because of their seclusion, their modest stocks of draught and saddle horses had a high degree of independence; but with the dissolution of the monasteries in the eighteenth and nineteenth centuries, almost all these breeding farms disappeared. One of the few that survived is the Benedictine Abbey of Einsiedeln in Switzerland. It was founded in 934, and right from the start had a stud farm under the charge of the monastery's 'marshal' (from Old High German *marah*, a horse), and was first mentioned in a document of 1064. In the list of duties to be carried out by the 'abbot's

marschalck', von Ripperswil, in the year 1090, it was laid down that on his travels the abbot was to be accompanied by twelve horses. Until 1920, the abbot himself always rode on horseback. Because horse breeding was practised intensively, the number of horses increased from year to year. As a result, the tenants had to pay part of their rent in oats and horseshoes.

During the fifteenth and sixteenth centuries, the Einsiedeln horse became increasingly well known and sought-after, particularly by the rulers of the neighbouring dukedom of Milan and Mantua. In a detailed historical study, P. A. Hubert writes: '. . . Many pretty little horses cross the Gotthard to the sunny south, greeted joyfully by their new masters as *cavalli della Madonna* (horses of the Madonna).' In 1655 the first stud book was written by Father Josef Reider, laying a solid foundation for further work with their stock of more than seventy horses. It contains a very informative inventory made at that time:

How many horses there were in stock on 1st January anno 1655:

firstly, horses in the royal stable	7 head
item of dray horses	4 head
item of pack horses	7 head
item of breeding mares	17 head
item of stallions	5 head
item of foals	31 head
total	71 head

In the eighteenth century the monastery was rebuilt to plans drawn up by Brother Kaspar Moosbrugger, with the monastery horses playing their part in transporting heavy slabs of sandstone from the quarry to the building site. Their reward was a new stable building 'the like of which is not to be found anywhere in the world', with cross-vaulting and arched windows.

As in other breeding centres, the introduction of Spanish, Neapolitan, Friesian and Oriental blood caused considerable fluctuations in respect of the unity and stability of the Einsiedeln stock, which could be eliminated only by breeding back to the older traditional Schwyz horse, so that by 1811 there were already fifty-three horses in the stables. The overgrown pastures were made fertile again.

With the construction of a road system at the start of the nineteenth century, the pack horse disappeared into the Alpine regions, so that in 1820 even the abbot rode out for the first time in a

A view into the stables of the ecclesiastical stud at Einsiedeln in Switzerland (Photo: Källn)

Stallion from the ecclesiastical stud at Einsiedeln

sprung carriage; some ten years later, the first 'chaise' was bought. This development led initially to the reduction of the Einsiedeln breeding stock. But shortly afterwards, intensification of agriculture, and the needs of the Swiss army that was being built up, brought about its definitive revival. There was also an upsurge of interest in horse racing and equestrian sport. The monastery stud farm adapted itself rapidly to the new demands, as can be seen from the register of Einsiedeln breeding horses for the year 1840 and the following years. Stud Book A covers the breeding horses from 1817 onwards. At this time, there were always 100 to 150 horses in the monastery stable and in 1841 there were 154. At the first Swiss horse show in Aarau in 1865, there was serious criticism of the unsatisfactory standard of the Swiss regional breeds of horses. As a result, the Einsiedeln authorities made efforts to improve the quality of their stock by purchasing stallions from abroad. Details of this are contained in Stud Book B. Quality was further improved by the use of English thoroughbred stallions (1890–1900), of Hackney stallions (1900–20) and from 1922 of Anglo-Norman stallions. Five old families of Einsiedeln mares still exist today and their lineage can be traced back to the middle or the beginning of the last century. They are the Quarta, Manda, Klima, Sella and Thea families.

At present, there are still about fifty horses in the stud. In conformity with the Anglo-Norman basic type, the Einsiedeln horse is a half-breed with a height of about 15.3 hands, a cannon bone circumference of 21 cm (8 in), and a weight of 550 kg (11 cwt). The mares live for an average of eighteen years. At annual horse shows, the Einsiedeln mares carry off top honours. Today, the Einsiedeln horse is still highly esteemed as a saddle horse and is much in demand. It represents the fulfilment of the pure tradition of breeding that has informed the work of the Einsiedeln foundation for more than a thousand years.

Arab breeding in Janów Podlaski

Inevitably, the development of the stud farm in eastern Europe was to take a fundamentally different course because of its specific aims and consequent dimensions, as will be seen in the example of the present-day Polish National Stud Farm at Janów Podlaski (Yanov Podlaski) in the district of Lublin. This establishment was founded on 3 January 1817, by a decree of Tsar Alexander I. At that time, Poland was a kingdom, and as 'Congres-

sional Poland' (in accordance with a resolution of the Congress of Vienna 1815), was linked in personal union with Russia, whose Tsar was at the same time King of Poland.

The stud lies about 125 miles east of Warsaw in impressive countryside, a mile from the former cathedral town of Janów Podlaski. Its arable lands and grasslands extend for 9 miles along the west bank of the River Bug, which at this point also forms the Soviet-Polish border. The farm owns some 2,000 hectares (4,900 acres) at present, which spread across the outlying estates of Wygoda, Zamek and Kijowiec, and, in addition, flourishing cattle and pig breeding enterprises. The agricultural production serves primarily to provide food for the extensive animal stocks.

Initially 90 mares and 25 stallions were introduced, but by 18 December 1817 the first director, J. Ritz, had in his charge more than 54 stallions of various breeds and 100 brood-mares, of which 63 were Danish, 30 English, 3 Mecklenburg, 2 Arab, 1 Turkish and 1 Neapolitan. In addition there were 33 three-year-olds. The stallions were stabled in what is today the breeding complex, while the mares were kept in Wygoda. Such a stock measured up to the ordinance of 6 October 1816, according to which a stud of just such a size and a stallion depot were to be set up in the interests of improved horse breeding. The choice fell on Janów.

The diversity of breeds within the stock reflects the typical situation in the eighteenth and early nineteenth centuries. It was only in the course of the nineteenth century that a certain unification of the breeding stock was brought about, in keeping with agricultural and military developments. Another factor here was that Janów functioned as the only state-controlled royal stud in Poland, and had to compete with numerous private studs, some of them very important and rich in tradition. From 20 April 1819, there existed in Poland a unified statute for the administration of studs (Dyrekcji Stad i Stacji Stadnych), to which not only Janów but also the royal stables in Warsaw and that belonging to the Grand Duchess were subject. In the years between 1823 and 1858, English thoroughbreds and Arabs were imported to Janów relatively frequently. They included the stallions Alabadzank and Tuissan, as well as some English part-bred stallions and English thoroughbred stallions such as the important Sorcerer (foaled 1818, imported 1825). At the time of the November uprising against Tsarist rule, and its suppression at Ostrojeka (as a consequence of which the Polish constitution was abrogated and Congressional Poland was effectively incorporated into Russia), the establishment had to be evacuated to the districts of Kalisz and Krakow for almost a year.

Between 1840 and 1850 there was considerable structural re-organisation of the main buildings. In 1841 the stallion stable was built, in 1848 the building known as the 'Clock Stable', with the clock tower that became the emblem of the stud farm. Among the most important acquisitions during this period were three English thoroughbred stallions—Albemarle born 1835, Northender born 1835, and Sir Harry born 1839—and some valuable thoroughbred mares. In 1857 four pure-bred Arabian horses, three mares and the stallion Dzelaby, were acquired from the Weil/Württemberg stud farm. By 1848 there was a total of 484 horses, including 100 brood-mares, 214 foals and 163 state-owned stallions. Taken as a whole, it can be said that, in spite of the conglomeration of breeds and types that were present when the stud farm was founded, by about 1880 the Anglo-Arab was the dominant breed. The same is also true of the other stud farms and horse-breeding establishments in eastern Europe, in contrast to the developments in central Europe.

From 1881 onwards horses were imported from England; this practice had already had quite modest beginnings in 1857 with 2 stallions and 5 mares of the Cleveland-Norfolk breed, continuing with the purchase of growing numbers of thoroughbred stallions which finally came to dominate the stud. From about 1900 the breeding of English part-bred horses became established and there was steady development in this direction until the beginning of World War I, when the stud had to be evacuated to the Charkow administrative division before the advancing German and Austrian troops who were occupying 'Russian Poland'. The horses were housed in the four Bielovodski studs of Derkulsk, Streletzk, Limarev and Novo-Alexandrovsk. During the covering season of 1915, 80 state stallions were brought back to Janów, and from there sent out to various covering stations. The entire stock of the stud farm and that of the stallion depot was lost during the war, including 115 stallions and 60 brood-mares with their entire offspring produced over three years. With the re-establishment of the Polish State in 1918, a completely new start had to be made on the main stud farm. The material basis had been completely destroyed. It was decided that breeding should concentrate upon: the pure-bred Arab; the part-bred Arab; the Anglo-Arab; and, subject to a time stipulation, the English thoroughbred.

For the stud, this implied the following tasks:

- maintenance and improvement of breeds by pure-line breeding, and selective breeding for the required physical and psychological characteristics;

- improvement of the Arab and Anglo-Arab was to be achieved without the introduction of foreign blood, ie, purely by selection of the best material in respect of type, appearance, lineage, constitution and performance, and by the intensive rearing of foals;
- indirect improvement of national horse breeding by the production of state stallions of the highest possible quality;
- the breeding of a true-to-type Arab with a healthy constitution, a powerful and harmonious appearance, and a high standard of performance, not necessarily with a very high running speed but with great endurance over long distances and while carrying a relatively heavy weight; the Janów Arab was to be a combination of the Kuhailan and Saqlawi strains.

In the expansion in the breeding of part-bred Arabs and Anglo-Arabs that took place between the two world wars, an important part was played by the progeny of the stallion named Shagya X, foaled in Radowce (Radauti/Radautz), which made an essential contribution to the reconstruction of the stud after 1945 and in obtaining international recognition for pure-bred Arab breeding. Under the outstandingly successful and caring direction of S. Pohoski (1899–1944), and with considerable good fortune in breeding, the Janów stud rapidly developed into one of the great international centres of horse breeding. It became the symbol of Polish and European success in the breeding of Arabs of that day. In the period between the two world wars, the work of the Janów Podlaski stud farm received international recognition and its pure-bred Arabs in particular were exported to many countries throughout the world.

Up to the beginning of World War II, the stables housed 9 senior stallions, 30 pure-bred Arab mares, 43 part-bred Arab mares, 23 Anglo-Arab mares, and 159 foals in all age groups.

But once again the cruel tide of war swept across this paradise in the lowlands along the River Bug.

With the total occupation of Poland as far as the Bug, Janów also fell under the regime of Fascist occupation. On about 17 September 1939, all 269 stud horses had been driven off, of which a few were found again in the immediate vicinity. The Soviet state stud farm of Tersk in the Caucasus (Balakshin) took 9 stallions and 53 Arab mares. Not only the buildings and equipment but also the stock of breeding horses had to be rebuilt. This took place gradually between June 1940 and July 1944, from stock provided by private studs in Poland, the pedigree of which could be traced back to the Janów breeds, from stud farms in German-occupied countries such as Yugoslavia and France, and from the few remaining young horses and a number of mares.

By 1944 the stallion depot once again had at its disposal some seventy state stallions, and in the stud farm there were 245 breeding horses including offspring. Some 80 per cent of this stock was maintained until after the end of the war. The Polish stud manager at that time, and from 1958 director of the stud, A. Krzysztalowicz, reports that with the retreat of the German troops on 16 July 1944, before the advancing Red Army, the order was given for the evacuation of the stud. All the horses, accompanied by a few stablemen, were moved by train to the administrative centre of Biala Podlaska some 16 miles away. They were then transported by way of the stallion depot at Lack to the remounting depot of Sohland on the Rotstein near Görlitz in Lusatia. Once again the Polish stud farm, including the residential buildings, was almost completely destroyed.

Before the rapid advance of Soviet troops, which reached the Oder in February 1945, men and horses had to leave Sohland in all haste on 13 February to make their way via Dresden to Torgau. They set out in two sections, moving on foot through storm and rain. Transport was found for 58 foals and 5 mares in an advanced stage of pregnancy. Led by Krzysztalowicz with Amurath Sahib, the section comprising the breeding horses got on the move, 90 horses harnessed in pairs, the mares with foals attached, the young horses led in hand. The streets before were jammed by refugees and columns of troops; it was dark before they could reach Dresden, and they had to spend the night in the open air, a circumstance to which, as it turned out, many owed their life. The second section—40 stallions each with a rider who led a second horse—led by von Bonnet, rode on, because it was impossible to halt the stallions.

Following a roundabout route, they reached the overcrowded city on the night of 13/14 February, where they were housed in stables prepared for them in Dresden-Neustadt (the cavalry barracks). It was the night of the massively destructive air attack. The Polish riders and their horses were caught unawares by the deluge of incendiary and high-explosive bombs, by burning houses, road surfaces and trees, by tons of fallen masonry, and caught up in the terror of the inhabitants. In spite of it all one of the stablemen managed to retain his hold on the irreplaceable stallions Witraz and Wielki Szlem that had been entrusted to his care. On 14 February, after the attacks, 18 stallions were recaptured and a further 38 found after several days of searching, but 21 were dead. Some days later, they set out again for Torgau. The Polish stallion de-

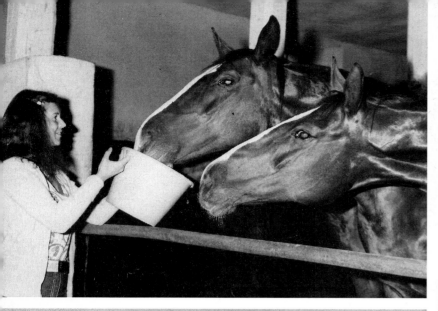

Previous page:
85 Greeting: contact is established by an analysis of scent which provides very detailed information

86 The equine eye reflects light and so vision is particularly sharp in half-light. This is the result of a zinciferous screen at the back of the eye that reflects incident rays of light back through the lens

87 For the horse, the most reliable source of information is the nose. But never blow into a horse's nose suddenly; it will only cause alarm and possibly an accident

88 A horse especially enjoys having its throat gently rubbed—it cannot reach it otherwise. The horse here is not impressed by the young woman's outward appearance, rather by her body scent and quiet, pleasant voice

89 The mare is no longer concentrating upon her foal but much more upon what is happening round about

90 Within a visual range of about 3—5 m (10—16 ft), horses perceive extremely fine movements. If they are trained to be appropriately attentive, they will react as required to slight signs made by the trainer that are almost imperceptible to the audience. By making use of the horse's well-developed optical-motory memory, it is possible to train it to perform quite complicated movements. This heavy draught horse has its eyes and ears fixed attentively upon its trainer; it will note and react to the slightest movements of his face, hands or whip

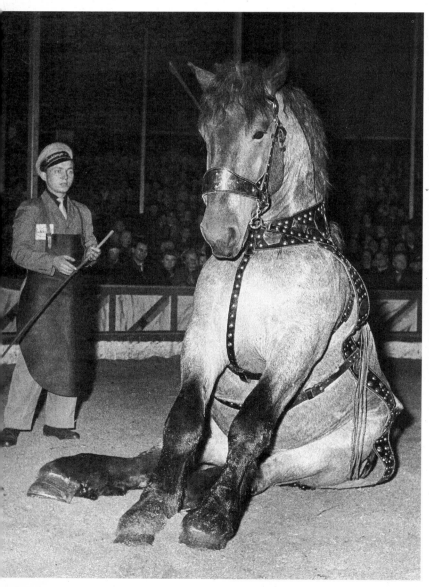

91 Centrifugal force develops with speed. Here in the circular arena of the Busch Circus, with a diameter of 13 m (42 ft), the horses adapt their movement accordingly. For this, long and thorough training is required

92 Horses can be trained to perform in response to hearing their
names—preferably of two syllables
—or to certain commands

93 Insects on the head, particularly on eyes and ears, can be very troublesome—head tossing is one defence

94 The beginnings of *flehmen* in a foal

95 'Sniff-tasting' or *flehmen* is displayed by foals as well as adult horses. By drawing the upper lip upwards and backwards, scents taken into the nostrils are intensified in the accessory olfactory zone. Towards the end of the process, the jaws are closed

Following page:
97 A horse always turns its head towards a source of interest in order to locate smells and sounds

pots of Biala, Boguslawice and Debica had also been moved to the barracks there, and were now joined by the state stallions from Janów, while the remaining 202 stud horses were taken by rail on 10 March from Torgau via Magdeburg to Schleswig-Holstein and to the remounting depot of Schönböken/Grabau, where they were put into the Nettelau section.

At the end of the war, a Polish administrative authority for the stud was set up to look after the interests of the breeding horses belonging to Poland in what was then the British zone of occupation. It arranged for the return of the horses to Poland (although without the top-ranking Witez II, which, in spite of protests, was removed illegally to the USA when the war ended). This stock was increased in the summer ot the same year by 14 brood-mares, some of the highest quality, from Bábolna. These mares were returned to Hungary in 1951. In the autumn of 1946, the Janów stud horses returned to their native country, being housed at first in the undamaged Posadowo stud in the region of Poznan. In autumn 1947 the Arabs were distributed among the newly-equipped studs in Albigowa (in the Rzeszów region), Michalów (Lublin region), Nowy Dwór (Krakow region), while the part-bred horses were the first group to return in the autumn of 1950 to the pastures along the Bug. It was 1961 before renovation work on the original establishment was sufficiently advanced for the Arabs to be brought back. Meanwhile the stock at Michalów had been transferred to the newly-founded Michalów Arab stud (in the Kielce region). In 1956 a start was made in Janów on research into problems of horse breeding, including the work of selection for the development of a small horse of the type known as the Kopczyk-Podlaski, although research was subject to a time limit.

Reconstruction of the destroyed buildings and re-establishment of the main centre at Janów as well as of the Wygoda branch was concluded in 1963. The principles that had guided the work of the stud in the pre-war period continued to do so from 1950 onwards, even though, after the great losses suffered, a new start required the highest standard of working efficiency. For the present and the foreseeable future, they can be summarised as follows:

- the breeding of Arab horses of the highest quality and of an internationally-recognised standard, which will achieve the reputation of the best in the world;
- the breeding of part-bred Arabs, especially stallions suitable for the state horse-breeding programme;
- the creation of a supply of horses of Anglo-Arab extraction intended particularly for export.

Work has continued purposefully towards the realisation of these ends. Particular importance has been attached to the carefully considered use of breeding stallions and to the rearing of the foals. A vitally important part was played in the period immediately after the war by the pure-bred Arabs Witraz, Wielki Szlem and the equally fine Comet, as well as by the part-bred stallions Equator, Wácpan, Shagya 33−2 and particularly Shagya 10−32. Since 1967, the stock of the stud has settled down at 350 breeding horses, including 7 principal studs, 4 trial stallions, 60 pure-bred

State stud farm of Janów Podlaski, Poland (Photo: Flade)

Arab mares, 70 part-bred mares, 35 horses intended for the Warsaw race-track and about 175 foals of every age group.

Considerable advances in the breeding of part-bred horses have been achieved by the stallions Shagya X-32 (Topolcianky/Czechoslovakia), Marten (Pruchna), Saumur (Great Britain) and Amper (Janów Podlaski). The Arabs from Janów are particularly sought after by breeding establishments in a wide variety of countries.

Since December 1981 brood-mares from the stud farm have several times taken the European or World Championship at the Paris Horse Shows. The aims laid down for the stud have undoubtedly been achieved. The standard of breeding attained for the pure-bred Arab is internationally recognised and emulated, that for the part-bred horse serves as a model for the whole country. The methods employed in looking after the breeding animals and rearing their progeny are exemplary. The decisive factor, however, is the commitment of management and workers which has made Janów Podlaski into one of the most important stud farms in the world.

Warmblood breeding in Neustadt (Dosse)

The state-owned stud at Neustadt (Dosse), situated some 50 miles west of Berlin, is one of four top-level studs run by the East German Central Office of Horse Breeding which have as their main task the producing and rearing of top-class prospective stallions and the constant improvement of their own stock of mares. Attached to the stud farm since 1978 has been the Central Institute for the Inspection of Stallions of the GDR, a new building which includes stabling for forty stallions, an indoor riding school and other training facilities. The state-owned horse-breeding administrative centre about a mile and a half north of the stud farm, which developed from the former regional stud at Neustadt (Dosse), with stallion depot, central sales agency and extensive riding stables, is an independent institution which is also under the control of the Central Office of Horse Breeding.

In the area west of Berlin, known as Havelland, the reclamation in the seventeenth century of the landed properties on the Prignitz, Havel and Rhin marshes created a substantial foundation for profitable agricultural development and so also for successful horse breeding. On the basis of documents still existing from the fifteenth century, Rössig reported in 1798 that 'in Thuringia,

Bohemia, the Mark, above all in Havellande, horse breeding and stud farming was practised on a considerable scale'.

The Thirty Years' War brought with it a number of setbacks, and an attempt was made to compensate for these by setting up court studs. The Brandenburg horses of that time are described as 'small, thick-set animals, modest in their requirements', and a report from the Office of the Crown Lands for the Mark of Brandenburg makes it clear that horse breeding there left much to be desired. Stallions and mares were put out to pasture together and no selection for breeding took place. In 1815 Sebald wrote that the common type of Brandenburg country horse 'is small, has a big head, often a sloping croup, its shanks are narrow and its stance slovenly'.

With the foundation of the state-owned stud farm and the introduction of the 'Prussian State Stud Farm Regulations', all this was changed. The intention was to mount the Prussian army without importing horses from abroad, and to ensure a supply of suitable home-bred animals. This must also be seen as the purpose behind the foundation of the stud farm and state-owned stud complex on the edge of the town of Neustadt (Dosse) in 1788. On this subject, Hutten-Czapski (1876) wrote:

> The old traditions of chivalry of the Teutonic Order of Knights marked all the institutions of state with this military character, which still today makes it impossible to say where the soldier ends and the citizen begins. This characteristic of the state had a powerful influence on all things hippic. The government's sole aim was to produce horses that were suitable for the army, and they saw to it that the country was in a position to satisfy all requirements in this respect. To this end, they set up central and regional studs. The first were to produce efficient stallions, while the second were to distribute the blood of these animals throughout the land. The studs at Trakehnen and Neustadt were the first ones, but soon breeding stations were established throughout the entire country [Prussia].

In 1694, the Elector Frederick II of Brandenburg, later King Frederick I of Prussia, acquired in exchange for land and office, the parish of Oebisfelde and the domain of Neustadt (Dosse), and set up a court stud there, while Rosenberg, founded in 1684, was added later. The horses bred there were destined primarily for the royal stables, and were the progeny of imported stallions, such as Danish, Friesian, Neapolitan, Spanish and Arab horses. Frederick I kept more than a thousand horses in his royal stables, and in

1724 there were 2,628 horses in his stud farms. For the coronation ceremonials of January 1701 in Königsberg, the royal household required an extra 30,000 trace horses in addition to the regular stable stock. The successors of Frederick I reduced the numbers in the royal stable somewhat, but maintained a lively interest in providing hardy riding horses for the army. In 1819, for example, the four principal Prussian stud farms at Trakehnen, Neustadt (Dosse), Graditz and Vessra housed 1,784 horses, in 1840, 2,052 and in 1850, 2,570 horses. The average stock held at Neustadt (Dosse) in the period from 1791 to 1796 was 400 horses (plus 234 stallions in the regional stud), and in 1840 there were 288.

At the beginning of the eighteenth century, only Neustadt (Dosse) and Rosenberg were still maintained to provide for the royal stables in Potsdam and Berlin. There were some attempts to encourage regional horse breeding, again in the interests of providing for the army, including a regional edict on the use of stud horses in 1713, and regulations for purchase and sale from 1715 onwards, such as those of 1716 governing the Magdeburg horse market, although none of these had a lasting effect. In 1718, male asses were imported from Italy, and Neustadt (Dosse) became a centre of mule breeding, with a stock of 125 animals, which ten years later had risen to 170. But because of the primitive conditions which existed generally, particularly under Frederick II (1740–86), the stud declined; in 1774 there were only eighteen animals left. 'Frederick the Great always damaged his stud farms by his economies, such as in letting his best mares and horses go for the sake of the money they brought in; he looked upon his stud farms more as a branch of trade.' (Wallmerode, 1797)

In 1787 his successor, Frederick William II, approved a plan of his senior Master of Horse for establishing a regional stud on the site of the Neustadt mule-breeding station that had been moved to Trakehnen. The main stud was built in 1788 in the late Baroque style, closely modelled on the buildings of the principal stud at Trakehnen, the 'Frederick William Stud' (main building and stables) in 1787–90, and the regional stud, 'Lindenaus Hof' (main building and stables), in 1787–91. By moving the Neustadt office to Dreetz and taking over Dreetz and other areas, including the domain of Neustadt (Dosse), the stud had acquired some 900 hectares (2,000 acres) of ground by 1797, but most of it was of very poor quality (Rohlwes, 1806, called it 'useless sandy shale'), so that extensive measures of soil improvement were necessary and these were quickly carried out, including those of the 'reed pond'.

Functionality and expediency of form characterised the new buildings. The stables were airy and light, allowing efficient ventilation. The floor was paved with clinker bricks. A fountain was built into the covering stable adjoining the main building to keep it cool on hot summer days, and it is still preserved today. The stallions were given a summer stable with open paddocks where they 'feel very much at home in the summer, and even the highly-strung, sensitive and delicate Arabians served their mares with greater enjoyment as soon as they were in this abode' (Ammon, 1818). Trees which were planted in the grounds of the stud and in the avenues leading to Lindenaus Hof when the buildings were put up still today lend the whole place a particular beauty. Residential accommodation, stables and a small indoor riding arena made up the fourth side of the square courtyard of the stud. In 1810 two more houses were built outside the square and some more at the beginning of this century. Most of the modern buildings have been added in the past ten years.

The brand-mark chosen for the new stud consisted of a snake entwined round an arrow, symbolising speed and dexterity. This brand was applied vertically on the right hind thigh with the arrow pointing downwards. When, in 1876, the stud was closed down and its horses distributed, it was passed on to the Graditz and Beberbeck studs. In 1895/6 when the stud was re-established in Neustadt (Dosse), it was reintroduced there, although in a slightly altered form, and placed horizontally on the right leg with the arrow pointing to the right.

The breeding stock that was in the stud when it was established was not suitable for use. Looking back on it in 1831, Lindenau wrote: 'At Neustadt on the Dosse I found a so-called royal mule stud with a few poor stalls of worthless mares and a pack of mediocre mules.' By varied purchases, a mixture of breeds was developed at first, until it became clear that the Oriental stallions and English mares—almost exclusively part-bred—were the most appropriate for achieving the aims of the stud at that time. In the early years, more and more breeding animals of this provenance were acquired: at first from England in 1787/9, in 1787 from Trakehnen and Mecklenburg, and in 1790/1 from Zweibrücken. Oriental stallions came from England, France, Spain, Italy and, after 1791, by special purchase from Arabia as well. Valuable horses were also imported from Austria, among which the most important was the Oriental stallion, Turc-Main-Atty (foaled 1792). We know today that this horse was a Turkmene and he exerted a very powerful influence; in 1839 his blood was still represented in all the Prussian studs and in many more elsewhere. In about 1800

there were 15 of his daughters in his own stable. Between 1792 and 1802, he sired 144 foals. The stallion was lost at the time of the occupation of Mark Brandenburg by the French in 1808; because of an injury to a fore pastern, he could not be evacuated with the stud.

In 1806 the stud had 103 brood-mares. A relatively uniform breed, the Neustadt horse had developed, although the horses were perhaps somewhat too small and delicate. The favourable influence that the stud exerted on regional horse breeding through the state stallions that it bred was unmistakable. Sebald (1815) wrote: '. . . those horses of the type that has been improved by the state stud are of medium size, and apart from a somewhat heavy head, have a rather pleasing figure; nor do they lack strength and endurance . . .'

Veltheim (1833) supported this view and maintained that the Neustadt horse constituted a breed which was 'not only in no way inferior to the Zweibrücken breed but, in the later generations, actually superior to it.' He went on to say:

. . . it should not surprise the connoisseur that here too [Neustadt], among the first generations, there existed many a horse that was too small, too delicate or in some other way not quite proportionate, partly because both the Oriental and English horses had first to survive a struggle with local and climatic conditions and also because those in charge of the stud still had much to learn by experience. But all this soon began to even out and regional breeding establishments could be provided with the services of quite splendid stallions, particularly since the excellent Anspach stud farm [Triesdorf] became the property of the Prussian state, and in addition, many noble horses found their way to other parts of Germany, particularly to Mecklenburg, where they contributed to the improvement of horse breeding. But unhappily these excellent prospects for the horse lover and patriot were, like much else that was good, in part destroyed by the wretched war of 1806, in part postponed for a number of years. With the rapid advance of the enemy troops, a considerable part of the Neustadt stud fell into their hands and was lost to its own country, while the rest had to be evacuated to Russia together with the Trakehnen stud, which move, naturally was of considerable disadvantage to that institute.

This was a fair appraisal of the facts. Due to the hesitation of the director of that time, evacuation before the French advance began too late. The first group reached Trakehnen and had to be

moved on to Schaulen (today Siaulilai) 60 miles south of Riga; in spite of new additions, it returned in the autumn of 1809 drastically reduced. The second group went to the French army, and a number of mares among them to the French stud at Zweibrücken. Almost twenty years of work in breeding carried out by the Neustadt stud was lost. After the Treaty of Tilsit (1807), order was gradually re-established in the stud. In 1811, seventy-nine mares were again housed in Neustadt; in 1813 there was a total of 242 horses, even though not of the best quality. Veltheim continued:

Already these establishments [the Prussian and regional studs] had begun to flourish again, when the 1813 War of Liberation made necessary, as a precautionary measure, the removal once again of the Neustadt stud to Silesia, which, as is inevitable in any hasty evacuation of a stud, halted progress once again, and then during the war there could be little expansion; there was some, however, when in 1813 a not inconsiderable portion of the Imperial French Stud at Zweibrücken fell into the hands of the Prussians [under Blücher] at the start of the 1813 campaign. Their transfer to Neustadt to increase the stud there was all the more advantageous because this breed was homogenous with that already there, since, as pointed out above, not only do some of these horses originate from the Zweibrücken breed but also because a number of the horses were taken to Zweibrücken from Neustadt by the French in 1806 . . .

Evacuation of the Neustadt stud took place between 21 January and 30 December 1813, and was completed almost without losses. In 1814, in addition to the Zweibrücken horses mentioned above (8 mares, 2 stallions, 39 foals), the stock again included 8 principal stallions and 76 brood-mares.

When the turmoil of war had passed, there was an upsurge in the quality of breeding in the Neustadt stud. This was partly the result of the acquisition of valuable Oriental stallions in 1816/17 from Asia Minor and Istanbul.

In 1829, in the course of his 'Nimrod's German Tour', the English journalist Apperley visited Neustadt:

The brood-mares of the Neustadt stud consisted of eighty, seventy of which are there called thorough, or full-bred and of Eastern blood . . . Among them were a few English thorough-bred ones . . . several were crossed with Eastern as well as English blood, and there were some Eastern mares. The foals were running by their side . . . The colts run loose summer and winter

until the autumn following their third year, when they are taken into the house and broken . . . The operation of breaking is easily performed, as there is a docility belonging to the horses of Germany which, on a large scale, is rarely met with here . . . They were lying in excellent pasture with large and commodious buildings to run into: and, by an arrangement which reflects great credit on the projector, a running stream of beautifully transparent water traversed each of the paddocks. We thought the colts looking well . . .

The paddocks at Neustadt contain eighteen hundred acres, and are divided by strong double posts and rails. A portion of them is mown every year, and, what surprised me, another portion is ploughed. In this country we are fond of the oldest pasture we can get for forcing any kind of stock; but Mr Strubberg [Director of the stud, 1808–49] informed us that he found it necessary to break up this land about every fifth year, taking a crop of barley off it, and laying it down again. Without this management, he said, the herbage became coarse . . .

. . . The economy of the stables appeared to be admirably arranged . . . There is one part of German horse breeding which I admire, and am a stickler for: this is, their aversion to what may be termed *natural blemishes*. The Jews at their festivals could not have been more careful that there should be no blemish or 'evil-favouredness' on the animals they brought for offerings; than the German horse-breeders are in their choice of stallions and mares for their studs.

In 1830 the stock in Neustadt (Dosse) included 7 principal stallions, 10 English thoroughbred mares, 77 mares of their own breeding and their foals of all ages.

Because of the demands of agriculture for stronger and heavier horses and so also for appropriate state stallions, there was a gradual reorientation of the Neustadt stud, which bred and reared these stallions, away from the breeding of Anglo-Arabians towards that of pure-bred horses, while the breeding of part-bred horses continued alongside. Today this kind of logic comes as something of a surprise, for on no account could a positive result be expected, apart from an increase in size and alterations in conformation. From 1839 onwards, only English thoroughbreds were used for covering; two stallions of this period were the chestnut Ganges (foaled 1831), used up to 1844, and the black Egremont (foaled 1833), used until 1843. Together with this trend towards English thoroughbreds—mares as well—there was also a move towards adopting organisational methods on the English pattern.

This included setting up a training farm in the neighbouring regional stud (main building with 28 boxes, 4 four-horse stables, indoor riding arena, a smithy etc) with a race-track. The first races took place there on 3 and 4 May 1847; but the track was closed again after 1858.

In spite of all the efforts made, no perceptible improvement in the size and conformation of the Neustadt horses was achieved in the forties and fifties. Wittenburg spoke of the 'tall and windy Neustadt horses'. The Berlin Central Authority in charge of studs thus

Neustadt (Dosse) stud (Photo: Flade)

decided in 1848 that the principal studs would specialise: Trakehnen and Graditz in breeding a carriage horse and Neustadt (Dosse) a saddle horse. Compulsory breeding programmes were drawn up. As part of this measure, Neustadt took over the entire stock of English thoroughbreds from Trakehnen and looked after them until 1866. In 1856 the stock of the stud was officially established at four to five leading stallions and 100 mares including progeny. The first foundation herd, to breed saddle horses, consisted of 28 English thoroughbred mares; the second foundation herd, to breed stallions for regional use, of 27 English thoroughbred and 21 part-bred mares. Nevertheless, Brincken (director of the stud 1849–66) was able to write in 1857:

The studs [ie the leading Prussian studs] have for some time allowed themselves to be led astray by their interest in horse racing to concentrate mainly upon racing blood in the breeding of stallions. But since, by following this path, we have produced many horses that are certainly noble but, at the same time, narrow, over-refined and small, whereas breeders everywhere are demanding large strong stallions, we are now seeking to cultivate as carefully as possible our earlier, more broadly and firmly based breeding practices, as if we were having to sweep them together again with a broom . . .

From about 1868 the production of part-bred horses was to be progressively consolidated by the import of warmblood stallions of Trakehner extraction. Neustadt (Dosse) was going to breed a 'firm-boned, compact, sound and serviceable horse which, in its breeding type and size, combines the advantages of nobility with sufficient weight to satisfy all demands made upon it' (Gunther, 1868). After the 1874 reorganisation, the breeding stock consisted of 87 part-bred mares, to which were added 2 English thoroughbred stallions and 3 part-bred stallions as the principal studs. Nevertheless, the attempt to achieve a decisive improvement in the quality of stallion that was bred did not succeed. Because of the small number of commercially useful stallions produced, high running costs and poor pasture, the stud had eventually to be closed down in 1876. Of the breeding stock, 44 mares and 58 foals went to Graditz, but the larger part (75 mares and 82 foals) was removed to the 400-year-old stud at Beberbeck which in that same year had come under the administration of the Prussian state authority for studs. Here it constituted the basic breeding stock, for although the mares 'for the most part failed to meet the required standard' (Oettingen, 1920) they were nevertheless ac-

cepted on account of their 'reliable capacity for hereditary transmission' (Mieckley, 1905). By 1883, only 38 of these mares with their female progeny still survived there, having had difficulties with acclimatisation. But the situation improved and in 1919, 57 part-bred mares out of a total of 112 of Neustadt extraction were being used for breeding in Beberbeck. In 1929/30 Beberbeck itself was closed down; most of the breeding stock was transferred to the Polish stud at Racot (Poznan district).

The closure of the Neustadt (Dosse) stud—the regional stud at Lindenaus Hof continued in existence—led to constant complaints. But it was not until 1894, the year in which William II demanded that Arabian horses should be bred to supply mounts for his hussar regiments, that breeding stock was returned to the stud farm, initially comprising twelve pure-bred Arabians; these, however, proved too small to satisfy demands. So the breeding of Anglo-Arabs was resumed; in 1895, 10 strong English thoroughbred mares were transferred from Graditz, and to serve them a dark-brown stallion, Young O'Bajan (foaled 1889), offspring of one of the most important of all Arab stallions, O'Bajan (foaled 1881), was acquired from the Hungarian state stud farm of Babolna. At the insistence of the farmers, the production of part-bred horses was also resumed, in addition to that of Anglo-Arabs, and for this purpose the first eight mares were purchased in the summer of 1896. At the same time, further capital was invested in the Anglo-Arab breeding programme with the purchase in 1902 of another pure-bred Arab, Dziaf-Amir, foaled 1897, from the Taurow stud (Ukraine). But, overall, there was a progressive orientation towards the production of part-bred horses, and although no final decision was reached in the contest between establishing the trend in the direction of the warmblood horse of Trakehner extraction or that of the Hanoverian horse, priority was given to the sturdy, highly-bred warmblood horse.

In 1908 the Neustadt stud again had 50 brood-mares, of which 35 were part-bred. Breeding of the Anglo-Arab was finally discontinued in 1916, and no more English thoroughbred mares were used. This represented a clear decision in favour of the production of robust regional stallions better suited to the requirements of agriculture.

It was a development that continued to dominate the period following World War I, when the demand for cavalry horses ceased. During this time, the leading stallions Mailand (born 1910 in Brandenburg, sired 33 registered stallions) and Sheridan (born 1907 in Hanover, sired 20 registered stallions) exercised a particularly strong influence on breeding, especially through their numerous

male descendants. But even in 1921, the 66 mares in the stud were basically warmblood horses of Trakehner extraction, and were of the most diverse origin (37 sires) with the result that 'this herd could not represent a single unity' (Henninges, 1921), even though quite a large number of them exhibited excellent qualities.

Fortunately the stud did not go along with the move towards the heavy warmblood horse of the Oldenburg type, in contrast to the regional breeding programme for which the regional stud at Neustadt had by 1923 acquired 73 Oldenburg stallions. In 1921 the stud farm had carried out experimental feeding and growth tests on Oldenburg and Hanoverian weaning foals, and discovered that the Hanoverians developed well, while the Oldenburgs lagged so far behind that they were quite unsuitable for stud breeding. In 1922 the Brandenburg warmblood breeders firmly directed their activities towards breeding Hanoverian warmblood horses, so that the use of Oldenburg stallions was progressively reduced until, by the beginning of the thirties, they had been discarded completely.

This tendency in breeding also affected the Neustadt stud. There, the aim was to produce a 'strong-boned, short-legged, warmblood horse with adequate depth of rib, straight and sweeping gait and with a quiet temperament'. In the coming years, this proved the right aim and, moreover, one that was realisable. Important aspects of it are still reflected today in the professional standard for the noble warmblood horse that is reared in the German Democratic Republic. In this sense, dependence upon Hanoverian origins in stud breeding was continued. Results were very successful. In 1929, Henninges wrote:

Nowadays, a good supply of effective, protein-rich fodder for the youngstock, together with extensive pasturing on well-kept meadows throughout the year, encourages the growth of offspring that are healthy, and which, in the strength of their bones, represent the peak of achievement in the breeding of warmblood horses, but without in any way lacking in nobility.

In 1930 the composition of the brood-mare stock was as follows: 11 warmblood mares of Trakehner extraction, 13 warmblood mares of Hanoverian extraction, 53 warmblood mares of mixed Trakehner and Hanoverian extraction in different ratios.

On the basis of subjective judgement, subsequent directors once again orientated their programmes strictly towards the pure breeding of a warmblood horse of Trakehner extraction; in 1940 only stallions of this breed were used as principal studs in Neu-

stadt, so that again the demands made on the stallions reared in Neustadt by breeders in the Province of Brandenburg were not fulfilled. The frequent change of director after 1930 was a further reason for the lack of expansion of the stud.

In spite of the great difficulties that faced the immense task of reconstructing the badly damaged national economy in the Soviet zone of occupation at the end of World War II, the Neustadt stud was reorganised under the name of the 'Arthur von Weinberg Stud Farm', and recovered rapidly, thanks to generous measures of assistance that were made available to a developing socialist agriculture. On 1 June 1949, 41 brood-mares were housed there, of which 8 were warmblood mares of Trakehner extraction, 23 warmblood mares of Hanoverian extraction, 7 warmblood mares of Brandenburg extraction and 3 warmblood mares of unknown lineage. In addition there were the leading stallions Fernab (foaled in Hanover in 1944) and Hexenschuss (foaled in Trakehnen in 1924).

In 1956 Neuschulz wrote that the stud 'raised the quality of the stock of mares to a very good level'. He continued:

Out of some forty mares, the pedigree of half of them can be traced back to Hanover. Brandenburg takes second place with the greater share and is followed by East Prussia. It is the task of Neustadt to conserve this blood that is so essential for national horse breeding by planned mating between these three great blood-lines, and to make it available in the quantities required and at the proper time for use in a national programme of breeding.

In the same year in which these words were printed, the state-owned stallion depot (former regional stud) and the Neustadt (Dosse) stud were placed under separate administrative and financial control, each existing as an independent unit. Neustadt continued to follow the breeding policy outlined above with, at that time, 47 brood-mares. The number remained virtually unchanged over the next fifteen years; in 1961 a herd of thoroughbreds with 35 brood-mares was added. As well as looking after this group, the stud was responsible for maintaining a number of racing stables between 1970 and 1974. This was a temporary arrangement that ended in 1977/8 when the thoroughbred herd was moved, half of it going to the thoroughbred stud farm at Lehn and half to that at Görlsdorf. Since that time, with full use of all the stable accommodation, the stud has been able to devote itself wholly to the task of breeding a noble warmblood horse of a very high quality.

In this task they have made constant and substantial progress. In 1965, for example, the brood-mares had an average height of 16 hands and their share of English thoroughbred and warmblood Trakehner lineage was only minimal; the 1981 stock—103 mares— had approximately a 30 per cent share of thoroughbred blood and an average height of 16.1 hands. A number of stallions had made a particularly successful contribution to the progress in breeding, such as the stud's Eberswalde, Duell II, Senatus and Adept (all of Hanoverian origin), Neumond and Drusus (warmblood horses of Trakehner extraction) and the part-bred stallion, Brack.

At the annual top quality stallion show of the German Democratic Republic at Magdeburg, held in connection with the Agricultural Exhibition at Markkleeberg, stallions from the Neustadt stud have, since 1967, regularly been highly placed in all classes.

The present breeding stock of 280 animals corresponds to the standard laid down in 1983, which reflects the aim of producing the best possible in breeding:

General attainments: a strong constitution, the legs having a particularly strong load-carrying capacity; high fertility; a lively temperament marked by sociability with great nervous stability and a keen readiness for work.
Special attainments: pronounced aptitude for all disciplines of riding and driving sports, as well as for recreational riding and trekking; a good aptitude for light draught work; well-timed action in all three paces, full of impetus and with a good length of stride, with energetic attack; a naturally upright stance combined with balance and agility.

Correspondingly detailed demands are made of the outward appearance of the individual breeding animal, including a height of 16 to 17 hands.

The main tasks of the Neustadt stud are to be seen in conjunction with those of other specialist and national horse breeding institutions. Basically they are:

• to produce breeding stallions through their own production of male foals and the purchase of male foals, which are to be reared together on the farm under optimal conditions;
• to develop their own stock of mares, which allows a great extent of individual mating, particularly in the interests of producing breeding stallions;
• to produce and sell sporting horses which satisfy the most exacting requirements in all disciplines of equestrian sport;

• to sell high-quality brood-mares to other breeding establishments.

In realising these wide-ranging aims, the stud farm at Neustadt (Dosse) exerts a strong influence far beyond its own boundaries on the development of warmblood breeding.

The Hanoverian stud in Celle

Celle, in Lower Saxony, represents a highly specialised regional stud which not only actively pursues the tasks of breeding in the area allotted to it, but also ensures the use of high-quality stallions in the covering stations subordinate to it.

Even before the stud was founded, farmers and horse breeders in their fertile lowlands between the Weser and Elbe could look back upon a sound tradition of horse breeding. It was not without good reason that the Elector Ernst August of Hanover (ruled 1679–98) introduced a leaping horse into the coat of arms of the House of Hanover (incidentally, at the suggestion of the philosopher G. W. von Leibniz, who died in Hanover in 1716). In 1714 Ludwig Georg of Hanover succeeded to the English throne as George I, and his mother country went to the English crown. In the possession of the Elector-King there were at that time a few small studs which had as their principal task to supply the royal stables with horses. The Memsen stud (1653–1838) became well known mainly because it provided the Hanoverian court stud at Herrenhausen with the basic material for their white horses (albinos with red eyes) and Isabella horses (biscuit-coloured or cream) that were so famous in the nineteenth century. Herrenhausen in turn provided not only ceremonial horses for London but, in the nineteenth century, reared more than two hundred stallions for use in breeding Hanoverian warmblood horses, of which some two-thirds were taken over by the Celle regional stud, including the very important founder stallion Adeptus (foaled 1880).

Perhaps prompted by the level of horse breeding in England, George II (who reigned from 1727–60) expressed his intention, in 1732, of employing a number of regional stallions 'for the purpose of improving horse breeding, for the benefit of our subjects, and so that so much money should not go out of the country in providing horses for the cavalry and dragoons.' In August 1735 a decree was issued stating that 'In the best interests of our subjects and in order to maintain horse breeding of a good quality in our German lands, We have resolved to establish a Regional Stud, initially

with 12 stallions . . .' In 1736, 13 stallions were purchased from Holstein and distributed. The horses, and the stablemen in charge of covering, were lodged at first with officials and later suitable accommodation was rented for them. The period laid down for covering extended from 1 March to 30 June. Branding was practised from 1735, the old Lower Saxon emblem of two crossed horses' heads probably being used as the brand-mark. Certificates of covering and foaling were issued, and selective breeding practised. By 1748, seventeen covering stations with more than thirty stallions had been developed; tenure of the land and buildings was established and from 1743 the director of the establishment was employed full time.

The regional stud suffered considerable damage during the Seven Years' War (1756–63), but by 1790, after much energetic work, over sixty stallions had been stationed in as many covering stations. Throughout the province, horse breeding had reached a high level and had become one of the most important branches of trade in Hanover's economy; between 1775 and 1780, 10,000 horses were exported annually from the breeding area.

The evacuation of the stud to Mecklenburg in face of the French advance (1803/4) by way of Neuhaus on the Elbe to Ivenack, and the ten-year period of French occupation, ending with another move to Hanover and Ludwigslust (1813), had disastrous consequences. After the war, it was a long time before the losses could be made good. Even in 1839 the services of some sixty stallions from the royal stables had to be called upon, although a large number of stallions had been purchased, including some from neighbouring Mecklenburg.

For the successful reconstruction and development of the stud farm, credit must go to the brothers A. and F. Spörcken in their capacity of Master of the Horse (1816–39 and 1839–66) who can be regarded as the true founders of horse breeding in Hanover. The 'Celle Races' were held (1838–63) during their period of office, using English thoroughbreds; but the danger of these horses exerting an excessive influence on breeding was recognised early and, after 1840, there was a rapid stabilisation. This was greatly assisted by the acquisition of valuable stallions: in 1848/9 Zernebog, Jellachich, Nordfolk and Flick. The stud was considerably extended under the Spörckens, so that the area that was owned in 1856 is still adequate for all today's needs. In 1866 Hanover became part of Prussia. The Prussian Stud Authorities took over some 220 regional stallions. In the years that followed the main aim was to consolidate regional horse breeding, to breed a warmblood horse that was rooted in the region, as strong as

Celle stud farm, Lower Saxony (Photo: W. Ernst)

possible and yet noble, a breeding target that was summed up by the Master of the Horse, W. H. Grabensee, in the phrase 'weight with nobility'. During Grabensee's period of office (1892–1915), the number of regional stallions rose to almost 370. The establishment of the stud book in 1888 (*Volume I* and *Aims of Breeding* 1893) had important consequences for the organisation of breeding. The Association of Hanoverian Warmblood Breeders, founded in 1922, took over the management of the stud book and, in co-operation with the administrative body in charge of covering stations and regional studs, guaranteed constant progress in breeding.

To accommodate the growing numbers of stallions, the complex in Westercelle, built in 1907 as a marketing stable, was leased in 1907 and bought in 1918, and since 1928 has been in use as a stallion testing centre. After World War I, the number of registered stallions rose so sharply (in 1925 there were 500), that although many of them were stabled privately, a further regional stud for Lower Saxony had to be established: it existed from 1925 to 1961 in Osnabrück-Eversburg. A measure that proved particularly beneficial to breeding was the establishment of the Hunnesrück stallion-rearing stud, which has existed since 1920 and is subordinate to the Celle regional stud; some twenty weaned foals are stabled there annually and raised together until the age of two and a half. Close links also exist between the Celle regional stud and the riding-horse auctions in Verden (Aller), held since 1949 by the Breeders' Association, which have achieved international importance and have increasingly influenced the type and model of the modern Hanoverian horse.

Equestrian Sport

It is only in the last few decades of this century that equestrian sport has developed for the general public, providing pleasure in and with the animal, recreation and physical discipline, and a two-sided training—for both horse and rider—which can lead to a high degree of perfection when horsemanship becomes an art. The influence of experienced riding and driving instructors is fundamental in the development of equestrian sport. They are also responsible for bringing on the next generation in this field. Among the many demands made upon them, they need to have an extensive theoretical knowledge and practical experience as well as a willingness constantly to add to their store of knowledge and consistently to put into practice their theoretical principles. Both instructors and adjudicators should at the same time be educators and should support and confirm this function through their own example. The broad social range covered by equestrian sport in many countries makes it imperative that careful attention is given to the training and fostering of a good many such people.

Driving

Even in an age of almost completely motorised and mechanised transport in industry, agriculture and forestry, the driving of horse-drawn vehicles has not only retained its importance as a sport and leisure activity but has increased its following. It is especially popular in the form of carriage and pair driving, the driving of a multi-horse team or of vehicles drawn by small horses or ponies, and provides an effective complement to riding events at horse shows. The physical separation of the driver from his horse demands considerable empathy, intuitive power and a particular degree of dexterity. An extensive knowledge of the theory of driving and expert handling of reins and whip are also needed. The sport of driving involves specialised and appropriate harnessing of horse and carriage, extensive preparations, particularly in the presentation of multi-horse teams, and a great deal of hard work, since horses, harness and carriage require lavish care and maintenance.

Horse and rider

The essence of riding lies in the concerted action of rider and horse, in which ideally the rider directs the natural inclinations of the horse with a minimum of coercion, in a way that achieves optimal sporting performances with a high level of harmony between rider and animal. This is the only way consistently to achieve peak performances in the disciplines of equitation, dressage, show jumping and cross-country riding. The foundation for this lies in providing the horse with sound basic training and systematic specialised training.

From the very start of training, the rider must gain the confidence of his mount, and must study the behaviour patterns and psychology of the horse in order to be able to shape its actions to his wishes. This was already recognised by certain very early hippologists who were interested in the subject of horse training, such as Kikkuli (fourteenth century BC) and Xenophon. They saw the importance of the rider's ability to encourage the desired reactions and to make them pleasurable for the horse, and at the same time to suppress undesirable actions and make them unpleasant for the horse. Seunig (1961) writes:

There are certain gifted riders who immediately and intuitively establish a degree of psychological contact with any horse, which defies rational explanation. This mysterious psychological process which transmits the will of the rider to his horse, so that the intentions of the two become fused into a single centaurian entity, is the fundamental basis for success in this sphere. An attempted explanation: as soon as the rider is in the saddle, he must force himself to adopt a degree of duality, an artificial schizophrenia. This splitting of his consciousness makes it possible for him both to feel as a human being and at the same time to experience the completely different sensations and emotions experienced by his other self, the horse (empathy), and to act accordingly.

Correct horse-rider proportions make for more successful communication between rider and horse
a Large rider, small horse
b Small rider, large horse
c Rider in correct proportion to horse

The secret, then, is to enter entirely into the behaviour patterns of the horse, to share its thoughts and feelings, and not to expect or demand of the horse that it should understand the rider.

In addition, the rider must be of an equable temperament. Xenophon wrote: 'Never approach your horse in anger, this is the supreme rule and habit in dealing with a horse. For anger is unpredictable, and frequently leads to some action that is regretted later.' The rider must have the ability to assess objectively his own performance and that of his horse in comparison with others. Great intuitive power, consistency, energy, courage, and judiciousness are other necessary characteristics for the rider, as indeed for the athlete in general.

A love of horses, perhaps starting in childhood, or else a genuine enthusiasm for sport are the usual motives for taking up riding. After basic training which lasts one to two years, the horse, and frequently the rider as well, specialises in one of the disciplines of riding, such as dressage, show jumping or horse trials.

Competitive riding and show jumping demand real talent on the part of the sportsman and an extensive knowledge of the theory and practice of riding. It takes years of strenuous training under a good instructor gradually to achieve reliability and proficiency in riding, whether it is undertaken simply for pleasure or for professional sport. The rider must be prepared for setbacks of all kinds.

Questions of this sort have occupied the attention of leading authorities in the field of equitation, such as F. R. de la Guérinière, who was director of the Académie des Tuileries from 1730 until his death in 1751, and who brought about important measures of reform in the theory of riding. His book *École de Cavalerie* (1733) was responsible for bringing order to the widely diverging theories of the time, for establishing a concerted move towards 'natural training', and for formulating this tendency clearly and systematically into a

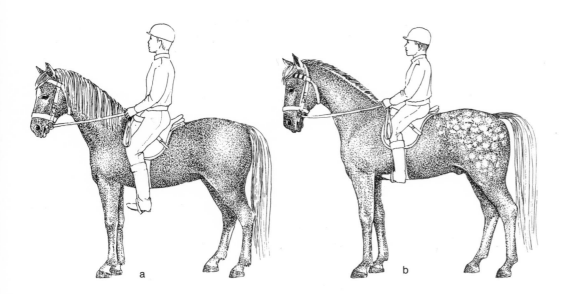

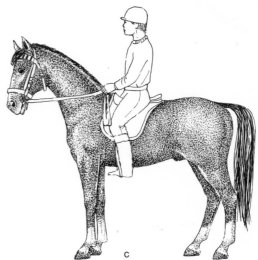

logical theory of equitation which effectively replaced outdated ideas. As the following extracts show, his experiences and conclusions are still relevant today.

Every art and science has its own fundamental principles and fixed rules. By following them, one achieves new knowledge and this in turn can lead to the peak of perfection.

The art of riding seems to require nothing but practical pursuit. But practice without fundamental principles means nothing more than skill gained by practice alone, that is, a superficial show, a deceptive brilliance which dazzles the uninitiated. The skill of the rider and the fascinating motion of the horse disguise the lack of training. That is why so few well-trained horses are found and just as few true experts in the saddle.

Because they lack theoretical knowledge, the pupils cannot distinguish between correct and incorrect. Regrettably, they always imitate a wrong action. It is easier to learn than the right one . . . Without theory there is no practice. In an art in which the body is so

closely involved as in riding, theory and practice cannot be separated. In equitation, difficulties are often met which can be resolved by sound theoretical knowledge . . .

Theory provides the correct fundamental principles. These must not be unnatural, but must rather help to make good the deficiencies of nature.

What theory teaches us, we should put to use in practice. To be able to achieve this skill, we must love horses. The rider must be strong and skilful and, in addition, warm-hearted and particularly patient. These are the essential characteristics for a good rider. There is hardly anyone who does not love horses . . .

The aim of training is, after all, to make the horse steady, skilful and obedient. It must be made to flex its haunches. Without this capacity, neither the military horse, the hunter nor training horse can walk with agreeable movements and in a manner comfortable for the rider . . .

Every rider must study in detail the natural tendencies of the horse. Knowledge in this sphere is particularly important and the result of long experience. Only over a considerable period of time is it possible to discover in this way its good and bad characteristics.

The fundamental principles of riding can easily be applied in the case of horses with a good, well-balanced conformation, strength and quickness to learn, and with good will . . .

What nature has denied, art cannot replace. This is especially true of horses with a poor conformation and lack of courage. But conformation and character are not the sole causes of obstreperous behaviour. Often it is simply that some action is required of the horse that it is as yet unable to perform. Excessive demands simply discourage the horse and overtax sinews and nerves. By the time training is completed, the horse's spirit is broken. Obedience is merely the consequence of weakness. It has become an abject, enfeebled creature. A different cause of weakness of the back, the limbs and of the whole horse can be too early a start with training. The development of the young horse is not completed, its strength is not yet fully developed. So it cannot perform the work demanded of it . . . Refractory behaviour and lack of attention are particularly common in young horses. The sense of freedom is still too much alive in them. The first training exercises are difficult for them. Only gradually do they become accustomed to submitting their will to that of

The walk, showing foot sequence

the trainer. People are always inclined to take unfair advantage of this supposed power. There is no animal with a better memory for punishment given at the wrong time.

In earlier times, when the unbroken foals left the stud, they were broken in by suitable horsemen. Riders were chosen who had great patience and skill and were, at the same time, bold and persevering . . . they would accustom the horses slowly to the presence of a human being in the stables, to having a leg handled, to being fitted with saddle and crupper. Calmly and patiently, they taught the horse to accept mounting and dismounting. Until every other conceivable means was tried, they never resorted to severity and force. With infinite patience, they made the young horses quiet, willing and obedient. And health and strength remained unimpaired.

In our own times [ie, some 250 years ago], fewer lame, vicious, intractable, stubborn, spiteful horses would be found if people would learn from the experiences of these great artists . . .

The trot, showing foot sequence

The demands made of the sporting horse

Sporting horses have to satisfy much more stringent requirements than do draught horses. So a planned programme for breeding entails considerably greater difficulties and is also much more expensive.

There is a series of requirements made of the type of horse that can be used for all sports disciplines in the sphere of driving and riding, that is, for the non-specialist horse. These demands were formulated long ago and are still universally valid today. Xenophon, for example, saw the horse's body initially as a unified whole, and considered the parts of the body from the point of view of their functional unity. He specifically took into account 'the soul' (by which he means character and temperament), of which 'the unridden horse [the foal before it is trained] does not yet offer very reliable signs'.

While E. Schiele was visiting Jordan in 1972, she was given an insight into the experience gained over thousands of years by people who even now are still nomadic. There she spoke to an Arab about the criteria they used in selecting the 'best' horse. He said: 'Before you are three very similar horses. They are of the same age, size, sex and colour and have

the same markings and conformation. So how do you determine which of them is the best?' The answer was as follows:

Listen and hear how the Bedouin do it. They send the horses out with three riders together with three more mounted on camels, and keep them on the move for forty-eight hours without food or water, sometimes walking, sometimes galloping. The riders are changed over on the way. Then the horses are brought to water, for their behaviour there is the touchstone. Scarcity of water is the Bedouin's worst enemy. The first horse rushes into it, bathes and rolls about, drinks with abandon and forgets everything around it. The second horse remains standing, bends one knee, drinks eagerly and will not be interrupted. The third horse bends its head, touches the water with its lips and drinks steadily. Then the riders produce a series of different noises. The first two horses go on drinking impassively; but the third pricks up its ears, stops drinking, lifts its head, looks round about it alertly and is ready for action. This is the horse that the Bedouin decides upon.

The fundamental aim underlying the training of a saddle horse or sporting

horse is that the rider should be able to master it with the minimum of force, without risk to himself, and giving full consideration to the horse. The basic training that the horse is given to this end comprises its schooling in obedience and the physical training necessary to achieve better performance, based on its natural tendencies. By means of constant repetition and systematic increases in intensity, motor skills, technique and locomotory characteristics, and condition are improved. The training stimuli employed should cause the organ, or the sections of muscle or tendon involved in the action, to adapt to the action demanded of it. The reactions of those areas of the body in which adaptation is brought about by training stimuli are, in principle, the same as those of the human athlete. But the fact that, in the sport of riding, two quite disparate beings carry out a common physical action in unison, presents added difficulties and gives riding a special position among all the sporting activities of man. The most essential feature of riding is the high degree of harmony between rider and horse in balance, movement, in psychological readiness for action and in the ability to direct all bodily activities to-

wards achieving the common goal. This explains the high demands that must be made of athlete and trainer in this sphere.

The more comprehensively the horse breeder can satisfy the requirements by modification of the horse's psychological qualities, by the deliberate modelling of type and by particular measures of rearing and early training, the more effectively and successfully can the aim of the sportsman and trainer be achieved, namely that of turning a 'raw' horse into a suitable sporting horse in the sense described above.

One of the tasks facing today's breeders of warmblood horses is increasingly to give consideration to specific criteria of selection that are important to the sport of riding, the main effect of which is to increase the effectiveness of basic training and to raise the level of specialisation in the horse. Even in the lowest class, the sporting horse must fulfil a series of basic demands (hence the concept of basic training); they include:

- general relaxation, absence of tension and rigidity;
- neat, even foot sequence in all paces;
- long-striding elastic gait (with a slow hoof-lowering phase), with active forward motion and precise timing;
- long intermediate stride;

- a lively trot, springy and 'rounded', ie the hooves must be lifted from the ground and not drawn low across it;
- the gallop, the most important pace for the show jumper, must be performed with perfect balance and with an active propulsive force, but without the horse shifting its centre of gravity to the forehand when increasing speed;
- with the rider's hand remaining passive, the horse must apply pressure equally to either side of the bit, without any compulsive distortion of the neck; there must also be an elastic see-sawing of the back with full rounding, known as the bascule, with the joints of the forelegs drawn in tightly in the jumping phase;
- the beginnings of 'handiness', ie responsiveness; active movement of the hind legs in the direction of the common centre of gravity of rider and horse, while keeping the poll (the highest point) mobile and held high;
- evenly muscled neck, ie equal distribution of muscles on either side of the withers;
- the beginnings of complete longitudinal flexion when turning while progressing forwards;
- abandonment of the horse's natural asymmetry in movement, and development of obedience to commands com-

The gallop, showing foot sequence

municated through the leg of one side only;

- weight equally distributed on adjacent feet when standing, with the head and neck at rest.

It is obvious that in the fulfilment of these demands, which of course are only the starting point of training, in addition to the inner characteristics (in the broadest sense), the horse's outward features also have a part to play. This is true both of the anatomical conditions which the rider should develop within the framework of the horse's training, or restrict if their effect is undesirable, and also of those that cannot be altered but at best can usefully be exploited; their specific nature must be taken fully into consideration in training.

Of course, all features and characteristics of the horse must be recognised, understood and exploited as soon as possible, but particular details can be isolated which are of particular significance if a horse is to be selected for the highest levels of competition. For example, certain features cannot be altered by the rider to any significant degree, such as:

- the height of the horse, and essentially the framework of the body, the massivity of the skeleton and with it the areas of muscle and tendon insertion and so in turn the muscle mass;
- the length of the horse including both total length from poll to tail root and also trunk length from shoulder to point of buttock;
- the position and length of shoulder and its musculature;
- the posture of the limbs and the flexion of the joints, ie the bending of the forehand and forehand limbs and that of the hindquarters and hind limbs.

Even from this brief and incomplete list, it is clear that the details of external appearance and their links with other features and with temperamental characteristics must be given careful and appropriate consideration by the breeder. These special features cannot simply be summarised in a breeding target or as a standard. More than ever before, it is essential to view today's warmblood as a sporting horse, particularly as a saddle horse, that is to say, in motion and with a rider. The earlier static way of looking at a horse must be replaced by a dynamic assessment. This is often forgotten and, in practice, means that there is still much adherence to earlier ideas of a draught horse, which in their time were entirely appropriate. Since the effectiveness of the horse's outward riding characteristics and inner riding qualities cannot be judged without also including the effect of the rider's presence and actions (including simply the weight of the rider), objec-

Clambering in cross-country conditions

tive assessment is no simple matter and demands sound knowledge and experience in the sphere of breeding and sport. Therefore isolated observations and generalisations must always be taken with considerable reservation and tested individually. Only a horse that is in motion or jumping can achieve the performance demanded of it. The starting point of all assessments carried out for breeding purposes must be the horse in motion or jumping, with a rider. Aim and methods must accord with this.

In 1953, the Swedish dressage rider Henri St Cyr formulated the aim of dressage as follows:

A horse that carries itself well, moves effortlessly and is light on the rein, all paces in perfect purity of stride and infallible regularity, a horse that can alter speed effortlessly at the request of the rider, perfect harmony between rider and horse, a rider who works with unseen aids, giving the impression that everything proceeds easily, without exertion for rider and horse.

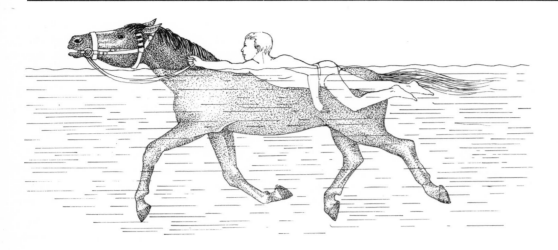

Swimming with the horse

Only a horse with a good basic training has a real chance of achieving its genetic potential and developing to the full its outward characteristics as well as its inner qualities in the course of specialised training.

In galloping and trotting races, the natural talent of the horse for speed, stamina and especially for frequency of action in these two paces plays a decisive part. This means that the breeding of thoroughbreds and trotting horses (pacers) is the decisive basis of performance in

Phases of the jump

this sphere. Planned breeding of horses for specialised tasks in show or competition work is not possible. Comparisons with the breeding of racehorses can be drawn only with reservations. But the breeder of show horses would do well to be guided by the general principles outlined above, and to recognise the problems which will confront the rider during the basic training of his horse, which, if it shows sufficient aptitude, will be trained for specialisation in dressage, show jumping or eventing.

The rider must be given a horse for training which shows natural promise both in its qualities and its physical characteristics, so that he can give it the sort of individual training that has been de-

scribed. On the other hand, the breeder can expect the rider to study closely the natural abilities of the horse, get to know them thoroughly, grapple with them, and make full use of the theoretical knowledge that is available in order to allow the horse, by the correct practical measures of development, schooling and training, to fulfil its potential. Riders and trainers without a sound grasp of scientific and theoretical method cannot hope to understand today's theories and literature concerning equitation, and so are unable to make use of it; as countless examples show, they are unable to develop the talents of even highly gifted horses. In recent decades, a high level of co-operation between breeders and riders has shown itself to be increasingly important and necessary. If we are to utilise, deepen and foster this liaison, it means that the foundation of equestrian sport at all levels, namely the suitable horse, should be made available at all times.

Equestrian events

A practice which has increased recently in equestrian sport is that of riders and horses participating in shows, exhibition work, exercises and various games of skill which are, however, not governed by

any strictly formulated system of rules. Participation in this kind of activity, together with the sport of performing vaulting exercises on horseback, is especially popular with children and teenagers. Here, no consummate equestrian performance is expected but rather skill, courage and lively riding within the framework of a collective activity.

Great demands are made upon the ability of horse and rider by cross-country riding of varying degrees of difficulty. Foxhunting, besides being a popular traditional sport in some countries, provides an excellent schooling opportunity for young horses and many a top-class eventer has had an introduction to cross-country work on the hunting field. In England, the season commences in November and ends in April. Drag-hunting, in which there is no quarry but where hounds follow a trail of strong-smelling chemical, also has its enthusiastic followers. The scent-line is laid across a predetermined route averaging 8 to 12 miles, taking in natural obstacles and hazards and making an exciting and stimulating course. These hunts provide excellent training for both horse and rider and a good schooling in discipline, level-headedness, quickness of reaction, camaraderie and co-operative action. At the same time, these are combined with a great sense of achievement.

Endurance riding and long-distance rides with fixed time limits require thorough preparation, a good deal of care and extensive specialist knowledge. The same is true of the sport of carriage-driving. Such activities are perhaps the best means for the rider or driver to get to know his horse and himself, and they create a particularly sound, enduring foundation for mutual trust and so for training towards a high standard of performance.

Cross-country riding, whether in the form of pony-trekking covering long distances through nearby or distant parts of the country, or as a member of a hunt, riding over ditches, fences and hedges and through autumn woods, is one of the finest experiences a horseman can enjoy.

Top-ranking equestrian performances are achieved only by the most persistent riders on suitable horses. Together with these horses, the rider develops the sport into an art, for example, the performances in the highest classes in dressage competitions which lead up from the individual lesson to the level of classical *haute école*.

The ability to master difficult show jumping competitions with a wide variety of obstacles of maximum permissible height and width, presupposes an almost acrobatic degree of body control in rider and horse. Because there are different methods of organising show jumping

competitions, there is scope for further specialisation within this sphere.

Horse trials (the three-day event or combined training) are for the rider what the decathlon is for the athlete, and are considered to be quite the most difficult of any test of horsemanship. They are deservedly called the 'crown of equitation'. Generally trials are carried out in three main sections on three consecutive days, and consist of the dressage test, the speed and endurance phase (comprising steeplechase and cross-country) and show jumping. The speed and endurance phase which follows the dressage test is a logically-composed sequence of tests leading up to the cross-country run as its real climax; the ability to negotiate it within an optimum time and with minimum penalties is a decisive factor in the three-day event. It is peppered with a large variety of typical and very difficult obstacles and ground conditions are usually arduous. The show jumping competition on the last day also tests the fitness and agility of the horse following its efforts on the cross-country course, and gives it the opportunity to keep penalties down towards overall placing position.

Just how exhaustive the demands made upon the potential of the specialised show jumper can be, are seen, for example, in the dimensions specified for the jumps, obstacles, combinations and

so on for international show jumping competitions as laid down in the Fédération Equestre Internationale's *Rules for Jumping Events*.

height	1.70 m (5 ft 6 in) max (except in Puissance or in Power and Skill Competitions)
width	2 m (6 ft 6 in) max; triple bars 2.20 m (7 ft 2 in) max; water jumps 4.50 m (14 ft 8 in) max
speed	350 m/min (383 yd/min) min and 400 m/min (438 yd/min) max; in indoor arenas this may be reduced to 325 m/min (355 yd/min)
length of track in metres	May never exceed the number of obstacles in the competition multiplied by 60

In jump-offs, record tests and other special tests of jumping, heights of well over 2 m (6 ft 6 in) have been reached. The world record is 2.47 m (8 ft 1$\frac{3}{5}$ in), and the world record for long jump is 8.40 m (27 ft 6 in). There are four independent endurance phases in a full three-day event and the Fédération Equestre Internatio-

nale has set the following guidelines for international senior competition:

Phase A: Roads and Tracks, normally carried out at the trot or slow canter
Phase B: Steeplechase, with obstacles, normally carried out at the gallop
Phase C: Roads and Tracks, normally carried out at the trot or slow canter
Phase D: Cross Country, with obstacles, normally carried out at the gallop

The phases follow one another and are designed to demonstrate the rider's knowledge of the horse's pace and stamina. The overall length of the course covered in phases A to D is 26–31 km (16–19 miles).

In extremely difficult steeplechase events, such as the Pardubice steeplechase held in Czechoslovakia since 1874, important elements are the great length of the course—in this case 6,900 m (4$\frac{1}{2}$ miles)—the degree of technical difficulty, the dimensions of the obstacles—for example, the 'Taxis' and the 'Snake Brook'—and their number (here about thirty), and the speed at which they are ridden, all of which make maximum demands on the horses' stamina, jumping power and speed, and may well prove too much for all but a few.

Equally high demands are made upon the horse specialising in dressage, in, for example, leg action, mastery of balance

and body control, learning ability and stability of the nervous system. This is especially the case in classical *haute école* as it is practised today by the Spanish Riding School in Vienna (founded 1572). This school bases its work on the principles of French classical equitation, which, as we saw earlier, itself evolved from the Italian. Training in the Vienna school today comprises three stages. The horse is ridden forwards in a straight line in a natural posture. After this, the 'collected' horse—that is, the horse already accustomed to a shift backwards in its centre of gravity—is ridden in all paces. It is after this that the true *haute école* begins, artificially developing and achieving an upright posture, increasing flexion of the haunches and going through its various airs. These are subdivided into two groups: airs on the ground—*piaffer* and *passage*; airs above the ground—*curvet* (*courbette*), *lançade*, *croupade*, *ballotade* and *capriole*. Airs above the ground may also include the following: *pesade*, *mezair* and *levade*. In this context, the basic paces of the walk, trot and canter are known as 'lower school'.

In principle, the Spanish Riding School works exclusively with Lipizzaner stallions which are particularly suitable on account of their quickness to learn, extremely pleasant temperament and certain specific anatomical features. Since 1919 they have been bred in the federal stud at Piber in Austria that was founded in 1798.

The English Thoroughbred— a Supreme Achievement

Together with the development of a system of state-managed stallions and studs, a further event, which still today has a fundamental influence upon and lays the foundation for the breeding of horses for high-level performance and modern equestrian sport, was the development of the English thoroughbred horse. It has contributed decisively to the establishment of warmblood breeds throughout the world and to their subsequent development.

It is difficult to give an exact date for the emergence of the English thoroughbred as a breed. Officially it is given as 1791, the year in which Weatherby published his *Introduction to the General Stud Book.* The forerunner of this fundamental work can be considered to be the entries in various racing calendars; the earliest records of racing performances had been drawn up regularly since 1709, although they covered only races that took place in particular areas of England. The first true racing calendar appeared in 1727 (J. Cheny), the next in 1751 (R. Heber), then in 1769 (T. Fawconer)—in all, there were forty-six volumes between 1727 and 1772. From 1773 onwards, the *Racing Calendar* was published by Weatherby as the definitive compilation of racing statistics. In 1793 the first volume of the *General Stud Book* was published, listing 237 mares and 169 stallions. Since that time, English thoroughbreds have been recognised as such only if their descent can be traced back in an unbroken line to horses that are named in this first volume; and racing calendars and the *General Stud Book* have been the basis and principal source of specialist information for the breeding of English thoroughbreds. The racing calendar provided a check on performance, the stud book knowledge about the relevant lineage of every English thoroughbred.

From 1793 onwards, selective breeding of the pure-bred horse was based entirely on the racing achievements of the individual animal; as a result, the English thoroughbred has achieved supremacy in racing performance. The various associated anatomical and particularly physiological and psychological features and characteristics are of considerable importance, not only for the horse's own achievements and that of its descendants within the English thoroughbred breed but also for the use made of English thoroughbred stallions in the production of high quality sporting horses from part-bred mares, and for the stabilisation and cultivation of all warmblood breeds.

As we shall see, there were three essential factors that finally produced the English thoroughbred:

- the existence of a stock of breeding mares indigenous to England and Ireland, based on native and Oriental horses, capable of performances that were already determined by breeding towards speed and endurance;
- the quite astounding effectiveness of a number of excellent Eastern breeding stallions; and
- the consistent practice of breeding on the basis of performance and the early use of documentation of 'own performances', that is, of the results achieved in races by the horses used in breeding.

As far as we know, the now extinct Galloway pony was the principal saddle horse used in the first century by the Britons, whose horsemanship was of such a high level that Caesar himself expressed surprise when he invaded the south of England in 55 and 54 BC. The Galloways were tough, untiring pack and saddle horses, well known for centuries for their speed, stamina and sure-footedness. At the beginning of the nineteenth century they were described as being mostly light or dark brown in colour, with a short neck and head, the legs 'black and predominantly flat and free from boniness'. It can be said with certainty that from the time of Caesar's landing in England the import of horses from the Mediterranean area and from the East has never ceased. Horse racing was also practised by the first Roman legionaries in occupied Britain, and tradition has it that during the reign of the Emperor Severus (206–10), horses were specially trained for racing in Wetherby, and that races were held in York.

King Athelstan (895—940) received from his brother-in-law, Capet, later King of France, gifts of horses that had been reared in Germany. In the twelfth century, English saddle horses, including Galloways, were often improved and refined by stallions of Eastern origin, and that at a time when, under Henry II, horse racing was increasing in importance alongside jousting. The monk William Fitz Stephen (twelfth century) described them in this way:

When a race between such trampling steeds is about to begin, or perchance between others which are likewise, after their kind, strong to carry, swift to run, a shout is raised, and horses of the baser sort are bidden to turn aside. Three boys riding these fleet-foot steeds, or at times two as may be agreed, prepare themselves for the contest . . . The horses likewise after their fashion lift up their spirits for the race; their limbs tremble; impatient of delay, they cannot stand still. When the signal is given, they stretch forth their limbs, they gallop away, they rush on with obstinate speed. The riders, passionate for renown, hoping for victory, vie with one another in spurring their swift horses and lashing them forward with their switches no less than they excite them by their cries . . .

Arabian mare, one of the Royal Mares imported into England from the Orient in the seventeenth century

Richard the Lion-heart brought two Eastern stallions with him from Cyprus, of which it was said:

Yn this worlde they had nu pere,
Dromedary nor Destrere,
Stede Rabyte, ne Cammele,
Goeth none so swifte without fayle.
For a Thousand pownd of golde
Ne should the one be sold.

Under Edward III a classification of breeds was already in existence, which expressly mentions the groups specialising in racing:

coursers—racehorses (from 1512 known as 'gentills', ie full-blood)
amblers—horses using an easy pace in which both legs on one side are lifted alternately with those on the other side
palfreys—ceremonial horses
nags—draught horses
ponies—horses of a small breed

The desire for efficient and fast saddle and racehorses led to the introduction of regulations which effectively directed breeding to this end; one important aim was an increase in height and overall scale. Henry VIII, for example, ordered that all stallions and mares that failed to reach the required minimum (stallions 15 hands, mares 13 hands) were to be 'eradicated'. He also ordered all noblemen and prelates as well as anyone 'whose wife wears a French bonnet or a cap of satin' to keep a stallion of the riding or racing breed, with a height of at least 15 hands. He himself had special paddocks laid out in his stud at Hampton Court for the breeding of racehorses. There is evidence that during his reign, racehorses were brought to England, most of which were Oriental or of Oriental parentage. In 1533, for example, Duke Frederick of Mantua presented to him a number of brood-mares from his stock of Oriental racehorses. The Duchess Catharina of Savoy also sent him some brood-mares from her stud near Turin, which at that time was considered to be one of the finest breeding establishments in Italy. From lists of the stock held in the English royal stud drawn up in the sixteenth century, it is clear that the lineage of the brood-mares, later known as the Royal Mares, can be traced back to these gifts.

In 1575 the Master of The Horse to Elizabeth I invited one of the most important equestrian experts from Naples to England for the

purpose of restoring order to Her Majesty's stud farms 'which had deteriorated badly as a result of the incompetence of those employed there'. His report, drawn up in 1576, clearly shows that all the breeding horses in the royal studs were of Oriental origin and a strict policy of pure breeding was maintained, for 'it is not advisable to mix two breeds of horses, since that would result in a half-bred horse'.

Charles I encouraged the spread of racing, with meetings held in Hyde Park in London and in Newmarket, the 'New Market' that had been founded in 1226 (to replace the 'Old Market' that had declined and fallen into disuse as a result of the plague) and which was well known as a racecourse from at least 1309, and gradually developed into a centre of racehorse management and a mecca for racehorse breeders and enthusiasts. In 1698 Tsar Peter I attended a race meeting in Newmarket. Windsor was one of the residences used from time to time by Charles I and horse races were also held there at Datched Mead. During his reign, the practice of racing for the prize of a bell carved in wood, decorated with flowers, came to an end; now the prizes consisted of valuable bowls or goblets each worth 100 guineas, on to which the name of the winning horse and its pedigree were engraved. Later the 100 guineas were paid in coin.

Gradually, breeding for speed and stamina was intensified in the existing population of racehorses, such as in the hobby, known since the fourteenth century, a variation of the Connemara pony which had certainly existed in the west of Ireland 200 years earlier; it differed from others in being particularly suitable as a riding horse, having a height of more than 13.2−14 hands, which for its time was considered large. Galloways, hobbies and the offspring of other English types from, for example, the period of Norman occupation in the eleventh century, can be looked upon as the indigenous group of English horses which as a result of more or less consistent selection for racing prowess produced the precursor of the English thoroughbred. The most significant genealogical contribution to the development of the breed was made by Oriental stallions, whose racing performance had a decisive effect.

The first 'authentic' Arabian stallion was bought for James I by a merchant called Markham. Unfortunately the Markham Arabian ran so poorly that he 'brought Arabians into bad repute'. This suggests that at the beginning of the seventeenth century, the native English racehorse was still superior to the imported Oriental horse. But this situation changed in about 1660, with the introduction of some particularly valuable stallions.

During the reigns of James I and Charles II, racing increased progressively in importance. Charles II himself participated in and even won some races, such as at Newmarket on 14 October 1671. He imported a large number of Oriental breeding horses, including thirty to forty mares. The term Royal Mares for the brood-mares in the royal stables dates from this time. It was also Charles II who in 1665 introduced the practice of presenting medals and silver cups, known as the King's (or Queen's) Plates, to the winner of certain races.

Compared with the usual distances covered today, the race-courses of that time were very long, normally 4−6 miles, sometimes even 10−12 miles. Weights to be carried of 56−76 kg (123−167 lb) were stipulated and initially only horses of six years of age or older were eligible to take part.

The races introduced by James I and Charles II remained the typical major competitive events for English thoroughbreds until the beginning of the nineteenth century. They were regularly held annually.

They correspond to the five racing classics held today: the Derby, dating from 1780, $1\frac{1}{2}$ miles (2,400 m) for three-year-old colts and fillies; the Oaks, dating from 1779, $1\frac{1}{2}$ miles (2,400 m) for three-year-old fillies; the St Leger, dating from 1776, $1\frac{1}{3}$ miles (2,400 m) for three-year-old colts and fillies; the 2,000 Guineas Stakes, dating from 1809, 1 mile (1,600 m) for three-year-old colts and fillies; the 1,000 Guineas Stakes, dating from 1814, 1 mile (1,600 m) for three-year-old fillies.

Over the years, distances, weights and the age of the horses participating have been reduced; it was recognised that races have a greater significance as tests of performance if speed can be increased, which can be achieved only by reducing distance and weight. In 1712 the first race for five-year-olds took place at York; in 1728 the first for four-year-olds at Hambledon; in 1756 the first for three-year-olds at Newmarket; in 1776 the first for two-year-olds at Newmarket.

Between 1660 and 1770, some 160 Oriental stallions were imported into England, resulting in improvements throughout the entire stock of racehorses. But only three of the stallions had a decisive influence upon the genealogical structure of the English thoroughbred.

First was the black stallion known as the Byerley Turk, foaled in 1680 and acquired during the regency of William II. During the siege of Vienna by the Turks, the stallion was captured by Captain Byerley, who rode it as his charger in Ireland in 1698. It was probably an Arabian of Turkish descent.

Next came the dark brown stallion, the Darley Arabian, 15 hands high, foaled in 1702 in the region of Palmyra (Syria) and imported in the reign of Queen Anne. It was bought by Darley, the British consul in Aleppo, in 1705 and sent to England in 1706 to his brother Darley of Buttercamb. The stallion is a direct ancestor of the outstanding stallion Eclipse (foaled on the day of a solar eclipse) to which the male line of some 90 per cent of the entire breed alive today can be traced back directly. The Darley Arabian was probably an Arabian of Syrian or Turkish origin.

The third stallion of this influential trio was the dark brown Godolphin Arabian, foaled in 1724 and standing 15 hands high, which was presented to the French King Louis XV, under the name of Sham, by the Bey of Tunis in 1728, together with some other horses. Because of the strain of the long journey, the stallion's health was brought so low that those responsible would not allow it to be housed in the royal stables, although it carried its family tree 'in a beautifully embroidered bag hanging round its neck'. After a temporary stay with a coachman in Paris, it was taken to England by an English Quaker, Cooke, where it was kept for a short time as a carriage horse by one Williams, then finally bought by the Earl of Godolphin, who in 1730/1 used it as a testing stallion for the English thoroughbred stallion, Hobgoblin. Because Hobgoblin, a descendant of the Darley Arabian, proved reluctant, the Godolphin Arabian was used as a substitute stallion to cover the mare Roxana, which gave birth to Lath, one of the most successful racehorses of that time, and so laid the foundation for the Godolphin Arabian's fame as a vital influence in the development of the English thoroughbred. He was a horse of difficult character and appears to have lavished all his affection on a particular cat with which he is usually depicted in engravings and paintings. He lived for twenty-nine years. According to his origins, he can be classified either as a Barbary horse (he is sometimes called the Godolphin Barb) or, more probably, as an Arabian born in North Africa.

Today, all English thoroughbreds can be traced back to these three stallions and some forty-two or forty-three mares. This, of course, does not exclude influences from other quarters. In 1881 Osborne named 475 stallions in extinct lateral branches that were listed in the *General Stud Book*. They were Arabians, Barbary horses, Persians and Turks (Turkomans), that is, all of them Orientals which were brought to England in the seventeenth and eighteenth centuries. But since the Byerley Turk and the Darley Arabian are represented through four generations and the Godolphin Arabian through two generations by only one male descendant each, one can also consider as the true heads of direct sire lines the stallions Matchem, foaled 1748, grandson of the Godolphin Arabian, King Herod, foaled 1758, great-great-grandson of the Byerley Turk, and Eclipse, foaled 1764, great-great-grandson of the Darley Arabian. The first volume of the *General Stud Book* names 23 daughters by the Godolphin Arabian, but only 9 by the Darley Arabian and as few as 3 by the Byerley Turk; therefore, of those stallions named as founder stallions, it was the Godolphin Arabian that, from this point of view, had the greatest genealogical influence, particularly through Matchem which was used for breeding purposes until thirty-three years of age. These considerations in no way alter the fact that all male representatives of the English thoroughbred can be traced back in a direct line to the Darley Arabian.

Examples of some breeding stallions are:

Touchstone
foaled 1831   13× King Herod   6× Eclipse   7× Matchem
  (ie King Herod appeared in Touchstone's pedigree 13 times)
St Simon
foaled 1881   144× King Herod   88× Eclipse   16× Matchem
Festa
foaled 1893   460× King Herod   265× Eclipse   218× Matchem
Dark Ronald
foaled 1905   823× King Herod   497× Eclipse   397× Matchem

Little research has been carried out into the development of the female line, particularly in the first 'pre-Oriental' period of English pure breeding in the seventeenth century. Views vary on the extent of the genealogical contribution made by native English mares. In any case, the initial basis of the true English thoroughbred in the seventeenth century was a group of indigenous horses which 'particularly in terms of strength and stamina, satisfied the highest requirements. With these animals we later laid the foundation of today's thoroughbred breed . . .' (Rice). It can be considered as certain that English thoroughbreds are not pure-blood Orientals, even though strongly suppressive cross-breeding with Orientals and intensive inbreeding in the stallions of the group carried out since the end of the seventeenth century makes it almost impossible to discover the true origin. Genealogically native blood is still present, however, and may well explain the occasional occurrence of a coarse head with a convex nose-line in English thoroughbreds.

The breeding of the English thoroughbred, then, is the breeding of modified Orientals brought about by selection for racing efficiency, which also led to alterations in morphological, physiological and psychological characteristics and features. Only horses that had successfully undergone racing training and competitive racing were used for breeding, and consequently were less susceptible to the potential dangers of inbreeding. From the original horses of varied extraction, a breed with consistent qualities of performance was produced within a short time. The development was such a rapid one that, as a result of excellent documentation, logical selection and passionate enthusiasm in the pursuit of breeding, further imports of Oriental stallions into England could in general be discontinued by the middle of the eighteenth century. From this time on, the extremely fast racehorse that had been developed could not be improved further, that is, made faster, by cross-breeding with stallions of this or other breeds. The situation is unchanged today, that is to say, the breed known as the English thoroughbred can be improved only by selection and not by hybridisation with other breeds. In the eighteenth century England was well ahead of other countries and exported breeding animals to a number of countries that did not have a stock of indigenous 'English thoroughbreds' of their own.

In the first hundred years of breeding, there was a distinct increase in height and overall size in the new breed. It is always surprising to discover how small even very successful horses of this breed were at the start of its development, and how great has been the variation in external appearance from the beginning to the present day; clearly there is no positive correlation between racing performance and outward appearance.

Today the average height in English thoroughbred stallions is 16.2 hands, in mares 16 hands, with extreme values between 15.1 and 17.1 hands. The average height of the stallions entered in the *General Stud Book* was:

1800–1825   15.2 hands
1850–1859   15.3 hands (known as the heyday of the breed)
1875–1900   16 hands

Between 1700 and 1900, the smallest English thoroughbred was Mixburg, foaled 1704, that stood at 13.2 hands, the largest Prince Charley, foaled 1869, standing at 17 hands.

Other characteristics within the breed show considerable variation. Touchstone, for example, had 17 pairs of ribs and 5 lumbar vertebrae, St Simon 16 pairs of ribs and 6 lumbar vertebrae, Polymelius 17 pairs of ribs and 6 lumbar vertebrae.

The change in height is the direct consequence of selective breeding for racing performance. In general, the larger horse carries weight better; other things being equal, it is superior to the smaller horse. The increase in height and overall conformation is therefore an indication of improved racing speed; the average speed of a racehorse today is some 37 mph. This has been achieved not only as the result of consistent selection for speed but also by certain technical factors such as improvements in the condition of the course and starting arrangements that have been carried out particularly in the last thirty years. In this context, the description given by Lawrence in 1809 of the racehorse Eclipse is still of interest today. He wrote:

. . . I paid particular attention to his shoulder, which according to the common notion, was in truth very thick, but very extensive and well placed, his hinder quarters, or croup, appeared higher than his forehand, and in his gallop it was said, no Horse ever threw in his haunches with greater effect, his agility and his stride being upon a par, from his fortunate conformation in every part, and his uncommon strength. He had considerable length of waist, and stood over a great deal of ground, in which particular he was of the opposite form to Flying Childers, a short-backed compact Horse, whose reach laid in his lower limbs; and if there be any common sense in forming such a comparative judg-

The Darley Arabian, foaled in 1702, one of the three founder stallions of the English thoroughbred. After a painting by Wooton

ment, I should suppose Eclipse calculated to excel over the course, Childers, for a mile. Eclipse was an excellent, but thick-winded Horse, and breathed hard and loud in his exercise. [At the post-mortem examination of the stallion in 1789, it was found that the heart was excessively large in proportion to body weight—almost 7 kg (15 lb)—obviously causing the animal considerable trouble.]

When viewed in his flesh, as a stallion, there was a certain coarseness about him but a critical eye could discover the high-bred Racer in every part . . .

Eclipse was undefeated on the race-track. His superiority was such that of all his opponents, only one, Bucephalus, forced him 'seriously to stretch himself' (von Wrangel). The significant contributions made to breeding by Eclipse include the foundation of the most influential blood-lines in English thoroughbred breeding through his sons Pot-8-os, King Fergus and Joe Andrews.

In spite of the breed being distributed among many countries throughout the world—in 1983 there were some 600,000 of them (1 per cent of the total horse stock)—it has retained its uniformity under very diverse conditions of climate and management.

For all breeding areas and breeding establishments, the description of the external appearance of the English thoroughbred is the same:

- a generally noble, dry, not too large head with large, unconcealed eyes and broad nostrils;
- long, majestically curved neck with little under-neck and good attachment;
- clearly marked, long withers;
- long, sloping shoulder;
- strong, muscular back with good carrying capacity, powerful loins;
- slightly down-sloping, strongly-muscled croup, even with a slightly projecting appearance, strongly-muscled hindquarters;
- clean limbs with short shanks (cannons), distinct tendons and hard, small hooves; metatarsal joints and hock joints should be big and flat, and splint bones are not always strongly marked;
- long strides in walking and trotting; the gallop stride is of maximum possible length and extremely elastic.

In the gallop, the back curves alternately upwards and downwards in rhythm with the feet as they come in contact with and leave the ground, and is supported and its weight-carrying capac-

ity increased by the nodding head movement, which is particularly strongly marked because of the length of the neck. As with part-bred horses (warmblood), the critical factor is not the length of the back but its ability to flex and arch, which, together with a good running action is the most important requirement in the racing and sporting horse, if a high level of performance is to be achieved. So any discussion of the 'square' or 'rectangular' overall dimensions of such horses can be relevant only from this point of view, since the length of the horse in relation to its height depends primarily upon the structure of the lumbar vertebrae, and therefore in turn has an effect upon the flexibility and arching capacity of the back.

In the course of the history of breeding of the English thoroughbred, selective breeding for speed has led to the development of an overall shape of horse that can be seen as a rectangle, that is, a development away from the original Oriental type of horse with a 'square' overall shape to a form which produces optimum length of stride in all paces. This was of interest at the end of the nineteenth century, and is still so today, in developing working and sporting breeds of horses. The modern inclination for the horse of 'square' overall shape is based on experience gained from the use of all-round working horses in sport, on average values, and also on the fact that stamina, fodder utilisation and hardness of constitution as characteristics handed down by Oriental horses, do, indeed, contribute substantially to high performances among warmblood horses. This is particularly evident in the case of all-round working horses used in horse trials and three-day events.

The main difficulty in selecting thoroughbred stallions for use in breeding warmbloods is that very rarely does an optimum level of performance on the one hand coincide with an external appearance suitable for the production of sporting horses on the other. Added to this is the distinctly limited efficiency in transmitting hereditary characteristics among those English thoroughbred stallions used for stock improvement, compared with the native stock of warmblood mares. The more consistently the native stocks of mares are used for breeding, the more difficult is it to find among the English thoroughbreds used any outstandingly good founders of a blood-line that can stamp their mark clearly and permanently upon the breed. This also explains the fact that at the beginning of the evolution of the warmblood breeds such as are indigenous today in central and western Europe, that is, from the middle to the end of the last century, English thoroughbred stallions featured relatively frequently in the early stages of warmblood breeding, as did, for example, Adeptus for the Hanoverian horse, Perfektionist

99   Among the many steeplechase courses in Europe, two have a world-wide reputation: Aintree near Liverpool, where the Grand National is held, and Pardubice in Czechoslovakia. The Pardubice steeplechase has been held since 5 November 1874, over 6,900 m (4½ miles) of varied ground, currently with thirty jumps, some of them very difficult

100   The three-day event, the most testing trial of all-round riding ability, is won at the gallop. The horse's stamina and reliability are demonstrated by the ability to jump, particularly in the cross-country section

101   An essential element of a jump is the powerful and rapid stretching of the hindquarters. Trainer and rider must provide the horse with the necessary technical and tactical schooling to achieve it

Previous page:
98   A young horse must first be put to low obstacles in order to gain experience and confidence

102 Rodeo: the Spanish name for rounding up cattle

103 In rodeo work, the sensitive mouth of the unbroken horse is treated with care. No bit is used, merely a simple halter

104 Children working with horses require courage, skill and stamina; the teacher needs a good deal of patience, expertise and a sense of responsibility

105 A good deal of practice and acrobatic skill is required to perform a pyramid on these swiftly-moving, fine, part-bred stallions

106 Moritzburg coldblood stallions are much in demand for forestry work, particularly in the mountainous regions of the German Democratic Republic

107 The multi-horse carriage drives off. At a gallop, nine stallions leave the arena of the Moritzburg Stallion Depot, Dresden. The horse's even pace makes this difficult exercise possible

108 Ponies make a good four-in-hand team—these are Haflingers from the foaling station at Ebbs in the Inn Valley

109 The sport of driving with fine part-bred horses is particularly fostered in a number of studs

110   Stallions in a dressage quadrille

111   In this phase of the gallop, none of the hooves is in contact with the ground. A return to the past—for the shooting of a film

112   The Stallion Parades at the
Celle stud farm in Lower Saxony
developed from modest performances in front of a few visitors at the end
of the nineteenth century into today's
event attracting tens of thousands of
spectators (Photo: W. Ernst)

113 The broad backs of these Haflinger stallions provide a good firm
base

114 The stallion testing station at
Westercelle uses a large tract of land
near Adelheidsdorf on which to train
its young stallions (Photo: W. Ernst)

115   In landing, balance is all-important if the horse is to avoid injury. The forefoot that first touches the ground transmits the load to the second foot which takes the full weight and is therefore most severely stressed

116   Where there are difficulties with the stability of the seat as a result of the horse's strong acceleration, the rider's action of clasping the neck of the horse is a perfectably acceptable means of regaining balance

117   Too much 'air'; if the link between rider's hand and horse's mouth is broken, the horse becomes uncertain. This specially-posed photograph clearly illustrates its discomfort

118   Obstacles higher than 5 ft can be cleared successfully only by a well-trained and experienced rider-and-horse partnership

119 A sudden relaxation of tension on the reins during a jump, which breaks the link between rider's hand and horse's mouth, can also cause premature lowering of the forelegs

120 This excellently handled event horse has its eyes fixed upon the point of landing

121 Training in rhythm and vivacity
in the trot is an important foundation
for dressage work and in proficiency
tests such as this young stallion
is carrying out

122 The high speed achieved by the racing trotter, some 30 mph, is the result of specific measures of breeding

Following page:
123 Centuries of consistent breeding for speed have made the English thoroughbred capable of a top speed of more than 40 mph

124　Cervantes leaves his mark in the Caribbean: the Don Quixote statue in Havana, capital of Cuba

125　'Flower horses' in Merano, Northern Italy

126　The type of heavy horse used in knightly combat was the model for the 'Golden Horseman' created by Vinach in about 1730; worked in copper-gilt by Wiedemann, it was erected on the Neustädter Markt in Dresden in 1736 on a plinth designed by Longuelune

Following page:
127　Brood-mares in the Neustadt (Dosse) stud

FRID. AVGVSTI II
DVCIS SAXON. S.R.I. ELECTORIS
NEC NON REGIS POLONIAE CVRA
PATRI ET ANTECESSORI
POSITVM.
A.D. MDCCXXXVI.

for the warmblood horse of Trakehner extraction, or Messenger in the breeding of the American trotting horse (harness racer).

It is a different matter when an attempt is made by using English thoroughbred stallions to influence in a particular way certain individual characteristics, as is done in certain fields of activity in connection with the production of racehorses. But here, too, the rule holds good that performance and outward appearance of the thoroughbred used must both be of an equally high level, and this is rarely the case. It is, and always has been, a valid principle that the brood-mare should come from strong indigenous stock that has been bred over many generations, and out of her by using appropriate stallions of a finer quality, including of course English thoroughbreds, the desired general-purpose horse for sporting use is bred. The breeder of warmblood horses must adhere to this principle, or else he will lose his solid, well-established stock of brood-mares, which he could rebuild, if at all, only after decades of selection through several generations of horses and by the use of 'booster stallions'.

An additional factor which further restricts the available range of possibilities for selection is that the basic stock from which selection can be made is very small in comparison with that available in other branches of animal breeding. The demand from riders for highly-bred horses with as much English thoroughbred blood as possible must also be considered from this point of view, and it is by no means easy to satisfy. But by laying down strict breeding targets, the breeders of warmbloods have gone a long way towards meeting the requirements, particularly in respect of height,

features of character and temperament, as well as quality of action, but on no account should they neglect to consolidate and stabilise their stock.

Within the framework of this book, it is not possible to give a detailed account of the development and significance of the English thoroughbred. In the present state of knowledge it is possible, however, to draw the following conclusions.

The English thoroughbred is the product of a development that has lasted for several centuries, during which time selective breeding for speed was the decisive factor.

In its extraction, the English thoroughbred cannot be considered to be of purely Oriental origin, because even before the import of Oriental horses for breeding there were running horses in England, which provided the foundation mares for the English thoroughbred. The origin of many of the foundation mares that produced the English thoroughbred is not known; the ancestry of all English thoroughbreds can be traced back in an unbroken line only to the ancestors entered in Volume I (1793) of the *General Stud Book*, and they included horses that did not come from the Orient.

Particularly in the nineteenth century, the English thoroughbred contributed much to the development of the warmblood breeds and of the trotting horse or harness racer. It is important today, and will remain so in the future, in its role as the fastest breed of racehorse, in the contribution it makes to the typical characteristics of the riding horse in today's warmblood breeds, and in the production of sporting horses by means of commercial cross-breeding.

Breed Standards

Akhal-Teké

This ancient breed is known to have existed for thousands of years. Its native home is Turkmenia. Because the oases there are so isolated, it was possible for the horses native to the south of the country to be bred for centuries without being substantially influenced by other breeds, and to develop particular, typical features and characteristics that are closely related to those of the pure-bred Arab. Today the Akhal-Teké is not only of great practical value as a saddle horse, but also of considerable interest to the zoologist and breeder. It is the most genuine and purest form of the ancient Turkmene horse and so the oldest whole-blooded breed in the world. The Soviet Union has done much to conserve and promote these valuable and unique animals, whose stocks are very seriously endangered; a programme of planned breeding has been carried out since 1921, mainly on the northern slopes of the Kopet-Dag Mountains near Ashkhabad; in addition, there is wider distribution in the Turkmen, Kasak, Uzbek and Kirghiz Republics.

The Akhal-Teké horse is particularly impressive for its ease and freedom of action, for the cleanly-defined lines of its body, joints and tendons, and for its powerful muscles. Its skin is smooth and soft, its coat short and glossy with usually a golden-copper-coloured ground shade (also dun-colour, biscuit-colour or reddish-brown), the hair of mane and tail is thin; forelock and mane may be completely absent. With a lively temperament, the Akhal-Teké has a good capacity for learning and a great affection for humans. Its hardiness and stamina are outstanding.

Height: about 15.1 to 15.3 hands.

Albanian horse

It shares a number of family characteristics with the Bosnian mountain horse. A distinction can be drawn between the Myseka-ja horse of the plains and the Albanian mountain horse. Attempts have been made since 1940 to improve the outward appearance of the Albanian horse by the use of Haflinger stallions (for the mountain horse) and of Anglo-Arabians, Lipizzaners and others (for the Mysekaja horse). Among the horses of the plains, many are proficient amblers; the mountain horse is noted for its load-carrying capacity and stamina. The two types differ primarily in size. The height of the plains horse is about 13.1 to 14.1 hands; that of the mountain horse up to about 12.3 hands.

Altér-Real

A southern Portuguese warmblood breed which evolved from the Spanish Andalusian horse in about 1750. These horses are aristocratic, tough and have good staying power; they are used mainly as saddle horses.

Height: 14.3 to 15.3 hands.

American saddle horse (Kentucky-Virginia saddle horse)

A breed indigenous to the United States of America which is derived from the horses of Canadian settlers, improved by English thoroughbred stallions and Morgans. It is met with principally in the areas of Kentucky, Virginia and Missouri and has been pure-line bred since 1891. It was considered particularly suitable as a mount for the American cavalry, and is held in high esteem today as an elegant, reliable and high-quality saddle horse, but is also used as a carriage horse. The horses are capable of a particularly fine trotting action and excellent overall performance in all paces. The breed divides into two groups:

Three-gaited saddle horse: the horse's mane and tail are cropped; the horse masters the three basic gaits.

Five-gaited saddle horse: mane and tail are left long; the horse masters the three basic gaits and, in addition, the amble and rack (racing amble).

Horses of this breed are exported in large numbers particularly to Central and South America.

Height: between 15.1 and 16.1 hands.

American trotting horse (Harness racer; American standardbred; Standardbred)

A North American breed, very proficient in trotting, used for trotting and ambling (pacing) races; it has exerted a strong influence on the other trotting breeds. It was developed in the eighteenth century in North America from indigenous breeds that showed good trotting ability and, from 1750 onwards, its aptitude for trotting was directed towards competitive racing in 'road races'. In 1789 regulations for the registration of this horse were laid down with specific minimum standards (hence the name standardbred). Contributions to the breed's development were made by English thoroughbreds, Orientals, Morgans, pacers (Narragansett, Canadians) and Hackneys. The breed was consolidated by the part-bred stallion Hambletonian-10, foaled in 1849. Trotting or pacing races have been carried out since 1800 under saddle, and since 1892 with horse-drawn sulkies. Selection is based exclusively on speed of trotting or ambling tempo.

The American trotting horse is extremely tough and shows remarkable endurance. But it is also an able draught horse, is very reliable and has a pleasing temperament. Its ability to learn is much higher than that of most other equine breeds. Typical external characteristics include great fluidity of shoulder movement and the specific hindquarters technique of the trotting racer. The walk and gallop are often poorly mastered, for which reason the use of stallions of this breed is usually avoided in the breeding of warmblood horses.

Height: between 15.1 and 16.3 hands.

Andalusian horse (Spanish horse)

A very old European breed that can be traced back to the old Spanish 'Iberian' horses that the Phoenicians probably brought to Spain in the first century BC, and which were praised by the Romans in the second century BC as the fastest horses in the world. In about the eighth or ninth century, the influence of Oriental, Barbary and Arabian stallions began to take effect. The true Andalusian horse developed after that, and in its heyday—the sixteenth to seventeenth century—it played a decisive role in the development of almost all the major European breeds, for example, Lipizzaner, Neapolitan and Kladruber horses, and through these breeds, exerted in turn a strong influence on the development of modern breeds of sporting horses. The breed divides into two groups:

Jennets, genettes (ginetas): a group strongly influenced by Barbary horses; they are agile, sure-footed, tough, light saddle horses, slightly less than medium sized, found mainly in Andalusia.

Villanos: heavy, powerful, ram-headed horses, frequently piebald, very little influenced by Barbaries and other Oriental horses; formerly used as war horses, nowadays used as draught and carriage horses.

During the eighteenth century, changes began to be made in the Andalusian by cross-breeding with English thoroughbreds, Norman horses and others; the result was a complete change in type. Today's Andalusian is a medium-sized, noble, light saddle horse (the jennet) with a pleasant nature and very lively temperament. Andalusians with a particular colouring and a tendency towards the Villanos type are often used for circus work.

Height: 15.1 to 16.1 hands.

Anglo-Norman horse

The forerunner of the Anglo-Norman horse, the ancient Norman breed, goes back to the Armorican horse of western France and is as old as the latter. As a result of unplanned cross-breeding and the use of valuable breeding animals for military purposes, the Norman horse almost became extinct in the seventeenth century. It is only since about 1830 that measures have again been taken to foster the breed by the use of English thoroughbred and part-bred stallions, and by a well-planned programme of breeding. There are three variants:

Carriage-horse type: an extremely elegant carriage horse with good trotting action, large in conformation, light in the legs.

Selle or saddle type: a noble saddle horse with excellent performance; well-muscled, slight rib arching, excellent galloping and jumping ability.

Cob type: a good all-rounder; a robust, short-legged, powerful, medium-sized carriage horse and working horse.

Stamina, speed and agreeable nature and exceptionally good leg action characterise this medium-weight warmblood breed, together with its notable charm and elegance. Especially in the nineteenth century, Anglo-Norman horses were used in almost all European studs, and also played their part in North and South America. The Anglo-Norman experiences certain difficulty in acclimatisation, and therefore is rarely found in pure-bred form outside its native region (exceptions included the original stud at Zweibrücken in the Rhineland Palatinate, and the development of the Nonius breed in Hungary). The breed is markedly late-maturing (at six to seven years of age). Measures of specialisation for racing prowess carried out in Anglo-Normans produced the Anglo-Norman trotting horse.

Height: 15.1 to 16.1 hands.

Arab

This breed has its origins in groups of horses living in the steppe belt of southern Russia (eg the Akhal-Teké and the Turkmene), northern Persia and possibly also Egypt, which were bred without any admixture of alien blood by nomadic Bedouin on the Arabian peninsula after the decline of the ancient civilisations. A high degree of reproductive isolation in the oases of the Nejd uplands, and selection determined by the desert climate and the demands made by man, created an extremely hard, frugal horse of great endurance; breeding was further promoted by the expansion of Islam after the seventh century, when it expanded beyond the narrow confines of its original home. For more than two thousand years, the Arab had remained cut off from other breeds by the inaccessibility of its narrowly restricted habitat, and had developed the typical characteristics of a desert horse. Always used exclusively as a saddle horse, it had forged close links with man. This undoubtedly explains its excellence as a riding horse, its aptitude for strenuous work and its marked fondness for human company.

Arabs have an overall 'square' outline, a particularly harmonious balance, with a long, flat croup, a high-set tail which is freely held, a fine head with the characteristic 'dished' profile of the breed, dry, clean-cut limbs and hard hooves. The texture of the coat, mane and tail is fine and silky.

A distinction can be drawn between: line-bred Arabians, known as Asil Arabians, which include the three classical types, *kuhaylan* (generally masculine), *saqlawi* (generally feminine), and since about the seventeenth century, the *muniqi* (racing type), together with their sub-groups; line-bred Arabians of mixed origin, whose Arabian extraction is certain; and other Arabians, among whose ancestors horses of other breeds occasionally feature.

The Arab has been involved in the development of all modern warmblood breeds as well as that of the English thoroughbred and is pure-bred in a number of countries.

Height: about 14.2 to 15 hands and over.

Ardennes horse

A very ancient breed which two thousand years ago was already living in the region that today is north-eastern France, and now has its major breeding area in the Belgian and French Ardennes and in Luxembourg. Further breeding areas have also developed in Sweden, South America and the USSR. The modern type shows the influence of the Belgian heavy draught horse, and in the Middle Ages and once again in recent decades, that of the Arabian. The Ardennes horse is a medium-sized, very willing and lively draught horse of excellent constitution and a good length of stride, particularly when trotting. The majority are greys.

Height: between 15.1 and 16.1 hands.

Armorican horse

The name of this ancient group of breeds is derived from the Latin *armoricus*, Gaelic *are-morici* (dwellers by the sea). The term is still used in the Romance languages to define the Atlantic coastal strip between the mouth of the Seine and of the Loire. It came to be applied to any coastal breed of horse so that, until the nineteenth century, the native area of the Armorican horse was designated as from Brittany to Skagen, or from Falmouth to the Tweed. The horses of this group were generally large and massive, therefore quite distinct from the Oriental and Roman breeds. Nor had they many points in common with the small Teutonic working horse.

The Armorican breed had its heyday in the south of France in the ninth and tenth centuries as a consequence of cross-breeding with Spanish horses which had been influenced by Oriental blood. Later, a number of important heavy breeds developed from it, such as the French Norman horse, the Friesian as the basis for Oldenburgs, East Friesians and Danish horses, as well as Belgian, Dutch and English heavy breeds. It is interesting that, until the sixteenth century, the heavy horses used by the knights in, for instance, Denmark and France, were exclusively Armoricans, and that they provided the foundation for all breeds of heavy draught horse and of heavy warmblood horses in western and central Europe. It is only in the last two hundred years that, as a result of cross-breeding and selection, the range of breeds found today in these areas came into being.

Arriegeois horse

A small breed of horse which lives in the upland valleys of the Pyrenees, and was mentioned as early as the first century. The horses are typical pack animals, very frugal and tough, of lively temperament and great agility. They have been bred under supervision since 1947. All the horses are black.

Height: about 12.1 to 12.3 hands.

Barbary horse (Berber or Barb)

This long-established breed, native to north-western Africa, the country of the Berbers (formerly Barbary, now Mauritania), provided the foundation for today's horse breeding in the north-west of Africa and parts of North Africa, Spain, Portugal and southern France, and had a considerable influence on the development of other warmblood breeds. It evolved in about the eighth century from native Numidian horses, an ancient breed from which the Carthaginians had already drawn the horses they required for mounting their cavalry. Numidian horses are often crossed with Arabian and with other Oriental horses. Nevertheless, the Barbary horse has retained its independence.

It is of medium height with a relatively heavy, almost coarse head with Roman nose, a short back, steeply sloping croup and coarse mane and tail hair. It is hardy and undemanding, and in spite of its lively temperament, very reliable. Over the past two decades, greater emphasis has been placed upon increased elegance, as a result of which the Barb is now very popular as a saddle horse. The Barbary is bred in Algeria and Tunisia.

Height: about 14.3 hands.

Bashkir pony

This small eastern European steppe pony has been reared for thousands of years in the south-western Urals, particularly in Bashkiria. Typical features of the Bashkir are also found in breeds that extend further westwards, eg in the Konik, together with its northern variants as well as in the Finnish horse. Depending upon habitat and origin, it is possible to distinguish between a mountain and a steppe type.

The Bashkir is a capable, undemanding pony with a great deal of stamina, very resistant to the enormous climatic fluctuations which are common in its native country. It occurs in many overall colourings; marks of different colour are rare. Breeders are working to produce an improved type alongside the original Bashkir pony by cross-breeding with stallions of the Don breed.

In addition to the Bashkir pony, there is a series of other breeds of typical steppe horses, such as the Czernomorsk horse (Crimea, the Ukraine) and the Minusinsk horse (the region of Krasnoyarsk, south-western Siberia).

Quite closely related to the eastern European breeds of steppe horses is a number of breeds that have existed successfully for hundreds of years and which are bred in the tundra regions of eastern Europe north of the 65th degree of latitude, such as the Pechora horse (west of the northern Urals) and the Mesen horse (in the region of Archangel/Arkhangelsk).

Height: Bashkir pony about 14 hands; improved breed about 14.3 hands; Czernomorsk horse about 15 hands; Minusinsk horse about 14.1 hands; Pechora and Mesen horses about 13.2 hands.

Belgian heavy draught horse (Brabant horse)

This breed originally evolved in southern Belgium, partly also in northern France, probably exclusively from the Ardennes horse

which developed very powerfully as a result of the extremely favourable grazing conditions there. In the period following the establishment of a compulsory stud book in 1866, there was a standardisation of type which was completely consolidated by the end of the nineteenth century. The horses are extremely powerful, very good-natured, easy to feed and they mature at an early age. Their ability to adapt rapidly to various climatic zones led to their distribution throughout many countries before the end of the nineteenth century, where they contributed to the foundation of a series of other heavy draught breeds. With progressive mechanisation of heavy agricultural work, the breed lost a good deal of its importance, even in the later breeding areas.

Size varies depending upon habitat. Because of altered conditions of work, a height of about 15.3 hands or less is preferred, though the range can be 15.2 to 16.1 hands.

Bosnian mountain pony

This breed played an important part as a post horse and a means of transport during the Roman occupation of the Balkan peninsula, and can be traced back to both eastern European breeds such as the Konik, and to Graeco-Roman breeds. Added to this there were Turkish and Oriental influences, particularly in the fourteenth to seventeenth centuries, so that in the seventeenth and eighteenth centuries there were already reports of considerable variations in physical structure. In the nineteenth and early twentieth centuries, an attempt was made to create a uniform type of mountain horse by the systematic use of pure-bred Arabians, but it proved unsuccessful: indeed, one result was the loss of some very valuable primary groups, such as the Veglia pony (from the island of Krk). Since 1900 the work has been entirely selective, and as a result there exist today four habitat-forms of this breed, all of which exhibit similar valuable character traits such as toughness, endurance, frugality and functional efficiency and, at the same time, differences in bodily form. The Bosnian mountain horse is bred in Yugoslavia, primarily in the region of Rogatica, Livno and Mostar, in Albania, western Bulgaria and northern Greece, where it is an integral component of the local breeds.

Height: about 12.3 to 13 hands.

Boulonnais

This breed of heavy draught horse has been a native of the fenland grazing grounds in northern France for several hundreds of years. It was repeatedly crossed with Arabians between the twelfth and nineteenth centuries. The Boulonnais is powerful, with a very good action, and it matures at an early age. As a result of its descent, it has an expressive, 'dry' head. Its double croup and especially strongly-muscled hindquarters characterise it as a coldblood. The long mane and tail hair is soft and silky. Greys predominate.

Height: up to 16.3 hands.

Breton horse (Breton draught horse)

A moderately heavy French breed of draught horse, native to Brittany. In this compact working horse, the coarse head and thick, broad neck (with double mane) are particularly striking. Dappled bays and greys predominate.

Two principal types of Breton are bred: the heavy draught horse which is just under medium size, very frugal, with good stamina (this is the native type which also contributed to the development of the Belgian draught horse); and further there is the light draught horse, which is known as the Postier Breton. The latter has good action, is deep-chested, and is easily maintained. It was developed from the Breton draught horse combined with Percheron, Norfolk and Hackney stallions, also a proportion of English or Arabian blood.

Height: both types stand at 15.1 to 16.1 hands.

Bujonny horse

This breed resulted from crossing the Don and Czernomorsk breeds with English thoroughbred stallions and has been bred systematically since about 1949. It is a particularly powerful, massive saddle horse with excellent qualities. Moreover, it is very suitable for keeping in large herds, and is very prolific. It is predominantly brown (russet and greyish-brown) occasionally shaded with golden-copper tones, and sometimes has markings of another colour. The major stock is concentrated in the studs of Simonowniki, Julowsk, 'S. M. Bujonny' and 'Erste Reitarmee' (First Cavalry Army) in the Rostov region in Russia and in the Issyk-Kul stud.

The horse can also be used for moderately heavy draught work.
Height: 15.3 to 16.1 hands and more.

Camargue horse (Camarguais; also known as *crin blanc* [white hair])

This group of horses, which can be traced back to the prehistoric Solutré horse, lives in a reserve in the Rhône delta, with an area of some 60 square miles, that was established in 1928. It was strongly influenced later by Barbary horses in particular and by other Oriental breeds. The horses were originally a domesticated herd that ran wild, and have now lived freely in this region for about two hundred years. The Camargue horse is hardy and shows great stamina. Semi-wild but supervised breeding is carried out at the Tour du Valat experimental station in herds of forty to fifty animals, known as *manadas*, and in some small wild breeding stations that have been established in the Camargue region in the Rhône delta. The stock is strictly protected; it has a well-known recreational function in providing riding horses for tourists.

Camargue horses are lively but good-natured. The head is coarse, often with a Roman profile, the eyes large and expressive. Characteristic features include the short, narrow croup, robust limbs and very strong hooves, a 'grass belly', luxuriant mane and tail, frequently a beard. Most of the horses are white.

Height: 13.1 to 14.1 hands.

Carriage horse

The name does not denote a breed, but a type of horse with a very powerful action in the trot as well as in the walk. Breeding this type of horse was fashionable in the period between about 1900 and 1930; such animals were highly esteemed and bred particularly from Oldenburg and East Friesian heavy warmblood breeds, as well as from other western European breeds. Because of the short length of stride associated with the high, showy leg action, breeding for this type of horse is now generally avoided.

Celtic pony (Celtic horse)

A very old native breed which already existed in a number of different types at the time of the Roman occupation of present-day France, Britain, Ireland, Spain and Portugal, and which was bred for speed. A number of primitive breeds developed from the Celtic pony, the precursors of small horse and pony breeds in western and northern Europe, which in turn had a considerable influence on the breeding of modern warm and coldblood horses. Particular mention might be made here of the Galloway pony which already had a reputation for speed in the fourteenth century, and which played a part in establishing a stock of foundation mares as a basis for the later English thoroughbred.

Cleveland Bay

Originally a uniform breed of English working horse that can be traced back to the Chapman horse known since the sixteenth century, it was developed in the eighteenth century in its native area, the county of Yorkshire, by using English and a number of Arabian stallions. At the end of the nineteenth century, breeding developments took two directions, continuing on the one hand with the old heavy working horse that was already in existence, and on the other, by an increased use of English thoroughbreds, moving towards a carriage type of horse that became known as the Yorkshire coach horse.

Today the Cleveland Bay is reared as an all-purpose warm-blood horse. It is dark brown to bay in colour; white marks are considered a flaw but black diagonal striping on the lower fore and hind legs is recognised as a former characteristic of the original Cleveland Bay.

Crossing the Cleveland Bay with English thoroughbreds produces the very valuable British part-bred hunter which is a reliable saddle horse on difficult ground.

Height: about 16.1 to 16.3 hands.

Clydesdale

An old breed from the south of Scotland which was improved during the seventeenth century by Flemish stallions and by Clevelands, to develop into one of the most valuable breeds of British draught horse. Before the breeding of heavy draught horses was restricted by the mechanisation of agricultural work, this breed was widespread throughout Scotland and large areas of England and Wales, and was also exported in large numbers.

These horses, which are predominantly dark brown, are of a lively temperament, with good action and a hardy constitution. There is some similarity to the Shire horse, but they are less heavy and not quite so large.

Height: 15.3 to 16.3 hands.

Cob

The term commonly used in Britain to denote a cross-bred, medium-sized working horse which is particularly suitable as a saddle or driving horse and as a steady hunter of a modest standard. It is usually a short, sturdy horse with a light head and elegant posture, and is particularly useful for carrying weight—up to 100 kg (220 lb).

Height: about 15.1 hands.

Comtois (Race Comtoise)

A very old breed that probably dates back to the ancient Teutonic working horse, and which is bred today in the extreme east of central France in the Besançon region. It is a medium-sized, swift-paced, hardy and lively coldblood horse, particularly suitable for working on hilly terrain. Its overall appearance is said to resemble that of the Ardennes horse of the nineteenth century. Chestnuts predominate.

Height: 14.3 to 15.3 hands.

Connemara pony

A breed native to the area north of Galway Bay (County Connaught) on the west coast of Ireland, probably of Celtic origin and already indigenous there in pre-Christian times. Its existence can be documented from the twelfth century onwards. From the fourteenth to eighteenth centuries, Connemaras were known as 'hobbies', or possibly this referred simply to a type variant ('hobby' meaning 'ambler'). To improve the stock, it was crossed with Oriental horses. For centuries the Connemara had the reputation of being a particularly powerful saddle pony with speed and stamina, and it helped to establish the genetic foundation for the development of the English thoroughbred in the seventeenth and eighteenth centuries. A number of herds of these ponies continued to live wild until well into the twentieth century.

Since 1924 breeding has been directed uniformly towards producing a hardy, strong-boned animal, well suited to dressage work and especially to hunting and show jumping. It is improved by Arabian and English thoroughbred blood.

Height: 13 to 14 hands, on average about 13.2 hands.

Corsican pony

This breed, restricted to the island of Corsica, is relatively elegant, with good strength and stamina. Its origins can be traced back to Oriental breeds such as Berbers and Arabs.

Height: up to 13.1 hands.

Criollo horse (Costeño or Crioulo horse)

In South America, especially in Argentina and Brazil, it is the native warmblood breed of the pampas, where it still lives semi-wild today. In Peru it is virtually pure-bred and provides tough, handsome saddle horses; in Argentina it is crossed with several European breeds and so lacks uniformity of type, although the majority are coarse and thickset. Here the Criollo is used primarily as a saddle horse and specialises in the walk and the gallop.

The Criollo can be traced back to Andalusian horses imported from Spain for the first time in 1535, and to this day retains certain ancestral traits. These include the convex nose-line, hardy limbs and a tractable nature. Added to these is great robustness of constitution, a characteristic undoubtedly acquired as the result of living semi-wild for a good many generations. All colourings occur including piebald (the pinto) and skewbald (the painted horse).

In true Criollos there are two groups of pinto horses: Tobianos, which are larger, and on the whole less spotted with white; and Overos which are smaller, but with white dappling over larger areas—usually the face parts are white and the animal is frequently wall-eyed.

In addition to the original Criollo horse, the Anglo-Argentino was developed in Argentina by crossing the former with English thoroughbred stallions.

Height: between 14.1 and 15.1 hands.

Dales pony

This breed emerged from the original population that also produced the Fell pony at about the end of the nineteenth century, after which the Dales pony was developed further as a draught horse. In particular, its natural ability in high speed trotting, and its size, were fostered. As in other breeds specialising in trotting, the steeply sloping shoulder is typical. The pony has very hard hooves and heavy feathering. The majority are black.

Height: on average 14 hands, maximum 14.2 hands.

Dartmoor pony

Since Roman times ponies have lived on the broad upland plains of Dartmoor in Devon, in the south-west of England. The ponies still live semi-wild and until the nineteenth century were allowed to breed without human intervention; as a result of later introductions of Shetland and other native pony blood the original pure-bred Dartmoor no longer exists on the moor, but is restricted to private studs etc. In spite of its small size, the Dartmoor pony has good riding qualities, such as its even gait and good natural aptitude for jumping. It is particularly suitable for children and also makes a useful driving pony.

Height: about 11.2 to 12 hands.

Davertnickel (Münsterländer)

A former breed from the Münster region of Westphalia, where as a working horse it was also known as the Low German Münsterländer or Münster pony. The horses were semi-wild; until the beginning of the nineteenth century they were hunted, the last hunt taking place on 14 September 1829. From the sixteenth century onwards, the Davertnickel was not without foreign genealogical influences, for instance, Oriental, Spanish and English stallions were used. It was strong, tireless and undemanding, with pace enough to gain it a good reputation as a saddle horse. Cross-breeding and the import into Westphalia of various breeds of coldbloods caused the disappearance of the breed towards the middle of the nineteenth century.

Height: just under 14.3 hands.

Døle trotter

The Døle trotter is bred by crossing trotting stallions with Gudbransdal mares. It accounts for some 16 per cent of Norway's total stock of horses. Døle trotter stallions are used for cross-breeding with the Gudbransdal, and so do not influence the Norwegian Fjord pony.

Height: 15 to 15.3 hands.

Don horse

This breed emerged in the eighteenth and nineteenth centuries on the basis of herds of horses belonging to the Cossacks living along the Don. It was developed at that time by crossing first of all Turkmene, Arabian, Persian and Karabach horses, later Orlov-Rostopschin, Streletzk and English thoroughbred horses with the horses of Mongolian origin native to the Don region. Since about 1805, an improved type has been bred in the Orlov Stud Farm, Streletzk, known as the Don-Streletzk horse, which was widely distributed in the area of the south Don. By well-planned selective breeding, the Don horse gradually became larger and developed into a tough, untiring, all-round horse of excellent constitution.

The hair colour is rusty or greyish-brown, often with a gold shading that results from an intermingling of golden-copper col-

oured hairs. The tail hair is strikingly thick and long. The Don's action is excellent, especially in the trot and gallop; the lines of the body are sharply delineated and the horse has powerful muscles. An even temperament and peaceful nature make it very reliable and willing.

There are now specialised breeding centres in the Rostov region; in addition, it is bred particularly in the Lugowskol and Issyk-Kul studs. It has exerted a considerable influence upon other breeds in the USSR.

Height: about 15.3 to 16 hands and more.

Dülmen pony

From the Middle Ages until well into the eighteenth century, numerous herds of wild horses lived in the area which is today Westphalia, and they can undoubtedly be seen as descendants of the Germanic horse as described by Caesar and Tacitus. Most of them were probably feral, formerly domesticated animals that had returned to the wild. As recently as 1875, there were reports of small horses living wild both in the Merfelder Bruch and the Tungeloer Bruch. Today only the Dülmen pony remains, living in an enclosure of some 250 hectares (620 acres), 12 miles west of Dülmen.

The breed has existed for more than six hundred years; particularly in the last two centuries, stallions of other breeds have been introduced, such as Welsh mountain ponies, Koniks (the Polish peasants' pony), and Basque ponies, as well as Arabians. The entire stock totals some 150 to 200 animals.

The Dülmen represents basically a noble type of pony; it has strength and stamina; its posture is not always faultless, it has a very sloping croup. In colour it is often mouse-grey, and may exhibit marks typical of the wild horse such as a dark eel-stripe along the back, a mark across the shoulder, zebra stripes and dark extremities. The pony has good learning capacity, is temperamental but good-natured.

Height: 12.1 to 13.1 hands, occasionally as much as 14 hands.

Dutch Harddraver (Hard trotter)

A breed with special trotting capacity bred in the fifteenth century in the Netherlands to take part in trotting races—a popular sport of the time—by mating Old Spanish stallions (see Andalusian horse) with native mares, probably of the Friesian type. Hard trotters played a significant part in the development of the Orlov trotter and the Roadster. The breed no longer exists.

East Friesian horse

A very old, heavy warmblood breed, based on the Friesian horse by the use of Andalusian, Neapolitan, Barbary and Yorkshire stallions, which has provided much sought-after carriage horses since the seventeenth century. The breed was consolidated at an early stage; since 1715, regulations have governed the selection of stallions, in 1814 centralised inspection of stallions and in 1859 of mares was introduced. After World War I, there was a move towards a more modern type of animal to suit the requirements of agriculture, and since 1945 measures of improvement have been intensified, initially by the use of Arab stallions. From 1960 onwards, there has been an increasing move towards breeding for riding qualities, and considerable convergence with the breeding trends seen in the Hanoverian, which meanwhile has replaced the East Friesian to such an extent that the latter seems to be close to extinction.

In outward appearance the East Friesian closely resembles the Oldenburg to which it has genealogical links. Because of the predominance of particular blood-lines, the majority are chestnuts.

Height: East Friesian without thoroughbred blood, about 16.3 hands or more, East Friesian with some Arab blood, about 15.3 hands.

English thoroughbred (French: *pur sang*; international symbol: xx)

This breed has developed as a result of consistent, planned selection for speed and endurance founded on a uniform process of selection carried out since the eighteenth century. It is based on mares of native origin (see Galloway) that had already been used for generations in England as running horses; since the fourteenth century, some of these horses have also carried a propor-

tion of Oriental blood. In the seventeenth and eighteenth centuries the mares were frequently mated with various Oriental stallions (see pp. 159–163).

The English thoroughbred is one of the fastest horses; it is reliable, capable of a fine performance and willing to work; in addition it has strength and stamina, it matures early, but is very exacting as to care and management. It possesses all the attributes and characteristics required for achieving maximum speed. The breed has been and continues to be a fundamental influence on the development and maintenance of all warmblood breeds and is indispensable in the breeding of specialised competition horses. Breeding of English thoroughbreds is carried out in many countries and is closely associated with horse racing.

Height: averages about 15.1 to 16.3 hands.

Exmoor pony

The pony is native to the high moors in the north-west of Somerset where it still lives semi-wild today. It is a descendant of the horse owned by the Ancient Britons. As a result of centuries of isolation, its outward form has probably changed scarcely at all; in particular it has retained certain colour nuances, for example, a mouse-grey ground colouring, sometimes with a dappled pattern of black, light underparts and light inner surfaces of limbs, and a

mealy (beige) muzzle; the colouring of the coat reacts to climatic conditions. The pony is able to adapt easily to extreme climatic fluctuations and is very robust. Its typical features are endangered because since 1960 it has not been possible to ensure the breed's semi-wild and natural way of life. Stallions of this breed are used for mating with English thoroughbred mares to produce riding horses.

Height: 11.1 to 12.1 hands, on average 12 hands.

Fell pony

This variation of the original Brythonic pony was already in existence between the sixth and first centuries BC. The Fell pony can be traced back to the same common group from which the Dales pony also derives. It lives in the north of England in the north-western part of the Pennines, on the Cumbrian fells.

The pony is extremely hardy, tough, frugal, sure-footed and docile, usually black. In appearance, it has typical pony characteristics, especially in regard to shape of head, short powerful legs and long hair in mane and tail. It has a gentle disposition, so it is a particularly suitable mount for children and also for use on difficult, rough terrain.

Height: on average about 13.1 hands.

Fredericksborg

An elegant saddle and carriage horse, originally bred in the Fredericksborg stud that was founded in 1562, the Fredericksborg was already held in the highest regard between the sixteenth and eighteenth centuries. The breed carries Andalusian and Neapolitan blood; from about 1800 onwards, and increasingly after the closing of the Fredericksborg stud in 1862, Arabians and English thoroughbreds were used. The breed, originally intended for the exclusive use of the Danish royal house on state occasions, later became widespread throughout Denmark, first of all as a saddle horse on the islands of Seeland and Bornholm, and later on also as a working horse.

Today the Fredericksborg is a medium-weight, elegant warmblood; to the typical features of the latter can be added a head that is 'dry' and not too large and often with a convex profile. Those horses with a particularly marked facility for trotting are used for breeding. Over 90 per cent of the breed are chestnuts.

The Knabstrup is a lighter-built sub-group of the Fredericksborg, mainly bred in Seeland and typically occurring with Appaloosa markings.

Height: about 15.2 to 16.1 hands.

Freiberg horse (Freiberger; Franches-Montagnes or Jura horse)

A breed found in the Swiss Jura which is based on the Jura horse that had probably been indigenous there for more than two thousand years; it was developed in the second half of the nineteenth century, using English coldblood breeds, Ardennes, Norman and Breton horses and, in recent times, also Arab stallions to produce an excellent, medium-weight easily-maintained draught horse. By increasing the preponderance of Ardennes blood in the Freiberg horse, the Burgdorf horse was produced.

Typical features are its animated, technically correct gait, great stamina and lively temperament. The Freiberg can be considered as a lightweight coldblood. Browns predominate, with few or no markings.

Height: about 15.2 hands.

French trotter (Anglo-Norman trotting horse)

This breed, specially bred as a trotting horse, developed from the Anglo-Norman soon after the first trotting races were instituted in France in 1836. In addition, the French horse has all the qualities of a good draught horse, and can also be used in harness. The horses have an attractive appearance and great stamina; because of these useful characteristics, they are employed in the French national breeding programme. In the course of their development, American trotter stallions were used to improve speed. Since 1937 the Stud Book has been closed. A special feature is that in some 30 per cent of all trotting races for this breed, the horses are entered as under the saddle.

Most of them are bays. Height: about 16.1 hands.

Furioso-Northstar (Furioso or Northstar)

A breed of English part-bred horses named after the original ancestors, the English thoroughbred stallions Furioso, foaled 1836, and The North Star, foaled 1844; it has been widespread in Hungary in particular for about a hundred years. The breed is also represented in Czechoslovakia and Austria. Equally worthy of mention are the two blood-lines in their own right, and the very successful combination of the two which gave the breed its name.

The Furioso-Northstar is a warmblood horse, useful for many purposes, extremely hardy and undemanding, which enjoys particular popularity as a 'good goer'. It is especially suitable as a reliable saddle horse. Chestnuts are common.

Height: 15.3 to 16.1 hands at the most.

Galloway pony

It developed from the small native British horse and lived on the mainland of Britain from the second century BC, primarily in southwest Scotland (the county of Galloway); from the first century BC onwards, it was the principal saddle horse of the Britons. It was a very hardy horse with great stamina, which for centuries had a reputation for speed and sure-footedness. Cross-breeding for improvement was probably carried out repeatedly from the twelfth century, and from the sixteenth century onwards was practised systematically using Oriental stallions. In the seventeenth and eighteenth centuries the Galloway played a part in the development of the English thoroughbred, but became extinct soon after the middle of the nineteenth century. (It should be noted that the word 'Galloway' was used by many to denote any medium-sized animal of riding type.)

Garrano pony

This breed is closely related to the small Celtic horse, and is bred today in two variations: the 'original' mountain type that was bred for centuries in relative isolation, especially in the mountains of northern Portugal; and the second type that shows much stronger Oriental influences. The Garrano pony is found in Portugal and north-western Spain, and is used as a draught, saddle and pack animal.

The ponies introduced into Central and South America in the sixteenth and seventeenth centuries by Spanish and Portuguese conquerors were of the same blood as this breed, which at that time had a considerably wider distribution.

Height: about 10 to 14 hands, on average between 12.1 and 13.4 hands, depending to a great extent upon habitat.

Gelderland

A medium-weight warmblood horse based on the East Friesian combined with the Groningen but, since the middle of the nineteenth century, also strongly influenced by Normans, Hackneys and Holstein warmbloods. Groningen stallions in particular are used for breeding today. The horses are mainly chestnuts and are reared predominantly in the south of the Netherlands. Like the Groningens, they have a stylish trotting action.

Height: about 16.1 to 16.3 hands.

Gidran

An Anglo-Arab breed, named after its original ancestor, Gidran II, foaled in 1820, son of a pure Arabian and a mare of Spanish origin. Since about 1830 the breed has been increasingly influenced by English thoroughbred stallions. Gidrans are native to Hungary, but also exert a considerable influence, directly or indirectly, on horse breeding in Poland, Czechoslovakia, Russia and other countries.

They are medium-sized saddle horses, capable of a high standard of performance, although individually somewhat difficult to handle. Most of them are chestnuts.

Height: about 15.3 to 16.1 hands, sometimes more.

Gotland pony

This is the genuine ancient Swedish pony, the eastern variation of the Norwegian Fjord pony. With minor exceptions (small numbers of Konik-like Livonian horses were imported in the eighteenth and nineteenth centuries), breeding has remained free of outside influences even in recent centuries, as a result of which the Gotland's form has remained virtually unaltered. The breed was probably widespread in large areas of Sweden, possibly also in southern and central Norway, and together with the Lyng horse (see Norwegian Fjord pony), represents a primary or parent form. Two hundred years ago it was still in existence only on Öland and Gotland, and for the past 150 years has been restricted to Gotland. Today the ponies live in semi-wild conditions, mainly in the forests of southern Gotland; for this reason they are also given the name of *skogrusset* (forest horse). The stock is small and is protected by law.

Gotland ponies are strong and sturdy with a coarse head, a back that is not too firm and a drooping croup (known as 'goose-rumped'), dry legs and very robust hooves. Chestnuts and blacks predominate, duns are rare.

Height: about 12.1 hands.

Groningen horse

Originally this heavy warmblood breed and the heavy warmbloods of East Friesland and Oldenburg had a common breeding background in the ancient Friesian horse. Because there was a rapid decline in the demand for heavy part-bred horses after 1960, the stocks of Groningen horses were reduced and, at the same time, measures of improvement were carried out. The Groningen is reared primarily in the northern parts of the Netherlands. It is well known for its particular trotting action and, in the original type, is especially suitable as a driving horse and all-purpose working horse.

Height: about 16.1 hands or more.

Gudbransdal horse

This breed has been developed as an independent group since about 1820, using Norwegian Fjord ponies crossed with Danish stallions. It is also known as the Doele (Døle) horse (valley horse), in contrast to the mountain horse; or Ostland horse, in contrast to the Westland horse. The Gudbransdal is of the coldblood type, but the use of trotter stallions and English thoroughbred stallions in breeding has given it toughness and stamina. It lives mainly in the south-east of Norway.

Height: about 15 hands.

Hackney (Norman: *haquenée*)

An influential and elegant breed of carriage horse, native to the English Midlands, that was developed from the Norfolk trotter. It evolved in the counties of Yorkshire and Norfolk and was first mentioned under the name of Hackney in 1303. It achieved uniformity of type in the course of the eighteenth century with the use of Roadster mares and Arab stallions.

Hackneys frequently have leg faults and lack a good length of stride in the walk and gallop, and are therefore specialised as trotters. In the twentieth century, their extravagant trotting action brought considerable status to the breed. Chestnuts with white markings predominate, though bays, browns and blacks are fairly common.

Since 1866 the Hackney pony has been developed from the Hackney horse, by systematic selection for trotting ability, in a programme of breeding based on the Dales and Fell ponies in association with Roadster and Yorkshire horses. The ponies are mostly brown or black and enjoy great popularity. They can be described as minor trotters but are not included among the recognised trotting breeds.

Height: Hackney horse about 15 to 15.3 hands, exceptionally as much as 16.1 hands; Hackney pony, about 12.2 to 14.1 hands.

Haflinger

The foundation of this breed was the primitive Alpine mountain pony which, in the original area of the Haflinger, that is, South Tyrol and the Merano-Bolzano basin, had been influenced by Oriental stallions since the era of the Crusades and the Turkish wars. In this way, the Haflinger developed quite individual characteristics and features compared with the Pinzgauer, Noriker or Freiberger.

This was probably a decisive factor when, in 1872, the breeders decided to import a part-bred Arab stallion whose son out of a mare of the native mountain strain became an outstanding foundation sire, to which all the stallions of this breed can still today be traced back in a direct line. The stallion was a light chestnut, having inherited that particular colour from both parents, and so stamped upon the Haflinger breed its characteristic colouring —chestnut with long flaxen mane and tail hair. The Haflinger is today a highly sought-after, all-purpose mountain pony with a high

level of breeding, very strong and willing, sure-footed and exceptionally good on hilly terrain, long-lived and very prolific. It has proved its worth both in mountain country and on the plains. Its pleasant temperament and strong, resistant limbs make it a particularly good choice for recreational riding and trekking. It is of a rectangular overall format which increases its carrying capacity and endurance when it is used for draught work and riding. It is found mainly in Austria, Italy, East and West Germany.

Height: about 13.1 to 14 hands; when improved by Arabian blood, up to 14.1 hands.

Hanoverian warmblood horse

This breed began its development early in the eighteenth century in the Hanover area, on the basis of heavy native mares whose origins can be traced back to the old Friesian horse (see the Armorican). It was developed further in the course of the nineteenth century by the use of the valuable stallions from Mecklenburg and Pomerania—named Jellachich, Norfolk and Zernebog—which can be looked upon as the founder sires. The breed is built up of blood-lines that are few in number but very widely distributed and therefore have considerable uniformity. With the emphasis on the development of saddle horses, increased numbers of English thoroughbreds and warmblood stallions have been used since about 1960, and today they account for a blood share of about 10 to 20 per cent.

The Hanoverian warmblood is a powerful saddle horse, with good all-round potential and, in general, a very high level of performance. In particular it excels in galloping and show jumping, has great tolerance and a quiet temperament. Horses of this breed are exported to many countries and so have also made their mark upon other breeds. In the present century, Hanoverians have exerted a substantial influence upon the Westphalian warmblood horse in particular, as well as the Mecklenburg and Brandenburg warmbloods.

Height: 15.3 to 17 hands.

Herrenhausen horse

This small breed of white horses (albinos) was named after the castle of Herrenhausen situated close to Hanover, where it was reared from 1844 for ceremonial purposes. The origins of the Herrenhausen horse go back to the year 1727, when a start was made in the Memsen stud (founded in 1653) on a planned programme of breeding for albinos, a quite rare colour-type, from Danish and Barbary horses. In 1803 breeding was continued in the Great Lodge in England and later, in about 1810, at Neuhaus (Solling) in West Germany. As a result of low fertility and poor survival capacity, the breed died out between 1892 and 1896. Its influence on the Hanoverian horse was quite slight.

Highland pony

The ancestors of this breed were small primitive horses that to some extent were kept as domesticated animals and to some extent lived semi-wild, in central and northern Scotland and the Western Isles (Hebrides), probably between the first and fourth centuries. Because of their poor environment, the ponies remained very small. In the Middle Ages they were known in Scotland as 'shelties' or 'shulties' (small breed), and from the sixteenth or seventeenth century also as 'garrons'. Between the ninth and thirteenth centuries, there was some interbreeding with larger horses from southern Scandinavia. From the thirteenth century onwards, selection for size was carried out among the ponies living in the Highlands; they reached a height of about 12.1 to 13.1 hands and gradually developed into a number of independent strains, most of which have become extinct today, such as the Barra pony (until 1900), Rhum pony (1888), Uist pony (1900), and Mull pony.

The Highland pony of today, living in the Scottish Highlands, is somewhat larger, very long-lived and is exceptionally sure-footed, therefore very suitable for riding in rough country, but is also useful as a draught and pack animal. Highland pony stallions in particular are exported for use in breeding hunters. The colour is mainly dun.

Height: about 13 to 14 hands.

Holstein warmblood horse

This breed is based on native stock and was already well developed by the twelfth century. During the sixteenth and seventeenth centuries, it was improved permanently by the addition of Andalusian blood. Since that time, the Holstein has been influential in the development of a number of European breeds. The breed itself was effectively consolidated during the nineteenth century by the use of English thoroughbred and Yorkshire stallions, as well as by warmblood stallions of Trakehner extraction and part-bred Arab stallions. From 1958 onwards, there was an increased use of English thoroughbreds and warmbloods of Trakehner extraction to produce a horse with even more marked riding qualities. Today's Holstein excels at show jumping and in endurance trials, is a good dressage horse with a lively temperament and an impeccable, well-balanced character. Most of them are brown. Breeding is basically restricted to Holstein.

Height: about 16.1 to 17.1 hands.

Hunter

This term does not denote a breed but is the generic name of a type of horse that is normally bred out of powerful, heavy English mares (eg Cleveland Bay) or Irish warmblood mares (Irish draught horse) by English thoroughbred stallions.

Hunters have a high level of performance, strength, good speed and balance; they show particular endurance in the gallop and are excellent jumpers. By nature, they are closely akin to the English thoroughbred, but have more powerful hindquarters and are heavier. There are three types, the lightweight (carrying up to 12 st 7 lb (79.3 kg)), the middleweight (carrying 12 st 7 lb to 14 st (79.3 kg to 89 kg)) and the heavyweight (carrying over 89 kg (14 st)).

In assessing the quality of the hunter, the decisive factor is type and not origin.

Hunters are bred not only in England and Ireland but wherever a hunting horse with stamina and speed is required.

Height: varies depending upon breeding background, generally between 16 and 16.3 hands.

Huzul pony

The Huzul is a small working breed living in the wooded mountains of eastern Europe. Both the Huzul and the Konik are descended from the forest tarpan, a subspecies of Przewalski's wild horse, but have developed differently as a result of dissimilar breeding influences in different environments. There are three basic types: Przewalski Huzul, the tarpan Huzul and the Bystrzec Huzul.

As might be expected in view of its origins, the Huzul is presently found particularly in the east of Czechoslovakia, the west of the Ukraine, the south-east of Poland, the north-east of Hungary and the north of Romania. Until the seventeenth century it still lived wild even outside this area.

Huzuls are used mainly in mountain regions. They are sure-footed, undemanding and very efficient. Both as draught animals and as saddle and pack animals they are completely reliable even in the most difficult conditions. They are long-lived, of relatively noble appearance, but heavily barrelled, short in the neck and croup, and very strong in the legs. All colours except white occur, including dun and mouse-grey. Markings are rare.

Height: varies depending upon the individual stallion's line, but in the USSR about 12.3 to 14 hands, elsewhere about 12.1 to 14 hands.

Icelandic pony

It is known that horses were taken to Iceland by the early settlers from about 874, and were predominantly of Scandinavian origin with a smaller number from the north of Scotland. These horses, with a height of between 12.1 and 14 hands rapidly adapted to the harsh environmental conditions by a reduction in size, to which the small Scottish horses may have contributed, although probably only minimally, since their numbers were few. A ban on imports imposed in 1200 remained in force until 1900, and the true Icelandic pony bred in conditions of reproductive isolation. The Lakagigir eruption in south-eastern Iceland in 1783/4 wiped out two-thirds of the stock (24,000 ponies). Because breeding proceeded entirely without external influences, there was an unusually high degree of consolidation of such features as physical toughness and efficiency, frugality and a harmonious balance in physical characteristics. The introduction of a stud book in 1920, and the establishment of breeding management in the mid-fifties, achieved results of persistently high quality which are reflected in high export figures.

The ponies continue to live a semi-wild existence, they are extremely sure-footed with a very hardy constitution. They swim well and safely, and—a rare feature in horses—survive long sea journeys with ease. They are very suitable mounts for children and equally useful as pack animals. In addition to the normal gaits, they also excel in the amble and the *tölt*, a very rapid walk which increases in speed to a canter. In 1982, there were about 35,000 ponies in Iceland.

Height: about 12.2 to 13.2 hands, on average about 13 hands.

Irish draught horse

An old native Irish breed, probably based on the Connemara pony and the hobby, so that distinctive breed-typical differences are difficult to define. Influences coming from Old Spanish horses and possibly also from coldblood breeds (the Irish draught horse has no feather on the legs however) make it in some ways reminiscent of a coldblood horse. The general effect is of a light draught horse, but certain physical characteristics such as its size, very good neck and shoulder development, good saddle position and strong legs make it particularly useful in the production of hunters, by crossing with English thoroughbred stallions.

Height: 15.3 to 16.3 hands.

Jutland horse (Schleswig horse)

As early as the twelfth century this breed was mentioned as particularly valuable. It was a native of the Danish peninsula of Jutland (see Armorican horse) and is related to the Fredericksborg horse. In the Middle Ages, the Jutland horse was exported in large numbers, and bred in various parts of Germany, in England and France. From the middle of the nineteenth century it has been influenced by Yorkshire and Shire blood. As a result, the breed has evolved into a heavy draught horse known today as the Schleswig horse, a medium-sized animal with a good action.

Again reflecting their origins, most Jutland horses are chestnuts. Height: about 15.1 to 16.1 hands.

Kabardin horse

This strain is the result of centuries of breeding, going back to the old Karabairsk horse which in turn was probably closely related to the Nogajsk horse. In the development of the Kabardin, an important part was played by Karabair, Turkmene and Arabian horses. By the sixteenth century it was already well known far beyond the boundaries of the Caucasus, in the northern part of which its native home lies. It is a very useful saddle, draught and pack horse, typically hardy, tireless and sure-footed.

The breed has a number of distinctive features such as a slightly convex nose-line, a steeply sloping croup and comparatively large and very strong hooves which are so hard that the animals never need to be shod. The characteristic colouring of the coat is brown, black or dappled dark brown; white markings are quite rare.

A finer type bred by using English thoroughbred stallions is the Anglo-Kabardin, reared mainly in the Malokaratschaewsk and Malkinsk studs in the northern Caucasus.

Height: about 14.2 to 15 hands; the improved type is somewhat larger.

Karst horse

A very old breed in the region of the Karst Mountains (today north-western Yugoslavia, the area round Trieste) that was already bred in the pre-Christian era by the Greeks and later by the Romans and which had excellent qualities. Karst horses were noble, but at the same time sufficiently heavy; they had strength, speed and endurance and were very good-natured. They were used as saddle and pack horses and provided the foundation for the Lipizzaner bred.

Kladruber (Old Kladruber; Kun starokladrubsky)

A horse bred for ceremonial purposes, it takes its name from the Kladruby stud in Czechoslovakia, founded in 1572 to provide the saddle horses required by the Viennese court. The breed developed following the import of stallions of Andalusian and Neapolitan type. Founder stallions include the Neapolitan named Generale, foaled in 1787, for the line of greys, and the Spanish stallion Sacramoso, foaled in 1799, for the line of black horses. The Kladrubers are still bred separately according to these two colours, the greys in the original Kladruby stud, the black horses at Slatinany. Kladrubers are strong, large, heavy warmbloods, of the carriage-horse type, lively in temperament, with a pleasant nature, late maturing but very long-lived. A particular feature is their high-stepping action in trotting.

To maintain the purity of the Kladruber breed, Lipizzaner stallions are used, mainly of the Favory strain. Pure breeding also ensures the preservation of the original Old Kladruber type which was consolidated in Kladruby in the eighteenth and nineteenth centuries. Typical features include the large head with an exceptionally pronounced Roman nose, large protruding eyes and broad jowls, the very upright neck, long back, long croup with a high-set tail, strong legs and large hooves.

Since 1932, breeding of the Kladruber has been guided by the interests of agriculture and sport, producing a part-bred horse. For this purpose, stallions of the breeds Furioso, Przedswit, Gidran Shagya and others have been used; stallions of the Kladrubers that continue to be pure-bred are used in the national breeding programmes.

Height: about 15.3 to 16.1 hands, sometimes more.

Konik pony (Polish Konik)

The Konik is the authentic primitive small horse of the forests of eastern Europe, while the Huzul represents the mountain form. Both have been established there for thousands of years and can be considered as the eastern European variants of Przewalski's

wild horse. The Konik lived wild for a long time in the east and north of present-day Poland and in Lithuania, and in the San area it persisted until the end of the eighteenth century. The last few specimens were placed in the Zamość Zoo in Poland; from there they were dispersed in the second half of the nineteenth century to areas in which they multiplied—although the breed no longer remained pure—at first in the Lublin district, where they were used as riding and draught ponies. In addition, quite large stocks were living in the Tarnopol and Lvov regions in north-eastern Poland and in south-eastern Lithuania at the beginning of the twentieth century. While there were no longer any pure-bred Koniks within these populations, deviations from the original form were slight, since conditions of climate and environment were unchanged.

Since 1936 experimental work using measures of selection has been carried out in the Bialowieża Nature Reserve, and since 1955, in the Popielno Experimental Station, to breed back to the typical characteristics of the wild Konik (the tarpan). In the Konik stud at Jeźewice, a programme has been under way since 1966 to provide Konik stallions for use in the breeding of hardy small horses in Poland. There are many eastern European breeds, which, because of their common origin, are closely related to the Konik.

The Konik has the typical wild colouring, together with all the characteristics, fine, long, dark tail and mane hair, little feather on the legs. In 'pure-bred' Koniks there are no markings. The overall format of the Konik is rectangular; they are sturdy and powerful and their hooves are small and very hard.

Height: 13 to 13.2 hands.

Landes pony

This breed lives on the Atlantic coast of south-western France. It is descended from North African horses, predominantly Barbaries, which came to the Landes *département* when the Muhammadan Moors from Spain invaded the area in the eighth century.

Height: 12.1 to 13.1 hands.

Latvian horse

This breed developed in the Latvian Republic from native breeds living there (for example, the Konik, Zmudic horse and Schweike), and particularly in the last sixty years, as a result of crossing with Oldenburg warmblood stallions, has become consolidated as an all-round, powerful warmblood. It can be used successfully both as a working and a sporting horse and is hardy and untiring. The horse's best paces are the walk and gallop, but it is also an efficient jumper.

Height: 15.2 to 16.1 hands or more.

Lipizzaner

This breed of heavy warmblood horse was developed in the sixteenth century in the Lipizza stud north of Trieste, based on horses of the old Karst breeds which already existed there, mated with stallions of Spanish extraction—foundation stallions included Pluto, Conversano, Maestoso, Favory and Neapolitano—and the Arab stallion Siglavy. The Spanish stallions came from the most important European studs of that time, such as Fredericksborg and Naples. In the course of time, Arabian blood was also introduced into the 'Spanish' strains of Lipizzaners. As a saddle horse for classical *haute école*, the Lipizzaner gained world renown and it is still bred today in the original type, in the Piber stud in Austria, for Vienna's Spanish Riding School which was founded in 1572 and built in its present form in 1735 and in its original home at Lipica in Yugoslavia. Lipizzaners are also bred in Hungary, Romania and elsewhere for use as all-purpose working and sporting horses. Like the original type, they are very reliable and enjoy considerable longevity, although they reach full maturity only at about seven years of age.

The horses are medium-sized, low, and strongly built with well-rounded quarters, short powerful legs and small, hard hooves. The tail is well positioned and carried with elegance. Typically the horses have an especially expressive head with varying degrees of convexity of nose-line. Particular features are the high-stepping action and the flexibility of the hindquarters. Willingness to learn, good humour and lively temperament, and complete absence of the difficult behaviour usually associated with stallions, all make the Lipizzaner stallion the supreme exponent of classical equitation.

Height: about 15.1 to 16.1 hands.

Masuren horse

Bred in the north-east of Poland, this breed can be seen as the direct descendant of the warmblood horse of Trakehner (east Prussian) descent, although since 1950 it has also been influenced by stallions of the Poznan warmblood breed. The horses have a variety of uses, not only in sport but also in farming. They are bred deliberately for riding qualities such as swiftness and jumping ability. The Masuren has an overall rectangular format, is adequately large and has good muscle development. Among its greatest assets are its reliability and stamina.

Height: 15.2 to 16.1 hands.

Merens pony

This breed, which is directly related to the Basque pony of the nineteenth century, lives in the extreme south of France. The ponies are very sturdy and frugal, and move swiftly with a good action; they are mainly used for riding. The stock is very small (about six hundred animals) but since the establishment of the stud book in 1946, careful attention has been given to its breeding.

Height: depending upon origin and conditions of rearing, 13.1 to 14.3 hands.

Mongolian pony

These typical steppe ponies are directly descended from Przewalski's wild horse which had its last biotope in the area which today is the Mongolian People's Republic. In the western part of this area, the wild horse was long ago incorporated into the stock of domestic animals owned by Asiatic herdsmen. Many breeds in neighbouring regions such as China, Japan, south-east Asia, India and as far as eastern Europe were influenced by the Mongolian pony, particularly as a result of the expeditions of conquest by the Huns, Magyars and finally the Mongolians, and the subsequent occupation, sometimes for centuries at a time, of vast conquered territories. Even until the nineteenth century, these traces were still visible in almost all breeds in these regions, and became accepted as breed-specific characteristics both there and elsewhere.

Today the breed exists as a stock of more than two million animals in the Mongolian People's Republic. The ponies are kept in herds of thirty to fifty individuals. As well as being used as saddle and pack animals, they provide a useful supply of mare's milk.

Typical features of the Mongolian pony are its extreme toughness, frugality, speed and agility. It is powerful with very strong quarters, a large head and sound legs. In many ways it still resembles its wild ancestors. Its colour variants correspond to those of other domestic breeds of horses; dun, combined with a black mane, dorsal stripe and shoulder cross, with diagonal stripes on the lower parts of the forelimbs—characteristics typical of the wild horse—occurs frequently.

Height: between 12 and 13 hands; on average, mares about 12.2 and stallions about 12.3 hands.

Morgan

This horse, native to the United States of America, is the earliest to have been bred to a uniform standard on the American continent. The breed derives its name from the foundation sire Justin Morgan, foaled in 1789, and provides saddle horses and driving horses that are good all-rounders of remarkable stamina. It has the reputation of being very reliable and is lively and receptive to training. The Morgan breed influenced the development of all later North American breeds including the American trotting horse.

Height: about 15.2 hands.

Mustang

Feral horses which until the nineteenth century lived in vast herds in North America, particularly in the extensive prairie lands along the Grand River. Mustangs are descendants of horses brought to America from the Iberian Peninsula from the sixteenth century onwards by the Spanish in the course of their expeditions of conquest. So they are not true wild horses, as is often wrongly assumed, but domestic horses that have returned to the wild.

The mustang stocks provided the foundation for the Amerindian pony which was bred by a number of Indian tribes, especially the Mohawks, in the region of the Grand River, and which was characterised by hardness, endurance and frugality. The somewhat larger Bronco horse developed in turn from this breed and itself was important as the basis of the American cow pony, and in particular of the polo ponies that are bred there. The various local groups of Bronco horses bear the names of the Indian tribes that

breed them; the horses of the Cayuse tribe are particularly well known.

Height: Indian pony 12.3 to 14 hands; Bronco horse about 14 to 14.3 hands.

Mytilene pony

Since time immemorial, there have been independent breeds of ponies on a number of islands off the Turkish coast in the Aegean Sea. A well-known one is the Mytilene pony, living on the island of Lesbos, a pony with great stamnina and a hardy constitution. This breed has existed for centuries in virtual isolation.

Height: about 11 hands.

Navarre horse

An old breed, the origin of which goes back to the Andalusian horse, it was bred in the Navarre region and in the area of the French/Spanish border, but no longer exists today. The Navarre horse influenced the Tarbes horse, a breed well known since the beginning of the nineteenth century and with many of the features of the English thoroughbred. As a result of the use of Anglo-Arabians, the Bigourdan horse developed about the middle of the nineteenth century. Today's Tarbes is a medium-sized, elegant horse of Anglo-Arabian type, and is an excellent saddle horse.

Height of the Tarbes horse: about 15.2 to 16 hands and more.

Neapolitan horse

A horse that was bred systematically in Naples during the sixteenth century on a foundation of Andalusian, Barbary and other Oriental breeds. Most Neapolitans were not too heavy, agile and, for their time, swift movers, particularly noted for their good action and learning ability. They had a long head with a Roman nose, a strongly-curved neck and particularly heavy hindquarters, rather poor legs with the hind legs shargly angled.

The Neapolitan laid the foundation for Italian equitation. The breed disappeared at the beginning of the twentieth century. The foremost among its descendants are the Lipizzaners and Kladrubers, but it has had some influence on almost all European breeds.

The Chigi breed, developed in the seventeenth century, was particularly famous; these horses were noted for an extremely high front leg action and a very slow and short stride, and were used primarily for ceremonial and display. They became extinct in the nineteenth century.

Marionettis, heavy working horses from central Italy, also developed on a basis of Neapolitan horses; genealogical links also exist with the Polesina breed that came from the Polesina district of Upper Italy and which also achieved a considerable reputation outside its own area in the fifteenth and sixteenth centuries.

New Forest pony

This breed of pony, descended from the small working horse of the Britons, has its base in the New Forest in Hampshire. Some foreign blood was introduced after the seventeenth century, and in the nineteenth century the ponies were systematically crossed with Arab stallions, and later attempts were made at cross-breeding with other native British ponies. Today standards are strictly controlled in private studs, but the forest ponies are largely cross-breeds. New Forest ponies are particularly noted for their sure-footedness, their aptitude for all forms of equestrian activity, their reliability and calm temperament. Because of their mixed breeding history, size and conformation vary considerably. All colours except piebald and skewbald are recognised.

Height: about 12 to 14.2 hands, according to type.

Nicaean horse

A breed of horse famous in antiquity. There were several variants of the breed, which reached its peak under Cyrus II and Darius I in the kingdom of Media (today, north-eastern Iran, north of Hamadan and the Province of Ardelan); it was said that 100,000 horses were kept in the stud farms alone. Nicaean horses can be seen as ancestors of the noble Persian horses; genealogical links exist with all Oriental breeds.

Nonius

A breed of warmblood horses that derives its name from its foundation sire, the Anglo-Norman, Nonius Senior, foaled in 1810 (La Rossières stud, France); the stallion served for twenty-two years and consolidated the typical characteristics of the breed. For more than a century, two variants have been produced. The continued use of Anglo-Norman blood and a certain proportion of Spanish blood developed the large Nonius, a heavy, elegant saddle and carriage horse; the head is large, the profile arched, the limbs long; it is a late maturer. The small Nonius was produced by the addition of English thoroughbred blood and a certain amount of Arabian blood; this is a medium-sized, hardy, tireless, strong, lively, light saddle and carriage horse.

Today, the large Nonius is bred more frequently. Most of them are black or brown without markings, very good goers and efficient showjumpers. They are bred mainly in Hungary but also in Yugoslavia and other Balkan countries.

Height: small Nonius, 15.1 to 16.1 hands; large Nonius, about 16.1, but can reach 16.3 hands.

Noriker (South German coldblood horse; Pinzgauer; Oberländer)

A very old breed of horses, named after the former Roman province of Noricum, bred initially in the region of today's Salz-

burg, and in the Middle Ages in the Grossglockner area ('Pinzgau'). Between the sixteenth and nineteenth centuries the breed was crossed with stallions of various breeds from Spain, and with Neapolitans, Belgian heavy draught horses, Kladrubers and Clydesdales, so that by the time of Charlemagne, when the important Noric breed was considered to be consolidated, it exhibited a great breadth of variation. It is only since about 1884 that the direction in which the various strains were developing has become clear. One type is the Oberländer, a light draught horse for use in the mountains, of compact build and very active. The other is the Pinzgauer, a heavy draught horse for use in the mountains; its principal pace is the walk.

In 1939, following considerable convergence of the two types, the term 'Noriker coldblood' was introduced, and changed in 1952 to 'South German coldblood'. The horses today are of medium weight, with good action; they are light feeders and mature early. The spotted marking typical of the Pinzgauer is no longer very common, bays predominate and there are some chestnuts.

Height of the South German coldblood horse: 15.2 to 16 hands.

Norwegian Fjord pony

To find the predecessor of this capable breed of pony one could well look to the old Lyng horse of northern Norway, which was of a type similar to the Gotland pony. In any case, the Norwegian Fjord pony is known to have existed in western and north-western Scandinavia since the earliest times, and it has the same origins as the Gudbransdal horse, although it is smaller.

These ponies have an overall rectangular format which ensures an adequately long back, making them very efficient at carrying loads for long distances over difficult terrain. Typical features of the Fjord pony include extreme willingness, quickness to learn and a friendly temperament. It is popular for riding, or as a pack and draught pony. It is very undemanding as to food and living conditions, and has an excellent constitution. Because it is such a good all-rounder, it has found its way into many countries in Europe.

Dun colouring is typical, usually light-brownish or brownish dun. Brown-dun is usually associated with the black markings typical of the primitive wild horse, that is, the dorsal stripe along the back—the 'eel stripe'—and diagonal striping on the forelegs, and also with a light-coloured muzzle, belly and inner leg area. Lower extremities and hooves show dark pigmentation. This

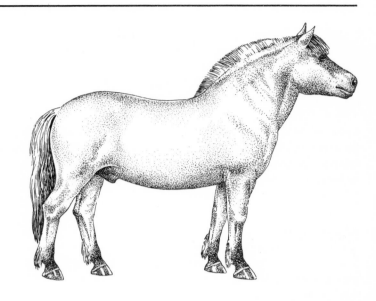

breed frequently lacks the horny knobs on the forelegs known as chestnuts.

Height: 13 to 14.2 hands; stallions on average about 14 hands, mares about 13.3 hands.

The Lyng horse (residual stock) reaches a height of about 12.1 hands.

Oldenburg horse

A very old, heavy warmblood breed based on the Friesian horse and using Andalusian, Neapolitan, Barbary and Yorkshire stallions; by the seventeenth century it was already providing carriage horses of high repute to the whole of Europe. By 1800 there was a uniform, closed breeding area; in 1819 regulations governing the selection of stallions; in 1861 a stud book; and from 1892 provisions for the inspection of mares.

Until 1914 the aim was to breed a heavy carriage horse with good action, but after that time there was a change in favour of a type of horse suitable for farming. In the mid-thirties, the first use was made of non-Oldenburg stallions, with an English thoroughbred being used from 1935 onwards, followed after that by an Anglo-Norman. Since 1952 efforts to improve the Oldenburg have been intensified, with the aim of making it more able to compete with the typical saddle horse type. It is developing into a medium-weight breed.

Additional large breeding areas have been established beyond the Oldenburg area, such as in the south and south-west of the GDR, in parts of Denmark and the Netherlands, and in Hessen and Baden-Württemberg, although some deviation of type has resulted. Breeding is directed towards producing a sporting horse.

The Oldenburg has a fine performance and boundless energy, a balanced temperament and a pleasant nature. It is low and heavy-barrelled, its legs are powerful with short shanks. The horses are predominantly brown and black.

Height: 16.1 to 17.1 hands.

Oriental breeds

A collective term for breeds of horses native to the Near East and Africa, approximating in type to the Arab, such as those found in Syria, Iraq, Iran, Turkey and the Caucasus region of the USSR. The name 'southern horse' is also commonly used.

Orlov trotter

A trotting breed, systematically developed by Count Alexei Grigorivich Orlov since 1775, which particularly bears the stamp of the stallion Bars I, foaled in 1784, a product of Arab, Dutch and

Danish blood. Since that time it has been perfected by inbreeding and systematic selection, although between 1810 and 1830 other trotting mares and other breeds were occasionally used. From 1845 onwards breeding was concentrated at the original stud farm of Chrenovoi (Chrjenow), and as a result of this, and consistent breeding practices, the horse was greatly improved. Heavy losses were suffered in the course of World War II, but in time they were made good. There are now at least twenty blood-lines. The most valuable characteristics of the breed, such as endurance, an equable temperament and excellent trotting ability, have been developed further, so that the Orlov trotter can be used both as a saddle horse and as a working horse. The most common colours are brown and black.

The Russian trotter represents a further development of the Orlov trotter, produced by crossing with American trotters (standardbreds), together with rigid selection for trotting performance. It is even faster, useful for just as wide a variety of purposes, and it makes up about 10 per cent of the total breeding stock of the USSR.

Height: Orlov trotter, 15.2 to about 16.1 hands; Russian trotter, 15 to over 15.3 hands, depending upon type.

Pacer

This term is used to denote warmblood horses in North America that have a natural inclination for and particular skill in the ambling and pacing gaits. In the early days of expansion in the USA and Canada, pacers were especially popular, since the easy pacing gait was much less tiring for the rider than the trot; this was an important consideration when great distances had to be covered. Pacing ability is an inherited factor and was consolidated within a quasi 'breed', the pacer, which later contributed to the development of the American trotting horse. There are different types of pacer, such as the Narragansett pacer, the Canadian pacer and others.

Height: about 15.3 hands.

Panje pony

This pony goes back to the Konik, but its efficiency as a draught animal was improved by the use in breeding of suitable stallions of other breeds such as Arabians, trotters and warmblood horses of Trakehner extraction as well as Belgian heavy draught horses. At the same time, valuable characteristics such as frugality, endurance and a robust constitution were retained. With the mechanisation of Soviet agriculture, the Panje lost its importance as a draught animal, and is employed today as a saddle horse or for light transport work, particularly in unfavourable weather conditions. The alternative name of Polesskaja horse is a better indication of its present location. It is widely distributed throughout the west of the USSR and large parts of the Ukrainian Republic.

Height: the foundation type, about 13 hands; the improved Panje, up to 14.1 hands.

Percheron

A very old breed of heavy draught horse native to the La Perche region of France lying to the west of Paris. It is descended from a regional breed which, over a period of a thousand years, was several times improved by Oriental blood, for the last time at the beginning of the nineteenth century. Also in the nineteenth century, it was influenced by Breton and Boulonnais horses. The Oriental element is still clearly visible in the outward appearance of this efficient, clean-limbed breed with its very free action, making it a particularly impressive horse. Percherons are hardy, tireless and energetic but of a pleasant, docile nature.

The Percheron provided the foundation for a number of other coldblood breeds in the USSR, Australia, USA, Britain and South Africa. Like all coldblood breeds, Percherons also suffered a considerable decline in numbers when the use of draught horses in agriculture was virtually abandoned.

By far the most common colours are dark-grey and black. Height: about 16.1, sometimes up to 16.3 hands.

Persian horse (Persian Arab; Plateau Persian)

The collective name for the breeds that have been living for several thousands of years in the region that is today Iran, and which were already held in high esteem in classical antiquity for their stamina, hardiness, speed and reliability. Their predecessor and at the same time most noble representative was the Nicaean horse which was much sought after as a saddle horse. The Persian exerted an enormous influence on horse breeding in Europe, and, with the Arab, on the establishment of the Oriental breeds. This happened particularly after the Arab peoples began their triumphant progress under the flag of the Prophet. They took their mounts from the abundance of horses they found in the conquered territory of Iran, and it was this alone that enabled them to move forward as large cavalry units and to cover vast distances in such a short time, and so to create the Islamic Empire. It can be assumed that at least during the first period of their conquests in the Near East and the southern Mediterranean area, thoroughbred horses of Persian origin were dispersed widely, and it was only later that the true Arabian horse, that had meanwhile evolved, came upon the scene. It is from this point of view that one can also consider the influence of the Persian upon the development of the many breeds of horses that were living in the area conquered by Islam.

The Persian horse, possibly with some contribution from the Persian mountain horse, was directly responsible for the establishment of the following breeds: the Bokhara pony, Kurdistan pony, Karadagh horse, Shirazi horse and Yamoote horse.

The Caspian pony (also called *mouleki*, *pouseki*—'small mouth'; or *kouzi*— 'the small one') can be considered as a direct descendant, living in isolation, of the Persian horse. Its height is 10 to 12 hands.

Pinto horse (Spanish: *pinta*—spot; American English: painted horse)

The collective term for piebald (black and white) and skewbald (any colour but black, combined with white) horses in North and South America, and so not the name of a breed. They are small riding horses, which, like all American horses, are of Spanish origin. Pintos were first kept by Indian tribes and were highly prized; they played a part in certain tribal ceremonies. Among the Criollo horses of South America, there are some groups of pintos.

So too among the breeds of North America and Canada, but here three-colour dappling also occurs. Since a stud book for pintos has existed in the USA since 1941, the North American pinto may, if certain breeding measures are successful, be developed as an independent breed.

Height: 14.1 to 15.1 hands.

Poitevin

This breed is probably descended directly from the Celtic horse that lived in relative isolation in the marshy regions of Poitou in western France, and is a very coarse, strong type of heavy draught horse. Gradually, possibly as the result of using horses from the Netherlands, a somewhat more refined variety evolved in the Mulassière. Mated with the large Poitou asses, it produces powerful mules.

Poitevins are large and big-boned; typical features include a Roman nose, long mane and tail, heavy feather on the legs and broad flat hooves. They are good-natured but lazy and slow and have a somewhat poor action.

Height: about 15.3 hands.

Polo pony

This term does not denote a particular breed but refers to the type of horse that is used in the sport of polo. Originally the horses came from the smaller native breeds of various countries which showed themselves to be suitable for this rigorous, competitive game by pronounced strength, stamina and agility. Until 1919, the height of the polo pony was limited to 14.2 hands. Because the game originated in Asia—it was played in Iran, India, China, Mongolia and Japan—there are still large numbers of polo ponies there today. Polo was first introduced officially into England, and so into Europe, in 1873.

Today the game is dominated by the specially-bred Argentine pony which, from the beginning of this century, has been greatly influenced by the introduction of English thoroughbred blood.

Height: while most countries aim for a height of between 15 and 16 hands, the majority of ponies are between 14.1 and 15.1 hands.

Poznan horse

This breed is closely related to the Masuren horse and therefore also to the warmblood horse of Trakehner extraction. Poznans are good all-rounders and of outstanding quality as saddle horses. They are bred mainly in the area round and south of Poznan in Poland.

Height: 15.2 to 16.1 hands and more.

Quarter horse

A specialised saddle horse and working horse used by cattlemen, originally a native of North America but also used in Australia, South and Central America. Quarter horses have proved particularly valuable in rounding up cattle on account of their natural turn of speed, particularly at a gallop over a short distance of about 400 m (a 'quarter' mile), in which they can achieve a speed of more than 40 miles per hour. These horses are enormously powerful, compact and broad. Their origin can be traced back to Spanish horses that were extensively modified by the use of Oriental and, in particular, English thoroughbreds. They are also known as cow ponies, ranch horses, cutting horses or roping horses, and can be classified under the general heading of Western horses (see p. 216).

Height: about 14.3 hands, also up to 15.1 hands.

Rhenish-German coldblood horse (Rhineland)

This breed was developed from about 1830 onwards on the basis of Belgian coldblood breeds such as Brabant and Ardennes horses, but was bred systematically and used extensively only from the end of the nineteenth century (the stud book appeared in 1892). In the 1920s it achieved full regional status and was bred in many areas. With the increasing mechanisation of agriculture and transport, stocks declined rapidly from about 1955, and now only small residual stocks remain. With the fall in numbers, there was a move away from the former, very large conformation to one of medium size.

These horses are strong, low and large-framed, with a high level of performance and a good action. They have an attractive temperament and good manners. The outward appearance corresponds to the demand for an all-round working horse for medium and heavy use. The most common colours are brown, bay roan and chestnut roan.

Height: about 15.3 hands, also somewhat less.

Roadster (Norfolk trotter)

A regional British breed that was bred in large numbers until the nineteenth century in the counties of Norfolk and Yorkshire. The horses carried a considerable proportion of Spanish and Dutch blood (Harddraver) and contributed to the establishment of various British warmblood breeds, the American trotting horse and others. They were notable for their skill in trotting.

Sardinian horse (Sardinian pony)

A mountain breed which has been influenced primarily by Barbary horses but also by other Oriental breeds. Depending upon the extent of this influence, it is possible to distinguish between the smaller ponies, known as *achettas* and the larger *achettones*. Reflecting its origins, the Sardinian horse is noble, late-maturing but very long-lived. It has a reputation for stamina and strength.

Height: between 10 and 14 hands; *achettas* up to 12 hands, *achettones* over 12 hands and up to 14 hands.

Schweike

The Schweike, which lives in the regions of Masuria, Latvia, Lithuania and Estonia, is descended from the Paustocaican ('brown horse of the wilderness') which still lived a wild or semi-wild existence there until the sixteenth century and, like it, belongs to the large group of horses that can be classified with the Konik. The Schweike, to some extent in conjunction with the Zmudic horse, provides the basis for the breeds of regional horses found in today's Baltic Soviet Republic, and the foundation for the warmblood horse of Trakehner extraction. It also influenced the Finnish horse by way of the Baltic breeds. At the end of the eighteenth century, it had a height of only 9 to 11 hands.

Senne horse

A breed that formerly existed in the Senne region south of Bielefeld in West Germany, it was first mentioned in a document in 1160, but is undoubtedly much older. These horses, that were just under medium size, were kept all year in a semi-wild state in forest pastures. They have genealogical and territorial links with the Dülmen and the Low German Münsterland horse. Because of their stamina, strength, speed and skill in jumping, the Senne horses were renowned as tournament horses, transport and war horses, from the fifteenth to the seventeenth century. From the seventeenth century onwards, they were influenced by Oriental, Spanish, Danish and English stallions. After 1680, Lopshorn Stud was the home of the Senne horse, and its stallions influenced almost all the breeding stations in central and western Europe. With the ending of forest pasturing in about 1870, and the rapid improvements in coldblood breeding, the Senne horse became extinct; in about 1880 probably the last of the Senne stallions were moved to the Beberbeck stud farm where they were incorporated into other warmblood breeds.

Shagya

A very hardy breed with a high level of performance, named after its foundation sire Shagya, foaled in 1830, a pure-bred Arabian that had been imported into Hungary in 1837. The breed provides reliable saddle horses with an excellent action. It is widespread in Hungary, Romania, Poland and Czechoslovakia as a result of the use of stallions of this breed in the national breeding programmes; in addition, it is pure-bred in a number of institutions.

Shagyas are markedly Oriental in type and most of them are greys.

Height: 14.3 to 15.3 hands and more.

Shetland pony

This breed, together with the Highland pony, is probably descended from the small primitive working horse from the north of Scotland. These small horses were taken to the Shetland Islands by the Picts, the ancient Celtic inhabitants of Scotland. In the ninth century, they were reinforced by small numbers of horses from southern Scandinavia, but any of these that survived were assim-

ilated into the breed. The ponies bred in almost complete isolation, producing this typical miniature breed by the middle of the eighteenth century. Attempts have since been made to develop a somewhat larger strain by cross-breeding and selection, so that today there are fundamentally two types: the original sturdy type of pony characterised by its dwarf growth, and the larger, somewhat more elegant Fetlar type. According to the official standards for the breeding of ponies on the Shetland Islands and in Britain, the first type is considered to be the 'authentic' Shetland pony, and may not exceed a height of 10.2 hands, while the Fetlar type reaches 12 hands. Since 1880 a number of studs have been breeding miniature ponies, using the smallest of the Shetland ponies and selecting for dwarf growth. For various reasons, the number of ponies on the Shetland Islands has declined in recent years (in 1982, some 700 to 800). The ponies are allowed to live semi-wild. There is a lively export trade.

Height: 'original' type, about 8 to 10.2 hands; Fetlar type, about 10.2 to 12 hands; miniatures, about 4 to 5 hands.

Shire horse

A breed of heavy draught horses originating in the shires of central England, already known in antiquity and famous in the Middle Ages for providing the enormously heavy steeds used in knightly combat. The breed became increasingly stabilised after the introduction of the stud book in 1878. Shire horses are the most massive and powerful coldblood horses in the world. They are adaptable and hardy. Striking features are the large areas of white marking and the very heavy feather on the legs. Bays predominate but blacks also occur. Since there is no longer a de-

mand for heavy draught horses in agriculture, their numbers have declined sharply since 1955 but they still remain in considerable demand for export, especially to the USA.

Height: at least 16.3 to 17 hands, often considerably more.

Sicilian pony

This breed can be considered as the last remaining residual stock of a small mountain breed which was influenced primarily by Italian and Barbary horses.

Height: about 13.1 hands.

Skyros pony

A breed of very small ponies found only on the Aegean island of Skyros, where for centuries it has lived an almost exclusively semi-wild existence in complete isolation. It is assumed that the ponies were brought to Skyros by Venetian travellers in the twelfth and thirteenth centuries. They are strong animals and in spite of the dearth of water and food, a small stock was able to maintain itself there without any admixture of outside blood. A special feature is the long fine hair of mane and tail, the latter reaching to the ground. Most of the ponies are brown, bay or chestnut, rarely black. They have only small white markings (star on forehead or spots in the region of the hocks). In 1928, 500 pure-bred ponies of this breed were living on Skyros and a group is reported to have been there still in 1940.

Height: about 9 hands.

Spanish horse

This breed developed in the eighth century, mainly in Andalusia, probably as a result of the increasing use of Oriental, Barbary and Arabian stallions that were mated with the native Andalusian mares, with selection being made for the Oriental type of horse. The same practice has continued until the present day, and the result is a very aristocratic, light warmblood breed which provides medium-sized saddle horses and carriage horses. A notable feature is the majestic bearing of the neck and the strong Arabian emphasis in type.

Height: about 15.2 hands.

Suffolk Punch

A strong coldblood breed, developed in the Middle Ages, known to have existed in 1586 in the county of Suffolk. It has been influenced by a number of other breeds; initially mares from the west of England were mated with Norman stallions. In the course of development, Yorkshire, Dutch and pacer blood was introduced. From 1877 there has been an obligatory stud book.

The Suffolks are large and powerful with good stamina and, in spite of their solidity, are relatively elegant. They have a minimum of feather. Almost all of them are light chestnut.

With the fall in demand for draught horses on farms, the numbers of this heavy breed have declined rapidly since about 1960. The same is true in its secondary breeding areas such as Ireland, North and South America and Australia. But the breed's future may after all be assured since very useful riding horses and show jumpers can be produced by English thoroughbred or part-bred stallions out of Suffolk mares.

Height: 16 to 16.2 hands.

Tennessee walking horse

A warmblood breed that has developed in the State of Tennessee from the former plantation horse used by the early settlers in about 1800, with contributions from English thoroughbreds, pacers and other breeds. It provides mainly saddle horses for use over long distances, with excellent riding qualities, including quickness to learn and a pleasant nature. Its action is superb, the horse having a particularly long, smooth stride. A typical feature is its slightly Roman nose. For its outstanding all-round qualities, the horse has earned itself the designation 'Everyone's pleasure horse'. Today the breed is found primarily in the south and southwest of the USA.

Height: 15.2 to 16.1 hands.

Tersk horse

This is still a young breed, developed in about 1925 in the region round Stavropol (stud farms at Tersk and Stavropol) in the Caucasus. It is based on Don and Kabardin breeding mares and Arabian stallions. With strict selection and a well-planned breeding programme, it was possible within a short time to develop the desired qualities of the breed, with particular stress laid upon outward appearance and the suitability of the animals for management in large herds.

The horses' origins are reflected in their basically Oriental type; they are hardy, with great stamina and good action, undemanding and very prolific. They are highly prized as saddle horses, and have a particularly marked learning capacity.

Height: about 14.3 to 15.1 hands, sometimes more.

Trait du Nord

A breed developed in northern France from a combination of Ardennes and Belgian heavy draught horses. It provides large, very powerful and strong coldblood horses of very heavy calibre. In spite of their great weight, they have a good turn of speed in trotting. With the general reduction in the stocks of heavy draught horses, this breed has almost disappeared.

Height: about 16.1 to 17.1 hands.

Ukrainian horse

This very young breed came into existence as recently as 1950 in the Ukraine, Alexandriski and Proval stud farms as a result of crossing native and Hungarian mares with stallions of Hanoverian and Trakehner extraction and with English thoroughbreds. It is essentially a breed of riding horse, being a very highly bred, aristocratic warmblood. Further development of the breed continues today in the Alexandriski, Jagolnitzki and Derkulski studs.

Height: between 15.3 and 16.1 hands.

Vladimir horse (Vladimir tractor horse)

This breed has been influenced since the 1920s by various heavy horses such as Ardennes, Suffolks, Shires and Clydesdales and was bred in its fundamental form until about the end of the nineteenth century in Russia on a basis of native regional breeds. In 1946 the breed was considered to be consolidated. The horses are powerful, untiring, hardy coldbloods, very willing as draught animals and with a good action.

Height: about 15.2 to 16 hands.

Voronezh horse (Bitjug)

The oldest breed of heavy draught horse in the USSR, developed in the area along the River Bitjuga (hence Bitjug) in the Voronezh region, later becoming very widespread. Its genealogical origins belong to the beginning of the eighteenth century when heavy Dutch stallions were crossed with the native peasant horse, the Lomovik, on the instructions of Peter I. Later, Orlov trotters and, in the second half of the nineteenth century, western European coldblood stallions, were also used. The breed achieved its final form and breeding stability in about 1936, after systematic improvement with trotters and warmbloods. Since then, it has been known as the Voronezh horse. The horses of this breed are medium-weight and, in terms of type, are on the border between the heavy warmblood and the coldblood horse. They have great stamina, a good action and are modest in their demands.

Height: between about 14.3 and 15.3 hands.

Warmblood horse of the German Democratic Republic

Since 1971, the breeding of warmblood horses in the GDR has been pursued with the common aim of producing riding horses with a high level of performance. In genealogical terms, the East German warmblood is based on the Hanoverian and warmbloods of Trakehner extraction, and before 1971, featured in the stud book under separate headings, as the Mecklenburg (almost exclusively on a foundation of Hanoverians) and the Brandenburg warmblood (a combination of the two foundation breeds). Since that time, English thoroughbred and warmblood stallions of Trakehner origin have been used systematically to improve riding qualities. As a means of raising the standard of breeding, preparation periods of a year have been introduced and testing of the stallions' performance is carried out centrally.

In keeping with the aim of breeding, modifications were brought about in a number of the heavy warmblood horses (bred on a foundation of Oldenburgs and East Friesians) that were present in the southern districts of the GDR, mainly by the use of English thoroughbred stallions and warmblood stallions of Trakehner extraction. Another group of heavy warmbloods continues to be pure-bred to provide the heavy draught horses required for use in forestry and agriculture. In general, these horses exhibit a hardy constitution, rapid regenerative capacity, high fertility, an amiable character and lively but stable temperament, making this valuable warmblood breed suitable for a particularly wide variety of uses.

Height: riding horse, 15.3 to 16.3 hands and over; heavy horse, about 15.3 to 16.1 hands.

Warmblood horse of Trakehner extraction

The breed developed in eastern Europe on a foundation of Konik-like regional strains of a type similar to the Schweike. It had already gained considerable status in the Middle Ages even before the first Oriental stallions had been used to improve the breed. From the eighteenth century onwards, and largely on the initiative of the principal stud at Trakehnen, this elegant, all-round, very hardy breed of saddle horse was developed. From 1787 the Trakehnen stud provided the necessary stallions which were bred on a foundation of Orientals and, later, on the basis of English thoroughbreds. At the end of the eighteenth and beginning of the nineteenth century, there was an important addition of Turkmene blood. After 1918, breeding was increasingly orientated away from the provision of horses for the army and towards the requirements of agriculture, and between about 1920 and 1940 the warmblood horse of Trakehner extraction fulfilled this need.

In spite of very heavy losses sustained by the breed—only about 6 per cent of the brood-mares survived World War II—it recovered, and today the horses are undoubtedly among the most highly-bred in the world, after the English thoroughbred, with a correspondingly high level of performance. Apart from the main breeding bases in East and West Germany, the horses are also bred in a number of other countries; in addition, the stallions are frequently used to improve other breeds.

The particular strength of this breed lies in its aptitude for dressage work and cross-country riding, and in its extreme reliability, its kindly nature yet very lively temperament.

Height: 15.3 to 16.3 hands.

Welsh pony

It is descended from the small Celtic working horse and in the nineteenth century was also known as the pony of Wales or Welsh mountain horse. It is known to have existed from as early as the twelfth century. The Welsh pony is one of the toughest and hardiest breeds of pony known. As a result of differences in environmental conditions, a number of variants developed within the breed, the independence of which was further increased by the use of Oriental and English thoroughbred stallions (eighteenth century), Hackneys and Norfolk trotters (nineteenth century) and Arabians and English thoroughbred stallions (nineteenth and twentieth centuries). The larger variants with good trotting ability, the 'hobbies', existed until the eighteenth or nineteenth century, but disappeared again during the nineteenth century as a result of changes in the manner of riding and through crossing with foreign breeds. The stud book, established in 1902, divides Welsh ponies into four types or sections:

Section A, the Welsh mountain pony: maximum height 12 hands; the typical foundation type for the other three groups.

Section B, the Welsh pony: maximum height 13.2 hands; a particularly useful riding pony.

Section C, the Welsh pony (cob type): maximum height 13.2 hands; an excellent, sure-footed riding and hunting pony.

Section D, the Welsh cob: minimum height 13.2 hands, but usually between 14.2 and 15.1 hands; a horse for hunting, cross-country work and driving, with stamina, strength and an outstanding talent for jumping. They are most famous for their spectacularly strong trot.

Western horses

A group of breeds belonging to various States in North America and Canada. All representatives are hardy saddle horses with great endurance. They include:

Western albino: a breed that is born white, with unpigmented skin, and weakly pigmented background to the eye with a pale blue or weak brown tone. Height: about 15.3 hands.

Appaloosa or spotted horse: a very reliable, good-natured saddle horse with great skill in galloping and jumping. This popular horse—almost in the pony category—is directly descended from the horses introduced from Spain by the conquistadores, and so carries Oriental blood. A typical feature is the striking spotted marking which occurs in several recognised patterns. The breed was mainly developed by Indian tribes who captured the ancestors of these horses and bred them as a pure strain, with special attention to markings. Appaloosa horses are also used as circus horses and in equestrian games. Height: about 14 to 15.1 hands. A variant developed from the Appaloosa is the somewhat larger, more powerful Colorado Ranger.

Palomino: a group of horses probably descended from the Spanish Isabellas, which were introduced to Central America in the sixteenth century. Because palominos are made up of a number of breeds they form a type rather than a single breed, with uniformity of colouring (a shimmering golden coat and silvery-white mane and tail); since 1932 a stud book has existed for their registration. They are sturdy saddle horses verging on pony status. Height: 14 to 15 hands.

The pinto horse (see p. 209) and the quarter horse (see p. 210) can also be included in the category of Western horses.

Zmudic horse

From the region of Kaunas (Lithuania), this breed has been known since the sixth or seventh century. Genealogical links possibly exist with the Konik, very probably with the Schweike. The Zmudic horse influenced the Schematukai horse (Szemaidic pony), as well as the Latvian warmblood horse and the Estonian horse. Today the breed divides into two groups depending upon size.

Height: the larger type, about 14.1 to 14.3 hands, the smaller, about 14 hands.

Bibliography

It is nearly impossible to give a complete survey of the literature concerning the 'horse' and it is steadily extended by new editions. The following survey is therefore limited to some basic studies or to those mentioned in the text which are to serve as further information. It was not possible to list articles in journals.

ALBAUM, L. I., and B. BRENTJES: *Wächter des Goldes.* Berlin, 1972.

AMBROS, C., and H.-H. MÜLLER: *Frühgeschichtliche Pferdeskelettfunde aus dem Gebiet der Tschechoslowakei.* Bratislava, 1980.

ANDRADE, R. DE: *Alrededor del caballo Español.* Lisbon, 1954.

APPERLEY, C. J.: *Nimrods German Tour. Sporting Magazine.* London, 1829. Translated by H. A. v. Esebeck: *Aus alten Zeiten (Nimrods Tagebuch).* 2nd ed. Berlin/Leipzig/Vienna, 1910.

BARMINZEV, I. N. et al: *Horse-breeding and horse sports* (in Russian). Moscow, 1972.

BOUCAUT, J. P.: *The Arab Horse, the Thoroughbred, and the Turf.* London, 1912.

BRENTJES, B.: *Die Haustierwerdung im Orient. Neue Brehm-Bücherei.* Wittenberg Lutherstadt, 1965.

BRENTJES, B.: *Von Schanidar bis Akkad.* Leipzig/Jena/Berlin, 1968.

BRENTJES, B.: *Die orientalische Welt.* Berlin, 1970.

BRENTJES, B.: *Die Erfindung des Haustieres.* Leipzig/Jena/Berlin, 1975.

BROWN, T.: *Biographische Skizzen und authentische Anecdoten von Pferden und übrigen Thieren derselben Gattung.* Weimar, 1831.

BUDJONNY, S. M. et al: *The Book on the Horse* (in Russian). Vol. 1. Moscow, 1952.

DENT, A. A., and D. M. GOODALL: *The Foals of Epona.* London, 1962.

DIESNER, H.-J.: *Die Völkerwanderung.* 2nd ed. Leipzig, 1981.

EBELING, E.: *Bruchstücke einer mittelassyrischen Vorschriftensammlung für die Akklimatisierung und Trainierung von Wagenpferden.* Berlin, 1951.

ENGELS, F.: 'Armee,' in: Karl Marx/Friedrich Engels, *Werke.* Vol. 14. Berlin, 1969.

ENGELS, F.: 'Kavallerie,' in: Karl Marx/Friedrich Engels, *Werke.* Vol. 14. Berlin, 1969.

ERBSTÖSSER, M.: *Die Kreuzzüge.* 2nd ed. Leipzig, 1980.

FILLIS, J.: *Grundsätze der Dressur und Reitkunst.* 4th ed. by G. Goebel. Stuttgart, 1918.

FLADE, J. E.: *Shetlandponys.* 5th ed. *Neue Brehm-Bücherei.* Wittenberg Lutherstadt, 1981.

FLADE, J. E.: *Das Araberpferd.* 5th ed. *Neue Brehm-Bücherei.* Wittenberg Lutherstadt, 1982.

FLADE, J. E. (under collaboration of H. Lenz): *abc—Pferdezucht–Pferdesport.* Berlin, 1968.

FLADE, J. E., and K. H. GLESS: *Kleinpferde.* 2nd ed. Berlin, 1984.

FLADE, J. E. et al: *Grundwissen für Pferdezüchter und Pferdesportler.* Berlin, 1981.

FLADE, J. E. et al: *Pferde—Zucht und Sport.* Berlin, 1983.

FÖLDES, L.: *Viehzucht und Hirtenleben in Ostmitteleuropa.* Budapest, 1961.

FRAISSE, F.: *Die Warmblutzucht in der Provinz Brandenburg.* Hanover, 1927.

GLESS, K. H.: *Das Pferd im Militärwesen.* Berlin, 1980.

GRABOWSKI, J.: *Hipologia dla wszystkich.* Warsaw, 1982.

GRAKOW, B. N.: *Die Skythen.* 2nd ed. (Translated from Russian). Berlin, 1980.

GRISO, F.: *Ordini di cavalcare.* Naples, 1550.

GROMOVA, V.: *The History of Horses in the Old World* (in Russian). Part I. *Palaeonthol. Inst. Series.* Moscow/Leningrad, 1949.

GROSCURTH: *Die Preussische Gestütsverwaltung.* Hanover, 1927.

GRZIMEK, B.: *Und immer wieder Pferde.* Munich, 1977.

GUÉRINIÈRE, F. R. DE LA: *École de Cavalerie.* Paris, 1733.

GURNEY, O. R.: *Die Hethiter. Fundus-Bücher.* Dresden, 1969.

HAHN-BUTRY, J., and H. J. KÖHLER: *Hannovers edles Warmblut.* Hamburg, Munich, Neuhaus-Oste, 1949.

HAUGER, A.: *Zur römischen Landwirtschaft und Haustierzucht.* Hanover, 1921.

HENNINGES, W. v.: *Stutbuch des Preussischen Friedrich-Wilhelm-Gestüts bei Neustadt (Dosse).* Hanover, 1929.

HUBERT, A.: *1000 Jahre Pferdezucht Kloster Einsiedeln.* Einsiedeln, 1963.

HUTTEN-CZAPSKI, M. v.: *Die Geschichte des Pferdes.* Berlin, 1876. Photo-mechanical reprint of the original edition of 1876. Leipzig, 1974.

JANKOVICH, M.: *Pferde, Reiter, Völkerstürme.* Munich/Basle/Vienna, no date.

KLENGEL, E. and H.: *Die Hethiter und ihre Nachbarn.* Leipzig, 1970.

KLIMKE, R.: *Grundausbildung des jungen Reitpferdes.* Stuttgart, 1980.

KNUST, T. A.: *Marco Polo—Von Venedig nach China, die grösste Reise des 13. Jahrhunderts.* Rostock, 1972.

KOSAMBI, D. D.: *Das alte Indien—seine Geschichte und seine Kultur.* Berlin, 1969.

KRZYSZTAŁOWICZ, A.: *Charakterystyka Państwowej Stadniny w Janowie Podlaskim.* Cracow, 1948.

KRZYSZTAŁOWICZ, A.: *Stadnina Koni Janów Podlaski.* Warsaw, 1967.

LEHNDORFF, G. COUNT: *Hippodromos, einiges über Pferde und Rennen im Griechischen Alterthum.* Berlin, 1876.

LEHNDORFF, S. COUNT: *Ein Leben mit Pferden.* Berlin/Paris, 1942.

LERCHE, F.: *Hlavní plemeníci státního hřebčína v Kladrubech n. L. v letech 1918–1948 jako podklad teplokrevného ohovu koni v ČSR.* Prague, 1951.

LERCHE, F.: *Starokladrubský kuň.* Prague, 1956.

LÖHNEISEN (also: Löhneissen *or* Löhneyss), G. E. v.: *Della Cavalleria sive de arte equitandi, exercitis equestribus et torneamentis.* Remm(m)lingen, 1609. Publ. by Valentin Trichter as *Neueröffnete Hof-Kriegs- und Reit-Schul.* Nuremberg, 1729.

MIECKLEY, E.: *Geschichte des Königlichen Hauptgestüts Beberbeck und seiner Zucht.* Berlin, 1905.

MOHR, E.: *Das Urwildpferd.* 2nd ed. *Neue Brehm-Bücherei.* Wittenberg Lutherstadt, 1970.

MORLAND, T. H.: *The genealogy of the English Race Horse.* London, 1810.

MÜSELER, W.: *Reitlehre.* 42nd ed. Berlin (West) and Hamburg, 1976.

NEUSCHULZ, H.: *Pferdezucht—Haltung und Sport.* Berlin, 1956.

NISSEN, J.: *Welches Pferd ist das?* 2nd ed. Stuttgart, 1964.

NÜRNBERG, H.: *Lipizzaner.* Berlin, 1980.

OESE, E. et al: *Pferdesport.* 4th ed. Berlin, 1982.

OETTINGEN, B. v.: *Das Vollblutpferd.* Berlin, 1920.

PLUVINEL, A. DE: *Le Maneige Royal—Die Königliche Reitschule.* Brunswick, 1626. Reprint Leipzig, 1969.

PRIZELIUS, J. G.: *Vollständige Pferdewissenschaft.* Leipzig, 1777.

PRSCHEWALSKI, N. v.: *Reisen in Tibet und am oberen Lauf des Gelben Flusses in den Jahren 1879 bis 1880* (Translated from Russian by Stein-Nordheim). Jena, 1884.

PRUSKI, W.: *Dzieje Państwowej Stadniny w Janowie Podlaskim 1817–1939.* Poznan, 1948.

PRUSKI, W.: *Hodowla koni.* Warsaw, 1960.

PRUSKI, W., GRABOWSKI, J., and S. SCHUCH: *Hodowla koni.* Warsaw, 1963.

RIDINGER, J. E.: *Vorstellung und Beschreibung derer Schul- und Campagne Pferden nach ihren Lectionen.* Augsburg, 1760.

ROHLWES, J. N.: *Die Pferdezucht oder die Veredelung der Pferde in dem Preussischen Staat in einer Darstellung des Friedrich-Wilhelm-Gestütes bei Neustadt an der Dosse.* Berlin, 1806.

RÜNGER, F.: *Herkunft, Rassezugehörigkeit, Züchtung und Haltung der Ritterpferde des Deutschen Ordens.* Berlin, 1925.

SCHIELE, R.: *Araber in Europa.* Munich/Basle/Vienna, 1967.

SCHIELE, R.: *Arabiens Pferde—Allahs liebste Kinder.* Munich/Berne/Vienna, 1972.

SCHWARK, H.-J. et al: *Pferde—Nutzung, Züchtung, Fütterung.* Berlin, 1978.

SEUNIG, W.: *Am Pulsschlag der Reitkunst.* Heidenheim, 1961.

SEUNIG, W.: *Marginalien zu Pferd und Reiter—ernst und heiter.* Heidenheim, 1961.

STAPENHORST, H.: *200 Jahre Landgestüt Celle.* Celle, 1935.

STEINBRECHT, G.: *Das Gymnasium des Pferdes.* 4th ed. Berlin, 1935.

SUMMERHAYS, R. S.: *The Observer's Book of Horses and Ponies.* London/New York, 1964.

TARR, L.: *Karren, Kutsche, Karosse.* Berlin, 1978.

TEMBROCK, G.: *Grundriss der Verhaltenswissenschaften.* 2nd ed. Jena, 1973.

TEMBROCK, G.: *Grundlagen des Tierverhaltens. Reihe WTB.* Vol. 215. Berlin, 1977.

TEMBROCK, G.: *Spezielle Verhaltensbiologie der Tiere.* Jena, 1983.

UNGER, W. v.: *Meister der Reitkunst.* Bielefeld and Leipzig, 1926.

UNGER, W. v.: *Die Ahnen des Hannoveraners.* Hanover, 1928.

VELTHEIM, R. v.: *Abhandlungen über die Pferdezucht Englands, noch einiger europäischer Länder, des Orients u.s.w., in Beziehung auf Deutschland.* Brunswick, 1833.

VOLF, J.: *Kone, osli a zebry. Ed. zvířata celého, světa.* Vol. 2. Prague, 1977.

VOSS, H.: *Homer—Ilias.* 6th ed. after 1945. Leipzig, 1960.

WALTHER, F. L.: *Das Pferd.* Giessen, 1819.

WALTHER, W.: *Die Frau im Islam.* Leipzig, 1980.

WERNER, J.: *Herodot—Das Geschichtswerk.* 2 vols. Berlin and Weimar, 1967.

WIDDRA, K.: *Xenophon—Reitkunst. Schr. u. Quellen der Alten Welt.* Vol. 16. Berlin, 1965.

WILLKOMM, W.: *Das Beberbecker Pferd.* Berlin, 1921.

WITT, O.: *History of Russian Horse-Breeding (XVIII–XIX century)* (in Russian). Moscow, 1952.

WITTENBURG, W.: *Beiträge zur Geschichte des Friedrich-Wilhelm-Gestütes bei Neustadt an der Dosse in der Zeit von 1786–1876.* Thesis. Leipzig, 1939.

WOLSTEIN, J. G.: *Marx Fugger: Von der Zucht der Kriegs- und Bürgerpferde. Aus dem Altdeutschen nach der Originalausgabe von 1578 übersetzt, mit Anmerkungen und einem zweyten Theile vermehrt herausgegeben.* 3rd ed. Vienna, 1805.

WOZEL, J., and J. KARPINSKI: *Turniere.* Berlin, 1979.

Index

Originally published in German as
Das grosse Pferdebuch

Published in the UK 1987 by
David & Charles Publishers plc
Brunel House Newton Abbot Devon

British Library Cataloguing in Publication Data
Flade, Johannes E.
  The compleat horse.
  1. Horses—History
  I. Title II. Tylinek, Erich III. Samková,
  Zuzana IV. Das Grosse Pferdebuch. English
  636.1'009 SF283

  ISBN 0−7153−8759−6

An Arco Horse Book
Published in the USA 1987 by
Prentice Hall Press
A Division of Simon & Schuster, Inc.
Gulf + Western Building
1 Gulf + Western Plaza
New York, NY 10023

PRENTICE HALL PRESS is a trademark of Simon & Schuster, Inc.

Library of Congress Cataloging-in-Publication Data
Flade, Johannes Erich.
  The compleat horse.

  Translation of: Das Grosse Pferdebuch.
  Bibliography: p.
  Includes index.
  1. Horses—History. 2. Horses. I. Tylinek,
  Erich. II. Samková, Zuzana. III. Title.
SF283.F4813 1986 636.1 85-28262

  ISBN 0−668−06530−3

Printed in the German Democratic Republic